Be
Healthier
Happier
and more
Productive

...

365 Inspiring Ideas

Leslyn Phelan Kantner

Published by Leslyn Kantner

Printed in the United States of America

First Printing, 2019

ISBN: 978-1-7334020-0-2

Dedication

I am forever grateful to those people in my life who are steadfast supporters; predominately those peeps who call me mom. And others, a couple of whom are now spirits tickling my aura. It is their non-judgmental acceptance of me that allows me to keep trying; reminding me the only way to fail is to stop.

And Elizabeth. I will always be ever-so-grateful for your daily scanning and correcting. Your two eyes are superior to my four. Thanks for being by my side all these years.

Perhaps mostly, I am grateful for all the lessons that life has presented, constantly offering me opportunities to choose my reaction. It is said that practice makes perfect.

Disclaimer:

While the author is a mental health provider, none of these suggestions are intended to act as therapeutic advice. Seeking local professional support is indicated if emotional disturbance is experienced in any capacity.

Forward

This book is a compilation of my blog ThisIsLeslyn.com and the year of daily posts that offered ideas for individuals to live a better life. I wrote them because even though my life has been difficult in many ways, I believe it's the 'little things' that help us to discover and sustain happiness. As you read, you may find a typo or misplaced preposition... I've chosen to allow this book to be imperfect for if I had waited until each small imperfection was discovered and corrected, it may never have come to fruition.

I am, first and foremost, human. I use the suggestions contained herein to manage life on a daily basis. As life throws challenges my way, I lean into fear (#348) and work to be vulnerable (#237). Many of my life experiences ended up being the springboard for my decision to become a mental health counselor in mid-life. I allowed curiosity (#172) to permeate every detail of my life as I sought to understand myself better (#309). I grew. Now, as a seasoned therapist, I have years of experience helping people grow happier and ultimately... healthier and more productive.

This collection of inspiring ideas comes from both personal experience and professional expertise. I share antidotes from my life and include research where it is applicable. It's not written with the intent that the reader will attempt to engage in an idea each day. I include 365 because my personal goal was to write every day for one year.

I chose not to categorize the ideas into happier, healthier, and more productive because many of the suggestions cover more than one base. If you get out and take a bike ride (#78), you'll be getting exercise (healthier) and increasing Dopamine levels (happier). Each category is interspersed throughout the book in no particular order. If you are needing a 'little something'... hold the book between your hands and randomly open it. My guess is that the page you open to will be a suggestion worth considering.

At the heart of who I am, is a Creative. I am curious about everything including behavior, human potential, and personal growth. I am inspired by people who have no fear; they motivate me to try.

Consequently, I've failed at a lot of things or decided that the 'thing' just wasn't a good fit.

With others, I've found joy; podcasting, painting, writing, biking, and traveling. It's important to keep in mind though, the only way I discovered what worked for me and what didn't, is that I tried. I keep trying; regardless of my age or station... I save what I need – making choices when necessary – and test the water on those things that interest me. You can too. Don't let circumstances or fear stand in your way. Joy is accessible when you believe it is within reach and many, many of the ideas herein produce joy with absolutely no cost and/or very little effort if your heart is open to receiving it. Truly, expressing yourself by writing a poem (#43), picking up litter (#72), spending the day nude (#109), or the simple act of visiting a cemetery (#228) cost nothing but offer something in return if you immerse yourself in the experience as I have outlined it for you.

If I were to pick this book from the store shelf and keep a hard copy, it would serve as a reference for those times when I needed some spice in my life, or a little pick me up. It would be accessible and bookmarked. My hope is that each reader will use it in a similar manner. Go ahead, read through... make a list and start your journey toward a happier, healthier and more productive life. If you love what you read, please consider leaving a review on Amazon or Goodreads. And, you can always reach out at thisisleslyn@gmail.com with questions or comments.

~Leslyn

Life must be lived, and curiosity kept alive.
One must never, for whatever reason,
turn his back on life.
~Eleanor Roosevelt

1 Challenge your beliefs.

Ask why – All. The. Time. Yes, this is relatively annoying when a 4-year-old echoes every one of your thoughts with "but, why?" and yet it seems as if that is when we stop asking ourselves. We learn (or assume) so many beliefs as we mature that often never again get examined and some of them are -in fact – simply untrue. I worked with a 20-year-old client once who held the erroneous belief that putting ice into milk would poison it. She was unaware of how she developed that belief; only knew that it was concretely woven into her knowledge system. I don't recall how we discovered that bit of information as it seems trite in comparison to her presenting problem but there were more mistaken notions lingering there as well that needed to be corrected to allow her a more accurate view of the world.

Even those things that we 'know to be true' today may not reflect our growth as the years go by. I find that people who were shy in their youth and developed beliefs from that perspective often need to reexamine those thoughts after developing mature confidence (i.e., "I can't do it."). Rules and ideas that were appropriate in one situation become implanted in our thought systems and then when the conditions change, we may fail to change our thoughts.

This concept is at the crux of all new discovery. If we fail to challenge our ideas about the world, science, medicine, and technology would standstill. It makes sense – a 'no brainer' – of sorts in that arena but it is just as important on the personal front. Take a step back and consider your personal, individual belief system. Validate what is fact from some acquired fiction. Distinguish what is still appropriate for your current circumstances and environment. Redefine as necessary.

Challenge your beliefs often!

#2 Set a timer/alarm

My mother used an old egg timer to monitor our 'corner time' when we were being punished. When my girls were young, I would set the stove timer and get everyone involved in a chore for 15 minutes – moving with the assumption that I could motivate them for at least a short period.

Today, I use the timer on my phone for a lot of different things. If I need to get out of the house at a particular time, I ask Siri to set an alarm for a particular time – reminding me to be in the shower by then or finished up a project in a timely manner.

If I am trying to remember a new thought or refresh something, I've lost track of (i.e. "breathe", "stay focused", etc.) I'll set an alarm on my phone so that it goes off at specific times throughout the day as a reminder.

Technology makes reminders easy. For all of us who have Alexa or one of her counterparts in our home, it's as easy as a spoken word to have an alarm remind us with those things, we need help remembering. It's as easy as that to set a timer as well. How many times have I started the tea kettle or put a slice of bread in the toaster just to get involved in something else?? Just the other day I came back into the kitchen to find my cast iron skillet ready to glow orange on my glass stove top. I had turned the burner on to dry it and then walked away – totally forgetting to come back to it. I'm lucky that the stove top survived and the house didn't burn down! A quick shout out to Siri or Alexa would have prevented that issue!

Use technology to set a timer and/or an alarm for reminders!

#3 Don't interrupt

Most of us learn a few basic social rules as we grow. We are told not to pick our noses in public and most of us remember this into adulthood. We learn not to interrupt someone speaking and yet we don't master that skill. How can we be good at one but not the other? They are both rather gross habits.

Being a good listener depends on hearing the entire context of what we are listening to. When we interrupt a speaker, we cut short the speaker's context. Often, we fill in the missing piece with a personal assumption as understood through our own lens, potentially misconstruing the speaker's intent.

When we interrupt, we steal energy from the speaker, diminishing the value of their comment; implying that it is less important than what we need to say. At the very least, it is a show of disrespect for what they are sharing. It may validate a sense of "I don't matter".

If the speaker – more so than 'what' the speaker is saying – matters to you; Don't interrupt. Even if the content is not your 'thing'… if your interest in the topic is nil… if it is emotionally charged… if it is controversial… let the speaker finish an entire thought before you chime in. Imagine the respect that can be demonstrated in a conversation if the entire exchange is transacted with complete thoughts and implied value!

Don't interrupt.

#4 One deep breath

Just one. A deep breath gives you a moment – often a necessary moment – to pause and collect. It can be used in almost every situation I can think of for that extra second, we may need to self-monitor.

Use a deep breath when you are a listener. Allow a breath to exist between the time a speaker stops speaking and your response. It provides the perception that you are intent on the speaker's content as well as offers your mind valuable time to process what was spoken, fortifying your ability to respond well.

Use a deep breath to reset your adrenalin as you feel it increasing during an arousal state in an argument or political conversation. Anytime I sense my energy increasing at an inopportune time, I utilize one simple deep breath to reset it and get present.

The time it takes you to deeply inhale and slowly exhale provides your mind with an opportunity to organize thoughts. It's an effective coping mechanism during a disagreement, a momentary memory lapse, or to calm an overwhelming flash. Our brain has an amazing ability to process tons of information in just those few seconds and can make the difference between over-reacting and staying silent.

Take one deep breath.

#5 Open your hands and let it go.

Coping literature and psychological dictates frequently make suggestions that are parodied into concepts which, insist we "just let it go", "forgive and move on", or "get over it", to name a few. The idea/concept is great and truly I think most of us attempt to follow any advice that implies we will move away from something that instils emotional pain.

I've talked to hundreds of people over time that have certainly heard and/or read that advice but have failed in finding peace. Eventually, the question is raised "so how is it done? How do you 'let go' of something?"

There are plenty of strategies but the one that has worked the best for me when necessary and is reported to be a successful option by many of my clients is the practice of holding your hands open flat when imagining that you are letting go (literally) of the thing that you wish to disappear. I must admit to the absence of any scientific evidence validating the efficacy of this gesture and yet I know enough about the way our minds organize rational thinking to believe that it simply makes sense.

In a closed position, our hands can 'hold' something. In an open position, they can not. Our brains just don't make the correlation of 'holding on' if we imagine it in our open flat hands. One caveat… letting go is not a one and done thing. The trick is to open your hands every time a thought / feeling you are attempting to diminish, presents itself.

Thought arrives > vocalize "let go" while opening hands.

As often as that thought shows up. Try it and let me know how you do!

Just open your hands and 'let it go'.

#6 Sticky notes

Use them everywhere! Students know this of course, and perhaps it was during my time as a graduate pupil that I discovered the absolute value of having a little piece of paper that would stay wherever I wanted it to be. Of course, it was great for books – I used them as bookmarks for important points, to keep track of research, and to denote piles of reference materials.

A short note on the door to remember my keys, phone, purse, lunch, yada, yada... the usual.

And then I discovered that I could use them to remind me of ALL The things I wanted to remember or more importantly... learn.

When I wanted to be more kind to myself the sticky notes would be little notes of inspiration; "you've got this", "do your best today", and "don't worry about it".

If I was trying to turn my inner voice into more positive and encouraging self-talk, the notes would say "Just do it!", "Your best is good enough", and "Keep going".

If I was working on a new mantra it would be posted over and over.... "trust", "be still", or "let go".

There wasn't just one sticky note. No... it was wallpaper. It was a whole pad of sticky notes displayed one after another in the places that I was most likely to see them several times throughout the day.

Over the kitchen sink.

On the wall in front of the toilet.

Near and ON my computer monitor.

The drawers in my closet.

The lampshade next to my bed.

Duplicates and bold colors to grab my attention.

Learning something new – retraining the mind takes repetition and time. I used sticky notes like hands free index cards and just glanced at them over and over until my brain automatically saw it without looking and I knew it was solidly there.

It's a technique I talk about often and I know many clients use it successfully... it's pretty basic but it works.

Sticky notes.

#7 Just do it

This is one of those little pieces of advice that I must remind myself repeatedly. It's something I know to do and yet I am resistant much of the time for a variety of reasons. It has been the Nike slogan for thirty years now and we still see it subliminally on television and in print media. Additionally, it's been the focus of a sticky note in my home through the years more often than not.

The inner voice I hear that says "just do it" isn't from a Nike commercial. It is a gentle and mostly loving – sometimes frustrated, innate reminder to move forward. It's the message I give myself when I feel hesitation; when I know I am resisting.

The vocal persuasion of "just do it" when it comes from an inner, strong voice is significant. It's more powerful coming from the self than from anywhere else if it is supportive and encouraging. As a dominant phrase in individual self-talk it can be a motivating reminder to stretch beyond your comfort zone, to try one more time, or to finish.

The next time you find yourself hesitating in a task, a creative effort, or an uncomfortable introspection be self-encouraging.

Just do it.

#8 Sing

As children, we sing songs to learn things and to just have fun. We sing with carefree voices regardless of our tone. We celebrate our birthday, our school loyalty, and our patriotism through song. As we move into our teens and young adulthood, we tend to associate songs with events such as first dates, key dances (prom), weddings, and fun times.

I recall singing along with favorite songs frequently in my lifetime, particularly when I was alone and happy. I never thought too hard about how good I sounded. I was just in the moment, enjoying the music, and expressing myself in unison with the beat; mostly.

When we sing, we literally send vibrations through our body and affect brain changes. Studies have repeatedly shown that people who sing experience less anxiety and have better quality of life. Think of the last time you saw someone in a car singing along to a song, perhaps alone and yet seeming to be in the process of intense enjoyment. Singing can produce higher levels of dopamine and oxytocin – both brain chemicals that are associated with happiness.

After a particularly challenging time in my life had started to settle, I spent a long weekend alone finishing a list of abandoned responsibilities that had been badgering my psyche. I turned on some calming music and set about the tasks at hand. Before long I realized that I was humming along to the familiar tunes and stopped for a minute because I realized it was the first time – in many years – that I found myself singing.

It was one of those things that you didn't notice was missing until you found it. It was a moment of realization that I recall because it was proof in my own mind that the changes I had just finished making were in part, survival for me. I was singing again.

I don't have a nightingale voice. Indeed, one of my vocal cords was paralyzed during Thyroid surgery a few years ago and since then, any ability I had to carry a tune has been impaired. Our brains don't care about tone – they care about the act of singing – the rise in happy chemicals. The point is to sing, with or without other people; with or without accompaniment; with or without the right lyrics...

Just sing.

#9 Keep a running list of to-do items

For years now, I've kept a running list of to-do items on my computer desktop. I keep it open so that it is easily accessible when I think of something to add. I add everything... even those things that are more wish list than to-do matters. When items are completed, they get deleted.

I acknowledge that this technique isn't necessarily advantageous to everyone. I often suggest it to clients as a method to be more organized and I see varying reactions. Perfectionists sometimes feel too anxious to leave something open and undone at the end of a day. People who think more concretely may react to the inclusion of 'wish list' items as too indefinite.

The benefits outweigh the objections in my opinion. I think we all have had moments when we can't remember what we wanted to do in reference to a particular project, or we've had the experience of doing one thing and then thinking we should have included another but forgot it had been a consideration.

I glance at my list when I head to Home Depot, the mall, or my local craft store... how many times have I returned from the home improvement store only to remember that I wanted to get spray paint for another project, a decorative knob, or a specialty light bulb? On a rainy Saturday afternoon, the list reminds me to look for a misplaced necklace, clean out the junk drawer, or fix the torn seam on my coat.

While I do sometimes use it for my day-to-day tasks, this running list is more about those obscure details that sit under our obvious awareness and, because they are not common in our thoughts, are easily forgotten.

Truth be told... some of the items on my list sit there so long they become obsolete. I had the intention of making a window seat cushion for years in my old house... it never got done. I have items like that on my list now. They are wish list pieces that keep me motivated and focused. They may or may not come to fruition, but the ideas sit there, and I don't stress about them. In fact – I appreciate that I have a forum to keep them in my consciousness. Try it!

Keep a running list of to-do items

#10 Jigsaw puzzle

I'm not quite sure why puzzles have such a bad rap. In my younger days we put puzzles together, mod podged them (wasn't that the original use for mod podge?), and use them as inexpensive wall art. After all, we spent all that time putting it together and it felt sinful to instantaneously break it back into pieces and box it up.

I guess that's one of the arguments against puzzles. Why bother if you are going to undo it? Furthermore, puzzles are like books for some - once you do it, there's no enjoyment in a repeat experience so it may feel rather futile all together.

I may argue however, that puzzles are a great tool in the pursuit of mindfulness. They encourage our attention and concentration unlike television or reading. They allow us to simultaneously converse and engage. They provide a common ground and, in some cases, allow for teamwork ("help me find this red piece").

Having a puzzle ready for assembly is a great tool for breaking habits. When it sits out and is available as a distraction tool, it can replace energy that might otherwise be directed toward a smoke or snack break. It's something that can be addressed five minutes at a time or in a five-hour stint without recourse. Indeed, it's a terrific - non-electronic - way to spend a rainy afternoon with a little Bon Jovi in the background and a glass of wine in the non-dominant hand.

I suggest the use of jigsaw puzzles to clients who are anxious as a means of helping them to slow down, focus, and learn to quiet. As one might imagine, this suggestion is frequently met with resistance and lots of objections. "I don't have time / space / patience..." - yada, yada. My rebuttal is a questioning rise of the eyebrows to challenge the rote response. There is not a legitimate objection (in my mind) as we all could benefit from giving up 30 min of television or Instagram time in favor of some mindful moments with a partner or child searching for the 'brown corner barn piece' or 'the inside of that pink flower'. Beginning your puzzle on a puzzle mat (a yoga mat works) so that it can be rolled up and tucked out of the way without disturbing your work typically nullifies the rest of the objections.

A simple way to increase your mindful activity, reduce anxiety, and increase family time is found in the pursuit of ... Jigsaw puzzles.

#11 Cry it out

On the long running television show Grey's Anatomy, the lead character Meredith has been known to "dance it out" with friends when full of intense emotion. That's great strategy but it's mostly great for fictional television.

Sometimes, in real life, we just must let the tears fall. We were born knowing how to emote. Babies laugh and cry when they have something to express and somewhere along the line, we are told to suck it up, dry up the tears, and pull up the bootstraps. We are taught to repress something natural and innate. I am not suggesting that we have a meltdown in the middle of a supermarket but taking the time to cry if we are sad, deeply disappointed, or full of other emotion in an appropriate environment can be a game changer.

Crying has its benefits. In fact, it is postulated that crying activates the parasympathetic nervous system which stimulates a relaxation effect. Crying may solicit attention from others, rallying our support system and generating a sense of belonging. Our bodies naturally release oxytocin and endorphins in emotional tears; chemicals found to relieve physical pain. Those same chemicals are known to promote better moods so the simple act of crying may indeed, lighten our mood.

Most of us who have had 'a good cry' with solid sobs would probably attest that even though it was exhausting, we felt better afterward. The energy (emotion is energy) that we feel when we are tempted to cry is best released. If we don't 'cry it out'… the energy remains in our system and may be redirected via anger, passive aggression, or a related negative expression. Perhaps worse, is the theory that proposes unexpressed emotions contribute to other major health concerns such as depression, anxiety, and even cancers.

It takes courage and strength to move against the cultural norm; to develop a productive coping mechanism; and to face down feelings. Allowing yourself to cry is an act of bravery. Tears don't have to be public to be productive so the next time you fill with emotion and get the urge to release it, remember to…

Cry it out.

#12 Laugh every day

Laughter really is the best medicine. The health benefits of laughter are well documented and the focus of legitimate scientific research.

A good belly laugh releases endorphins similar to crying that are known to promote healthy functioning. One study indicated that people identified to have a good sense of humor literally live longer. A sense of humor is defined as being able to see the funny side of things and to appreciate jokes or funny things. The people known to have a good sense of humor may burst into laughter over something as simple as a pun…

…What do you call cheese that's not yours?

… Nacho cheese!!

But one doesn't necessarily have to be a comedian to experience laughter in the ways that it becomes a benefit. We all can laugh; we just have to connect to the things that we find funny. Perhaps it's a television show (or their YouTube clips) such as America's Funniest Home Videos. Sometimes it the spontaneous moments of innocence and/or ignorance that we can all relate to that are the funniest. Or, perhaps it's the variety of programs that dupe us as in Candid Camera. Personally, those get me almost every time!! I laugh so hard that I cry. (I wonder if that means double the endorphins?)

Or for those of us who laugh at just pure cuteness of babies and/or animals, YouTube is full of compilations that will bust your sides with laughter. Technology makes it super easy for us to include laughter in our lives today. At any point, we have instant access to videos or a plethora of websites with jokes. We have memes and gifs in our streams on Facebook, Twitter, and Instagram. Laughter is only a swipe away at any time we want it.

The trick is to include it. Sign up to receive a Joke a Day with the LMAO app for iPhone or the LOL Jokes app for Androids. Instead of surfing Facebook – spend a few minutes on YouTube searching funny videos. Check out Reader's Digest collection of humor – some of the funniest written jokes I know of. Make it a habit!

Laugh every day!

#13 Friend time

This is one of those happy life tips that we innately 'know' and yet it is the one most frequently thrown on the back burner. As we build careers, family, and homes it seems that friendship moves steadily down to the bottom of our priority list.

I say... move it on up!

I postulate that the reason our friends stay our friends for so long is that we don't live with them 24/7. Unlike our life partners and children, our friendships get space. When we are frustrated with our friends, we go home. When we are disappointed, we let a few days go by before we call. If we aren't really on the same page- we take a break until the memory fades. And then, regardless of the pejorative infraction, we rally back together to enjoy the connection that is often impervious to the daily stressors we experience in our familial relationships.

Our friendships 'feed' us because they are often without expectation. They can be a 'resting ground' where we go to step back and gain perspective. Our friends are almost always a voice of reason while simultaneously having our back. Spending time with friends allow us to regenerate and realign our attitudes. They provide a platform for fun and laughter; for stillness and acceptance; for reflection and honesty. And spending time with them needs to be more important than weeding our garden or changing the sheets.

Best friends call us out on the shit we dish up for ourselves. We tend not to defend ourselves to them the way we may our spouse or partner. Because we don't question their love for us, we generate very different reactions by their challenges, and we take in more of what is said.

If your life is short on time (like it is for many of us), double duty some of your errands by asking a friend to tag along and have lunch or dinner along the way. Chores are more fun and often more productive when shared with a friend and laughter. Some of my favorite memories are those everyday tasks that were shared in friendship. One's ability to be a better parent, partner, and worker is elevated when friendship is also valued and incorporated into life.

Pick up the phone and schedule a little...

Friend time.

#14 Read fiction

I've included reading several times throughout this book but it's important to mix it up a little. At the core of this suggestion is the inclusion of 'trash' fiction; you know – the stories that may or may not be terribly well written but in a weird way, take you into another mental space free of any daily life stressors. The stories that whisk you away to a faraway island or planets in another galaxy.

It may be a national best seller or on an obscure list of sci-fi thrillers. It could be an epic trilogy based on real historical events or an unrealistic saga of Zombie rampage. No matter the genre, fiction has a way of whisking us onto a different plateau where reality is temporarily displaced, and our imagination can run amok.

A good story not only allows for us to step out of our lives momentarily, it helps us to foster empathy as we are transported into the perspective of a character who lives and thinks differently than us. Additionally, it creates a space where we can imagine ourselves interacting with a variety of circumstances and personalities; potentially improving our own relationships.

The brief disruption from stressors allow our mind and body a 'break' … a mental nap of sorts. It provides an opportunity for reset, which is proven to increase our overall sense of well-being. It quiets our mind by distracting us from our daily grind. Reading fiction before bed is indicated for people with insomnia. Reading fiction opens our mind to creativity by stimulating our imagination. It fosters our ability to produce mental images and it builds our vocabulary.

Dust off your library card, download Audible, and/or charge your Kindle and spend a little time with this one daily goal…

Read Fiction

#15 Explore

This tip is subject to individual interpretation. My favorite type of exploration involves an automobile and a map. Waking up on Sunday morning, packing a snack bag, and heading out to discover treasures on a road never before traveled.

It's a tradition started by my father and one that I've carried on to this day. I've found quaint villages, amazing diners, quiet spots, and captivating historical nuggets simply by traveling down a road that I've never investigated. It's true that as time goes by, I need to travel further out but the discoveries continue, and the pleasure of new information and charming revelations has yet to be exhausted.

Of course, exploration doesn't have to mean a car - it can be applied to people as in meeting new friends. It can be information as applied to learning something new. It can be an expedition through YouTube.com or a University library. Explore anything that is interesting to you. The point here is to motivate and enhance curiosity and interest so that life doesn't get stale.

All too often we fall into the trap of routine and favorites without adding intrigue anywhere in our life. Exploration protects against stagnation. Grab a friend or explore alone... step into that little shop you've been curious about or stop for desert in that restaurant you've wanted to try. Is there a park you've been meaning to walk through?

Don't wait until a moment of boredom overtakes a hot summer weekend. Make exploration a part of your journey in some form. Add this one word to your to do list today...

Explore

#16 Face the sun

This tip is specifically for those winter months or rainy grey days that may plague our mood or drain our sense of well-being. At those times - when the sun isn't shining or is only accessible for a short time - our exposure becomes limited. It is likewise restricted for those of us who work indoors 7 to 8 hours a day, regardless of the time of year.

Exposure to sunshine helps our body produce vitamin D. Healthy vitamin D levels are essential to feeling good and when the sun is stubbornly hibernating, supplements may be helpful. An additional benefit to absorbing sun rays is the recent discovery that they promote immune function. Furthermore, sunlight supports the production of serotonin, another chemical that induces feelings of happiness.

When the sun IS shining, a helpful trick is to sit as close to a window as possible - assuming it is too cold to be outdoors - and position your face (eyes closed) toward the rays. Sit there as long as possible so that your skin can absorb as much of the vitamins and energy as possible. If the weather is nice of course, go outside so that there isn't any barrier between you and the sun's rays. I'd be remiss if I didn't remind you to wear sunscreen for this exercise regardless of the time of year. For people with limited access to daytime sunshine due to working conditions, I often recommend that they eat lunch or take a break in their cars utilizing the same techniques. If making time to 'face' the sunshine is literally unfeasible for some reason, a sun lamp is a fair alternative.

It's important to note that people who are afflicted with Seasonal Affective Disorder (SAD) have probably been advised of these techniques and yet they are advantageous for all of us - all year long. For all of us, grabbing a little more Vitamin D and purposefully manufacturing natural serotonin is as easy as being sure to turn and...

Face the sun.

#17 Spread kindness

This 'life hack' is a no -brainer. It's as old as time with the essence of 'do unto others as they would do unto you...'".

We 'know' to do this; some call it chivalry - others call it good manners. But... how much attention do we really pay to distributing kindness - especially when people are neutral or worse, unkind to us?

Our lives are busy, and we are increasingly finding it difficult to pay attention to our individual family members, let alone complete strangers. And yet, the simple act of extending a kind gesture carries an impact that may extend far beyond either of the parties involved. This 'ripple effect' is mostly silent and unseen.

Suppose I take a grocery cart from an elderly gentleman in the parking lot and return it for him, smile brightly and wish him a good day...

I have no way of knowing how lonely he felt that morning and my comment lifted him. He goes to the bank and feeling lifted - comments to the bank teller about her beauty.

He had so way of knowing that earlier that day her drunk husband called her a pig and she was still reeling from the insult. Because her esteem was slightly lifted, she extended a courtesy to a customer and credited back a bank fee.

She had no way of knowing that the bank fee she was crediting made the difference that allowed that customer to afford extra groceries to make a dinner for a neighbor who was sick.

And on... and on... and on... it goes.

Performing acts of kindness on a regular basis has tremendous health benefits. It appears that extending kindness contributes to happiness, slows aging, improves heart function, improves our relationships and is reportedly - contagious.

And... it's mostly free! The only thing it takes to extend kindness is effort & attitude. If you have a few extra bucks it doesn't hurt to treat people now and then to random surprises but mostly... kindness is pure heart driven. Pick up a piece of litter, pick something up that has been dropped, open doors, smile, say kind things, let someone go first or jump in line, run an errand, cook a meal, clean a room, take in garbage cans, loan a book, etcetera, etcetera... it doesn't matter what the effort, just look around and... Spread kindness.

#18 Bake

Who doesn't love the smell of freshly baked cookies and/or bread rising in the oven? For some of us, it immediately evokes memories of mom or grandma's kitchen, holidays, and favorite recipes. As such, taking time to bake something can be a great way to induce calm, comfort, and security.

It turns out that the smell of baking bread specifically, may make people kinder by conjuring pleasant memories.

Don't know how to bake? Grab a cookbook or browse online and choose an easy recipe, something that makes your mouth water. It doesn't have to be complicated or fancy - even boxed brownies smell and taste amazing (add a few chocolate chips to the brownie batter for double chocolate delight).

Don't need the extra calories? Bake anyway and share with a neighbor, friend, or coworker. Imagine how popular you'll be at work if you show up every Monday with a plate full of tasty goodies. No one must know they are the result of your personal happiness regiment.

Next time you need a little pick me up or you just want to relish in great memories...

Bake.

#19 Declutter

Minimizing is a thing these days. From the tiny home craze to the amazing success of Marie Kondō's book, The Life-Changing Magic of Tidying up… we are beginning to connect to the concept of 'less'. Retirees are 'downsizing'; families are embracing a 'minimalist' lifestyle; and an entire industry has risen on the concept of 'decluttering'. After decades of acquiring, people are finding peace in the concept of 'letting go'.

Reducing clutter relieves anxiety. We simply feel better when things around us are in order. Indeed, less stress about our environment allows us to sleep better, particularly when the decluttering is in the room where we sleep. The benefits of decluttering include increased happiness… when we are happier, we are more productive and creative.

Years ago, when I had an estimate for house cleaning, the woman said she had to charge me more for all of the 'choochkies' she would have to dust. That's a fair disadvantage to collecting random baubles.

In order to successfully declutter we have to be conscious of what we truly need. How many junk drawers do we have to have - really? Take a good look around at all those knick-knacks you've been collecting in the pursuit of making the cover of Good Housekeeping and assess their importance. Are they things you'd grab in the event of a fire? Would you miss it if it was gone?

Start small. Clean out the drawers you rarely dive into. Try the back of the closet and thin out the clothes you didn't wear this year. Do the basement, the attic, and the garage. By the time you get through those spaces you will have more discernment and can attack the main living spaces.

Think of how much time you'll fee up when you don't have to dust/clean all those nooks and crannies after you…

Declutter.

#20 Educate yourself

The expectation of education is motivated from a very early age. In several cultures the idea of education includes post-secondary instruction without question and many of us are groomed to attend a trade school, Community college, or University before we are fully able to comprehend the extent of that commitment.

Our pursuit of knowledge is primarily vocation driven; we learn what we need to know in order to produce the income that sustains our lifestyle. Some of us expand our competencies in the pursuit of secondary incomes or hobbies. We amplify that expertise over time so that our proficiency is deeply rooted but perhaps not especially broad.

And yet in reality, the entire world is a classroom. Indeed, our very lives are a continuous curriculum of material offering educational content. Each failure, each joy, undeniably - each day - brings us information that we can attribute as educational and learn from if we choose.

Perhaps it is this education - this kind of learning - that proves to be the ultimate training. While acquiring 'data' or 'information' allows us to answer trivia questions and fix things around the house, I contest that it is far less meaningful than what we achieve if we 'learn' about ourselves and the world around us.

Yes, academic education has value and its continuous pursuit is desirable; do as much as you can regardless of your age or position. The public can utilize most college libraries for little to no cost; offering motivated learners unlimited opportunities and the internet can perhaps match that offering.

Self-knowledge is just as accessible with introspection, mindfulness, and reflection.

Read books on emotional development, emotional intelligence, communication, relationships, and spirituality. Be curious - about everything and stay open to new ideas. Take advantage of wisdom where you can find it; older relatives, friends, counselors, & clergy. Don't let teachable moments slip away unnoticed or unappreciated. Use them to...

Educate yourself

#21 Paint

Paint is relatively cheap - at least to other types of hobbies and/or decorating fixes. I'll talk about painting in three different arenas:

Paint as art - Painting, regardless of your ability level is good for your health and happiness. Just the act of holding a paintbrush can spur our creative juices, help us enter a state of flow, and promote feelings of happiness. Many of us might agree that the subjective nature of abstract art allows us to be true contenders on the international art scene with the simple act of throwing paint laden brushes of primary colors against a large blank canvas. Whether it is that technique or a purchased paint-by-number selection from the local craft supply center - painting an art piece will lend to lower stress levels and enhanced memory.

Paint furniture - have a piece of furniture that needs updating? If not, score a bargain at a local garage sale or flea market and then go ahead and give it a new coat of paint. You can be creative and paint something 'artsy' or go traditional and with the flow of your existing decor. It can be a big piece that you sand down to bare wood so that you have a fresh pallet or something that needs a little scraping, a bit more sanding, and then a fresh coat of a new color. Furniture can be painted to match almost any decor at all. From country chic to glossy sleek - the painting industry has your needs covered.

Paint your house - Maybe not the outside (but hey, if you're game - got for it), but give your inside a clean fresh look with a gallon or two of new paint. For less than $100, your entire family room can have a clean, crisp feel or your kitchen can be more modern. Painted kitchen cabinets are currently in fashion and while they certainly take patience and technique, the payoff is a whole new look for pennies in comparison to new cabinetry. Be brave with your paint selection - it's only color and it can be changed with a little effort if it turns out to be not-your-thing. Creating a space you feel good in can make a big difference in your attitude about being there. If home is where the heart is, then let your heart show there with colors that highlight you.

Don't be intimidated by paint - regardless of the modality you opt for - as the cost/benefit analysis is almost always positively slanted in its direction. Create a Pinterest board of ideas for inspiration and you'll be ready when the time comes for you to… Paint.

#22 Photographs

Many of the photos we take these days are digital and hence, stored on our mobile devices, in the cloud, or on a hard drive. Photos older than ten or so years are yet undeveloped, in a shoebox under a bed, or tucked into albums buried on the bottom of the bookshelf behind the sofa in the Den. If you're lucky, someone with much patience and creativity created an album of cherished shots with stamps, paper, stickers and jovial comments.

How often do you peruse these memories?

We take photographs to capture moments that are important to us - in that time. The photograph enables us to savor the experience; not only in the moment, but at any time that we revisit the photo. Research tells us that savoring increases psychological well-being.

Browsing old photographs of family and friends can remind us of people who were central to our youth, perhaps acting as a reference for our value system or center of strength. Remembering Grandma via a snapshot of Thanksgiving dinner might elicit memories of family and traditions; re-centering our concepts if or when we get sidetracked. Additionally, recalling times of love and belonging or times of pleasure and joy can be soothing and comforting.

As I go through old photos, I am reminded of all the amazing friends I've had along the way. I may not have kept up with them or know anything about their life currently but looking at the memories stimulates great gratitude for their presence in that time of my life. Those thoughts often evoke smiles and laughter which, motivates feelings of well-being.

At the center of this message is the direction to keep taking photos - but more importantly… look at them frequently. Take time to scroll through your phone or tablet when you need a little pick-me-up. If thoughts of missing someone arises… go with it. Honor the memory, honor the missing, and savor the experience that the photograph captured. Embrace your past and savor the memories in your…

Photographs.

#23 Fresh sheets

The mention of fresh sheets brings a sigh of 'ahhh' whenever it is considered. Memes suggesting fresh sheets and shaved legs are heavenly experiences float through social media with happy puppy faces and satisfying smiles. As I investigated people's thoughts about sheets, I found a variety of practices as it pertains to how frequently people do change their sheets. From "weekly, duh!" to "umm.... I really can't remember", it seems that only some of us have a hard-fast rule.

There are all kinds of reasons that we might consider a more regimented protocol for clean linens, but this post is not about hygiene. Perhaps the most compelling reason to change our sheets is the sense of comfort and pleasure that fresh sheets compel almost Every. Single. Time.

Have a rough day at work? Change your sheets before going to bed.

Feeling lonely? Change your sheets before going to bed.

Need to be your best tomorrow? Change your sheets before going to bed.

We are programmed to associate cleanliness with good health and/or a sign that things are 'right'. The act of going to bed in an environment that smells and feels clean, tricks our brain - if only momentarily - to believe that everything is in place - in order - and good to go.

To make the experience as good as it can be, I strongly recommend that we all have at least one set of amazing sheets. While the experts vary in their opinion of thread count, they all seem to agree that Egyptian cotton is by far, the best. As long as the thread count is at least 200 and European Egyptian, you will be sleeping on some of the most comfortable fabric in the world. An 800 count EE sheet is some of the most luxurious bedding to experience. It compels nudity for an entire sensate experience. Think about it tonight and treat yourself the experience of …

Fresh sheets.

#24 Turn should to could.

From the moment we become aware, rules guide us. We learn about standards, values, and expectations before we learn to talk. These elements become the list of 'should's in our life. I should make my bed; every morning; I should eat breakfast; I should finish my dinner; I should do my homework; I should be nice; Etc. These should's establish the base from which our life is guided and some of them are quite central to 'who' we are.

The problem with should's is that many of them fail to make sense outside of the environment in which they were originally established but we continue to hold on to them.

One of my favorite stories is of a woman who began preparing dinner one morning while her mother – who was visiting – sat in the kitchen to keep her company. The woman was readying a large roast for the crock pot. She cut a healthy slice from each end, threw them away and placed the roast in the pot. Her mother, looking wide-eyed questioned the action "why would you throw away perfectly good meat?" The woman, looking perplexed at the inquiry explained "that's what you always did...". With a stout laugh, the mother quickly responded, "but honey – that's because my pot was too small."

This story exemplifies the all-too-familiar behavior that many of us are affected by from day to day.

By the time we are adults in our own homes, raising children, working jobs, and trying to maintain our relationships – the list of 'should's' is longer than the day is long. We are striving to meet demands and expectations which have piled up through the years, without questioning their validity for this period of our lives, this day, or this hour.

Of course, we all have responsibilities and obligations that are important to us and we want to accomplish them. However, instead of commanding yourself to do something because you SHOULD.... First examine where it is coming from.

Are you taking down the curtains and washing them because it is important to YOU? Or is it something your mother did because she lived on a dirt road and the windows were open all spring?

Are you making a casserole for your sick neighbor after work today because that's what the other gals who are at-home moms did? Or because you want to help your friend?

Are you saying no to lunch with a friend because you 'should' stay home and get the laundry done?

Rephrase your 'should' to *'could'*.

I should do the laundry today instead of having lunch with my friend.

I COULD do the laundry today instead of having lunch with my friend.

When you rephrase the thought with *could...* does it have the same pull?

When you use the word *could* – your brain understands it as if you are *choosing* something rather than engaging in a behavior which is expected.

The psychological difference is dynamic. You've created *choice* in your life instead of an expectation that is not authentic to you just by ...

Turning should to could.

#25 Start a new tradition

It's great to honor old traditions, be it finding Easter eggs and baskets, going to Church and celebrating Christ's rise into Heaven; or drinking mimosas and eating lamb. Perhaps you dress up and spend the day with family. Maybe you have ditched all the standard traditions and wonder how to make this Christian holiday one that is meaningful to you.

It's a great day to start a new tradition. Focus on brunch instead of dinner. Make ham sandwiches and go on a picnic. Fill plastic eggs with treats and distribute them in a pediatric ward of your local hospital. Maybe it could be a day when you all 'unplug' from electronics and spend the day playing games with your family.

Regardless of whether you acknowledge the religious aspect of Easter, it's a great day to begin doing something meaningful - to add a new element, a different spin - on the day.

Traditionally, Christians celebrate the ascension of Christ into the Kingdom of Heaven. If Christianity is your thing - really celebrate! Throw a party. Do something in the spirit of Christ.

If you follow a path other than Christianity but find that most of the world is shut down and you have the day off... do something a little different. Celebrate your family, your faith, or your community. Begin a tradition of your own - one that takes advantage of your day off.

Start a new tradition.

#26 Spontaneous letter

Remember when we used to get 'real' mail? Think of how you feel when you get a card in the mail these days... it's so nice to pick something up from the mailbox that is sent from an actual human being and isn't asking for money, right?

Why not offer that feeling to someone you are thinking of and write a little note - or a long letter - and send it via snail mail? Really... even a short note that is handwritten for no reason other than to say "hello, I am thinking about you". Imagine how that gesture would brighten someone's day.

In particular, an older relative or friend who isn't as proficient with electronic communication. While I believe we all miss that personal touch a bit, it is the older generation who is most affected by our reduction of using paper mail. They know what they are missing! And... they haven't mastered the substituted forms of communication that connect the rest of us to the world.

It doesn't even have to be fancy to be impactful. Just grab a piece of paper... share a few kind thoughts... fold and slip into an envelope... address & stamp... and let the postal services do the rest of the work. For the price of a $.50 stamp (in the US at least), you're sure to brighten someone's day because for no particular reason you wrote a ...

Spontaneous letter.

#27 Change your routine

How often do you feel you're in a rut? Do you ever get the sense that life is just full of habits, routine, and rituals? Perhaps mostly unconscious? Has your daily routine become mundane?

You see, moving along in the rut of routine can impact our ability to notice life. It becomes so rote that we enter autopilot mode and tend to fall asleep at the wheel, so to speak. Remember that time when you arrived at your destination but noticed that you had no recollection of actually driving there? That's how easy it is for our brains to check out... to shift into unawareness.

What doesn't grow, will eventually die and so when you notice monotony settling into your day to day life it's important to be aware. It is then that some element of your routine needs to be rearranged. Perhaps you go for a walk after breakfast instead of before. Maybe you eat your largest meal around noon and lighten it up in the evening.

Either rearrange your perfunctory behaviors or add something significant. Beginning something new is effective especially when it is constructive to personal growth. Begin a gratitude journal or take a class; learn a new language or how to play an instrument.

Deleting habits that aren't productive can also be beneficial. If you habitually wake up, pour coffee, and light a smoke, try waking up - meditating (or praying) for 5 minutes - and shower before grabbing your coffee. Set the alarm 30 minutes earlier and take a walk, go to the gym after work, or make dinner from scratch. Making even these small changes to your daily activities can produce enough variety to kick you out of the doldrums. Getting out of that rut may be as simple a tweak...

Change your routine.

#28 Speak kindly to yourself

It's still a bit amazing to me when I become aware of how difficult it is for some people to engage in kind 'self-talk'. From little put downs such as "I know this is dumb but…" to looking in a mirror and thinking "you stupid idiot" in a loud critical internal voice, some of us engage in self talk that is demeaning, shaming, and downright hateful.

People who struggle to feel 'worth it' are the most frequent offenders and may simply be repeating condemning assertions that were absorbed over time from critical or abusive parents, bosses, or partners. Rarely, do I find that the statements represent truths, yet many of them do underline belief systems.

Entire industry segments of publishing and psychological research have built up around this problem from books such as Shad Helmstetter's What to Say When You Talk to Yourself to Dr. Kristin Neff's Self Compassion lab at the University of Texas at Austin. Both of which, are resources I use with clients who experience antagonistic inner critic aggression.

Self-awareness and self-compassion are essential components of splitting up with that judicial speaker. Each time you hear the criticism begin to drown out your more rational loving voice… put your hand over your heart and imagine that you are speaking to someone you love. Begin a supportive and compassionate conversation that is empathetic and loving - the way you talk to a friend who is having difficulty. Be intentional with this practice and you will foster the ability to more consistently…

Speak kindly to yourself.

#29 Smile

When was the last time you smiled without a reason? It turns out that the practice of smiling - randomly for no actual reason - increases happiness. The muscles stimulated by smiling triggers a release of dopamine, serotonin, and endorphins - the chemicals that, when activated, allow us to feel happy.

In a landmark study with college students, Kraft and Pressman (2012) validated that students who produced a smile were able to recover from stress more effectively than students who were instructed in the opposite. This concept has been further probed by leaders in the Positive Psychology field and substantiated. We know that the more people smile, the better they are to cope with stress and that they report higher in life satisfaction.

Especially interesting is that we don't have to smile spontaneously for this effect to be present! Indeed, just the act of smiling produces some affect.

The goal then, is to try to smile more often whether you feel like it or not. Smile in the car on your way to work. Smile in the shower or while you are dressing. Smile at strangers just for the heck of it (many of them will smile back - perhaps initiating the ripple effect). Smile for a full 60 seconds before you get out of bed in the morning and notice the difference.

I assign the task of smiling to The Elevate Class students and they report overwhelmingly how surprised they are when it really does make a difference. It's like a water-soluble vitamin though... it's only in your system for a day or so after you take it... you have to smile every day for the effect to be in place.

Experiment a little and for no particular purpose...

Smile.

#30 Play with puppies (or babies)

Playful puppies and happy babies are two of the most smile inducing things on the planet. The joy we experience by engaging with either is equivalent or better than Christmas morning for many.

While some of us know firsthand, the mental and physical health benefits of having a pet, others may not have the lifestyle or the ability to house an animal full time. And yet, the mere act of playing with a puppy brings a smile to even the most disgruntled canine averter; especially if none of the responsibility is imminent. There is an innocence and a joy that is exuded without effort from a young pup; one that is instantly absorbed into our hearts and perhaps reminiscent of our own youth.

Likewise, a content baby delivers a shot of happy with every coo and giggle. The delight broadcasted from a tiny human with no worries in the world reminds us of the purity of life... the time before the world tried to tell us who we needed to be, how we need to be it, and then disapprovingly - suggested that we may fail.

I'm not suggesting that we run out and adopt puppies or babies (although if you have the desire, time, and resources - by all means...) but it IS a suggestion to volunteer with either population in the capacity of a sitter, a helper, or rescue. If nothing else - hang out at PetSmart for an hour with the intention of petting a puppy or two. The next time you find you are having a bad day or if you need a little pick-me-up, find some space that allows you to ...

Play with puppies (or babies).

#31 Take a class

What do you want to learn? Is there a hobby or a language that you've coveted an interest in? Is there a craft or a skill that you'd like to develop?

From JoAnn Fabrics to Home Depot; from community colleges to community centers; learning opportunities abound. Perhaps you've wanted a new wreath for your front door or a fresh tile backsplash in the kitchen... you can learn to do that. Maybe you've wanted to learn American Sign Language (ASL) or the history of the Vatican... you can learn that too!

Some travel organizations such as Road Scholars offer combined adventure and education in their group itineraries. Or, you could teach English and travel through organizations such as TEFL. That's a little more involved than taking a class but it most certainly offers an amazing 'learning' opportunity.

At the very least, taking a cycling class at your local YMCA or an intermediate yoga class at your resident studio is forward progress; if we aren't growing - we will die - just like every other living organism on this planet. Always seek to find momentum in the advancement of your knowledge ...

Take a class.

#32 Make love (slow and deliberate)

What's better than an hour of slow, deliberate, sexual, intimate time with someone you care deeply for? In this day and age of fitting in work, kids, activities, house stuff, and relationships… the time we allow for connecting intimately is significantly reduced. The time an average couple spends engaged in the act of 'sex' ranges from 5.4 minutes to 19.2 minutes and that probably does not include the 'quickies' that exist in some relationships.

Let's face it… wake up sex is generally a good way to start the day but it's typically not romantic, soft, & slow. We tend to get right to the tasks at hand. Copulations that take place at bedtime during work weeks are also typically somewhat perfunctory; meeting the most basic of needs. Can you remember the last time you took an hour or more to savor the experience of sensual pleasure with your partner?

Research indicates that having sex once a week with a caring partner will increase happiness. Imagine the happy boost if that once-a-week interaction is fully engaging and completely satisfying. Imagine if you were to make time for titillating foreplay and afterglow snuggling on a regular basis. Can you fathom the cohesion that develops between you and your partner?

Take the initiative and the time to engage with your mate the way that you did in the beginning of your relationship. Get to know one another again in an intimate way… double check assumptions about pleasures and preferences; introduce something sexy and new. Demonstrate your affection, desire, and dedication by…

Making love (slow & deliberate).

#33 People watching

Whether we are in an airport, on a train, standing in line, or sitting on a park bench... we are likely to be watching the people surrounding us. Sometimes we are absentmindedly observing, not paying any attention. Sometimes we are sitting there unwittingly passing judgements. Sometimes we are trying to ascertain the life story of an individual, couple, or family in our sightline; curious to know if our observations have any merit.

People watching can help you develop mindfulness habits; tuning into the acute details of your environment. People stop being random subjects in our space and we begin to notice their humanity. When we pay close attention, we can discern worry, joy, hesitation, and humor in people's facial expressions and body language. An astute observer can decipher how an individual identifies (by the way they dress, condition of fingernails, jewelry, makeup, hairstyle & color, etc.), their self-esteem (do they stand tall with confidence or crouch small with insecurity?), their emotional state, their level of 'niceness' (do they smile back or hold the door open?), and perhaps even their level of extrovertness.

The big caveat of course, is that what we see isn't always what it *is*. Some people are experts at hiding their truest feelings. Some people walk through life 'faking it until they make it'. Some people have developed defensive personas for their public engagements. While we can't know 'for certain' without checking our assumptions, we can hone our perception skills by taking the time to pay attention to details when we are passing time in public and ...

People watching.

#34 Start a group

Groups of likeminded people are fun, powerful, & meaningful. We are happier humans when we are connecting to people who share similar interests be it literature, games, athletics, or any particular interest. As we mature and change, our interests may also evolve; effectively diverging us from the interests of our existing social circle. While we don't have to completely disengage from those established connections, it is important to engage new ones where our shifted ideologies can be supported and grown.

The internet makes this especially easy with online groups that connect people in almost any stake one may imagine. If personal interaction is more desired, the internet again can introduce us via sites such as Meetup.com where people with a variety of interests can connect in their locale.

Groups allow us to experience connectivity. We problem solve, when necessary, when we have the ability to draw from different perspectives. Group membership grows our tolerance and acceptance attributes. We learn how to receive and open our opportunities to give when we belong to a group.

Instead of sitting at home feeling lonely and isolated, anyone with a computer and the ability to type can begin a group to share their aspirations with kindred spirits. No matter the topic - one thing for sure is that we are not alone. We just may not have been introduced to another person who shares our taste for adventure or fun. This issue is easily rectified, and fun awaits just as soon as you...

Start a group.

#35 Write your story

If your life ended today, would people really have known you? Is there a truth you want told? Is there a perspective you've wished to share? What are the messages and ideas that you'd like to have be a permanent part of your story?

Writing your story is not only a great way for future generations to know you but it is a good way for you to put your life into perspective - to see it as a whole; a living, flowing creation.

The most important element derived from writing your story is that it most likely will demonstrate great resilience. Most of us have endured pain, heartache, disappointment, despair, and fear. By describing those times in conjunction with the resolution and emergence into something different, we can see the entirety of the cycle instead of staying focused on the more noxious elements.

Your story gives your life a living voice, one that others may connect to, and one with which others may resonate. It may offer hope to others experiencing similar adverse events; showing them how to move toward the other side.

Writing your story allows your voice to be articulated; to have shape. It demonstrates your side, your perspective, your focus; delivering context that has only been available from your view. It allows you to see the connectedness of events, time, and learning in a way that is only available in retrospect.

It may help you to reaffirm your values. Often when we see our lives from a deep, rich, linear perspective, it validates our choices; affirms our position; cements our belief system. It helps provide clarity of the things we declare as important in our life.

Ultimately, writing your story has the potential to provide a great sense of peace that where you are now is the result of a winding road and regardless of the bumps... it led here. Even if 'here' isn't where you want to be, you'll likely notice that this isn't the first difficult challenge you've faced, and you've demonstrated the resources in the past to move through. You may find new energy to persevere.

No time like the present for you to put pen to paper or fingers to keyboard as you begin to...

Write your story.

44

#36 Befriend someone

Do you know someone who doesn't have a big social circle? Do you know an older person who is lonely or actually… alone? Are you aware of someone who recently experienced a traumatic loss? Is there someone in your environment, at work or at church, who appears to be alone more often than not?

Are you able to share a piece of yourself? Do you have an hour a week to make a difference in someone's life? Perhaps they could use a friend.

While carving out an hour from your week may seem cumbersome or downright impossible, imagine bringing a summer of sunshine to someone else's grey cloudy life. Imagine that someone chooses to live - makes the decision to stay alive - because you take an hour from your week to share kind thoughts and a little light. Imagine that someone counts the hours that pass by until your presence graces their path again next week.

Maybe it's a kid who doesn't have anything to go home to… or a widower who is tired of eating alone night after night. Your kind gesture to behave in a friendly manner to this person who may feel isolated and alone could mean the difference between a life of loneliness and a life of hope.

Be mindful of the people in your periphery. Pay close attention and then offer your friendship. It's free to give and relatively cheap to maintain. The benefit is amazingly immeasurable when we take the time to…

Befriend someone.

#37 Acceptance

My mother used to say, "It is what it is." She said it so much that it became rather like fingernails running down a long chalkboard when I heard it. Almost simultaneously, she would quietly recite the Serenity prayer, "God grant me the serenity to accept the things I cannot change, courage to change the things I can, and the wisdom to know the difference." Each time I heard either phrase, I imagined her throwing her hands in the air as if she was surrendering and it infuriated me because I wanted to have more control than that.

For anyone with 'control' issues - accepting our inability to create the reality we want to have is challenging. It is imperative therefore, to learn acceptance. It took me decades to realize that courage and determination were instrumental in learning how to 'accept' that I am powerless to change some things; other people for example.

Some of us spend way too much time thinking about how the world or people in it 'should' be or what 'could' have been done and far too little time seeing things as they *are* so that we can make a difference where it is possible.

If I have a yard sale planned and it is raining - *any* time I spend lamenting about the rain and its effect on my plans is a *waste* of *energy*. I can be disappointed for sure but anything outside of that is non-acceptance. If I've made a mistake and feel embarrassed or ashamed, moving forward from it requires acceptance - not avoidance of what is.

And... in order to change anything we have the power to change - we must see it clearly *as it is* - not worse or better than it is - in order to change it accurately and reliably. If we want to turn sadness into something different, we must stop resisting the sadness and accept its presence. The first step to anything is quite simply...

Acceptance.

#38 Embrace difference

Like acceptance, embracing differences is a specific contributor to feeling better about yourself and about the world in general. Embracing differences requires us to step out of our comfort zones, to 'accept' that our worldview is only one perspective.

We know this intellectually of course. We 'know' that there are 'different strokes for different folks' and yet we often struggle with the reality that the way I think or what I think is vastly different than someone else.

The solution, or the strategy for embracing differences is directly correlated to the concept of 'right' and 'wrong'. If we simply let go of the notion that what I think is 'right' - by definition, making the other 'wrong' - then we can see other forms of thought as merely different. The struggle comes with our belief that I may not be 'good enough' if I am not 'right'.

In reality, there are perhaps dozens of 'right' viewpoints - all contextually unique. Consider the act of burping. The act of belching loudly while sitting around a dinner table would be regarded as quite rude in most of North American households, particularly if you were a guest or at a business function. However, in India - it is a demonstration of having enjoyed a good meal.

Instead of thinking of someone or something as being right or wrong as a general principle, explore the idea that it is simply different. This uncomplicated distinction eliminates a lot of judgment and unnecessary degradation. Over time, even the most extraordinary variations of our personal likes and dislikes can be appreciated as we...

Embrace differences.

#39 Try Za'atar

I mean… we all have to eat - so why not make eating adventurous and tasty all at the same time? While some of my readers may already know and love za'atar - I'm rather new to this lovely concoction and I thought it necessary to encourage ya'll to try it.

Za'atar is a blend of spices with a middle eastern origin, popular throughout the Mediterranean. As a spice blend, it is a mixture of dried thyme, oregano, marjoram, toasted sesame seed, salt, and sumac - some or all in various percentages depending on which part of that region you come from. In fact, families often had their own recipes and handed them down through generations; keeping it a secret. I didn't have any trouble finding a recipe for it on the internet and a bottle was quickly found in the Mediterranean section of my local specialty grocer.

It's often served with olive oil and pita, which is the middle eastern equivalent of garlic and spice with hot Italian rolls - really anything that you can dip in flavorful olive oil has me sitting quickly down at the table. My ah-ha yum-yum moment came with za'atar smothered all over a roasted chicken. Just thinking about it now - my mouth is watering.

I would be ever-so-happy to hear of your special recipe or standard inclusions for this lovely new addition to my flavor cabinet; or even a quick story of how and when you decided to…

Try Za'atar

#40 Let someone else be right

Or, I could say... let go of trying to prove your point. I know for some people - this will be a big challenge. You know - our ego simply gets in the way at times. Ok, maybe more than 'at times'... and it's necessary to realize that's all it is - an ego.

I'm not sure the proportion, but a HUGE percentage of arguments escalate simply because someone is determined to be - right. We need to win. When both (or all) parties in the conversation determine that 'they' must prevail, it is likely that someone will eventually be verbally beaten into submission; ending the exchange with feelings of defeat and a sense of failure because they were unsuccessful proving their position.

I ask ... "why?"

If we have the knowledge, or perhaps proof to substantiate our point... why must we shove it down the proverbial throat of those who don't know? Or, perhaps have a valid - but different - perspective? Why is it so necessary to demonstrate the lack of knowledge in someone we converse with?

If it is not life changing, a national security issue, or harming anyone - why not just ... let it go? How many ego wins does one person need to feel big or secure? If necessary... Google it and quietly validate the question/answer for yourself but keep it close... allowing someone else to believe what they believe; assuming it doesn't overstep the above referenced boundaries.

I wonder how many challenges you'll save yourself from if you were to ...

Let someone else be right.

#41 Try yoga

Unless you've been under a rock or tucked away in a cave for the last several decades, you've heard - ad nauseum probably - about the benefits of practicing yoga. Kudos if you practice a form of yoga on a regular basis... pass this post along to someone you know who doesn't and come back tomorrow. If you have wanted to or have been confused about it - read on.

Yoga is one of those things that you have to try a few different times to find the kind you like, the teacher you prefer, and the environment that is conducive to something you want to do regularly. How do you choose between the 11 different types? Try 'em all and keep doing the one you like the best. Here are a few of the most popular and easy to find...

Hatha yoga - generally refers to any yoga practice based on the practice of physical movement. It's generally where people start.

Iyengar yoga - Here the focus is on alignment and precision. A teacher is a necessity for this type of yoga because the workout is in the precise pose with controlled breath.

Kundalini yoga - combines spirituality with your workout. It's fast paced and may include meditation.

Vinyasa yoga - Known as the most athletic form of yoga, movement is deeply coordinated with breath and movement is designed to flow from one pose into another.

Bikram yoga - If you like to sweat, this 'hot' yoga may be for you. There are 26 poses, performed sequentially in a room that is 105 degrees with low humidity.

I've never known someone sorry they took a yoga class. It's a generally affordable way to get in shape, relax, manage breath, strengthen cardio, and improve flexibility. Once you've learned the poses and develop good form, participating in a yoga class is as easy as opening a YouTube page or tuning your TV one of the many channels offering a selection of classes.

Why not take the time to treat your body and your spirit to one of the world's oldest and most helpful forms of exercise...

Try yoga.

#42 Host a party

When was the last time you entertained for no particular reason?? We celebrate birthdays and anniversaries, promotions and retirements, and weddings and babies. We come together for Tupperware, candles, baskets, kitchen knives, bakeware, leggings, and lingerie but when was the last time you had a party for no reason other than you wanted to party with a few of your friends?

We don't 'need' a reason to celebrate friendship or to get to know acquaintances better. It's as easy as setting a time and date; run the vacuum and swipe a dust rag (if you must); and pick out a great playlist. It can a BYO beverage, chip, app, chair, etc., or whatever you want it to be. It can be themed (think s'mores and a backyard fire), adults only, or a girl's night out. I'm sure some of us can even make it totally impromptu - making a same day invitation.

Parties - or lessor defined 'gatherings - can remind us that we belong; that we have a tribe, that people care. They can offer a needed diversion from stress, an opportunity to relax and unwind, and the potential for humor and camaraderie. If formality is more your thing... send invites, polish the silver, and pull out your most elaborate serving dishes.

Either way, the value is in assembling your peeps, winding down, and engaging in the social interactions that are deeply rooted in our humanity when you...

Host a party.

#43 Write a poem

Poems stand alone in a variety of forms and sometimes, they are set to music and become song. They rhyme or not... they are rhythmic or not... they are short or not. They cite heartache, fear, joy, and hope. They are stories and parables.

How would a poem about you begin? What about a poem of your life? Would it be silly and childish like those of Shel Silverstein? Would it be inspiring like Maya Angelou? Would it be tragic or hilarious?

Poetry can be as simple as a collection of your visions and/or inner thoughts, strung together with or without subjects and verbs or punctuation and grammar.

Photograph
I see it there, moving
Me
Reflecting time, gone now-
You
Captured e-lec-tricity,
Us
Colored memory.
Ghost

Or they can be more vividly representative...

The ONE
The day you left me long ago
The angels came to say
They would take you home to rest
You wouldn't be far away.

I listened to their wisdom
I tried to let it be
And I was looking for the day
When they returned for me.

The days and nights are lonely
Now that we're apart
But I have always saved for you
A piece of my heart.

The rest has gone to one so small
You hardly knew
He's the apple of my eye
He has the best of you.

We will live without you now
And try to go on
But rest assured my dear sweet love
You'll always be my ONE.

A poem is *your* heart... *your* voice... and may promote freedom of expression and emotions where they might otherwise not work. You can use metaphors or describe literally... grab a notebook or open a document and give it a try...

Write a poem.

#44 Fix something

As you look around your house, do you see something that needs fixed? Are you frustrated that it doesn't work? Is it more of a hassle to think about fixing it than the actual 'doing' of fixing it?

A few years ago, I got tired of not being able to drain my bathroom sink - the sink stopper had broken months before and it was that kind of thing that you completely forgot about until you need it. I opened YouTube.com and searched 'fix broken sink stopper' - which is actually called a 'Pop-up Drain Assembly' and found a dozen explanations - with videos - on how to repair it. After a quick trip to Home Depot for the part - it literally took 5 minutes!! I must have complained about it being broken for more than 5 months and it was a really super easy and quick fix.

My neighbor fixed her leaky toilet 'innards' in a similar manner without any significant effort. It seems that almost anything you need fixing has a tutorial available online. It may take rewinding and repeating a few times as we 'catch on' but technology makes that super simple and no matter what you want to repair… there's a video to guide you through.

The sense of satisfaction that comes from fixing something yourself runs deep. Becoming your own handyman for those little things that are more nuisance than not is empowering - especially for us women who are sometimes less exposed to 'repair' experience than our brothers. Certainly - sexism in NOT intended here - only demonstration of typical norms; which, are definitely changing as years go by. Thanks perhaps to those videos that offer teaching moments for those of us who didn't get it by way of life. The point is - regardless of gender or experience, YouTube offers a tutorial so that you can …

Fix something.

#45 Build something

If fixing something offers a sense of accomplishment, then building something magnifies that tenfold. Starting from scratch is satisfying in so many arenas and construction is no exception. I'm not suggesting that you get all motivated and decide to build yourself a house - you may want to try something basic like a birdhouse - to make sure that something you build is inhabitable. Frankly, even birds wouldn't nest in the first birdhouse I attempted; but it looked cute and rustic in my flower garden.

I was fortunate enough to have a dad that could fix almost anything and allowed me to get comfortable with a hammer at a young age. My little brother was so good, he took out part of a wall with nothing more than a Fisher Price plastic one. It caused Dad to be more discerning about what he was teaching us!

As a joke, I received a tool belt one Christmas because I was apt to place a nail with my shoe or a stapler; whatever hard object was close at hand. It worked - but no doubt, jobs are easier when you have the proper tools. A tool belt kept everything I needed reasonably handy.

My first big project was a wall of built in bookcases. I wasn't overly anal about how square they were but at least I made sure they were level! A talented carpenter I know once told me that "a little caulk and a little paint - make a carpenter what he ain't" - so I knew that the imperfections of those shelves would be hidden away; mostly.

Each time I sat in that room I could hear a faint rendition of Helen Reddy's "I am woman, hear me Roar" and smiled a grin of pure satisfaction. I built something I wanted, and it looked and performed the way I hoped it would. I haven't been as successful with other projects, but more than anything I have the sense of accomplishment that came from trying.

What would you build if you were to …

Build something?

#46 Stand up straight

At the risk of sounding like your mother, I think we can all use the reminder to 'stand up straight'. The number of Americans who complain about back pain at some point in their life has crested over 80% and it is suggested that poor posture is to blame for a significant percentage. Since we've transitioned to desk jobs and electronic browsing - our shoulders curve and our heads are bent - throwing the natural alignment of our spines out of whack.

Bad posture is the culprit for more than back pain. There is evidence that it promotes Asthma (restricted breathing), heart disease, joint degeneration, and higher levels of stress. It is a leading cause of missed work and worldwide - back pain is the leading cause of disability. Improving posture strengthens the musculature surrounding the spine, keeping aligned properly.

I am particularly mindful of my own posture when I see a television news anchor or an interviewer sitting in perfect alignment (how long so they practice that so that it appears naturally?) It's a reminder for me to square my shoulders and pull in my abdomen while simultaneously raising my chin Aligning myself perpendicular to the floor.

There are a number of products marketed to help you remember and/or strengthen the back muscles but in a recent review, the writer declared that they were mostly annoying and that the only significant solution was to pay attention and practice. Essentially - include it in your mindfulness regiment. It's a little thing that can make a world of difference. Remember...

Sit up straight.

#47 Find a great hairdresser

How many times have you seen a photograph of yourself and lamented about your hair? How many days do you glance in the mirror and feel a slight sinking feeling because your hair just isn't how or where you want it to be? Have you ever browsed a series of photos, realizing that you've had the 'same look' for waaay too long?

Hair is an important part of our overall appearance - unless of course you have none. One look at a photo of DT boarding Air Force One on a windy day is all we need to understand the significance of good hair. A good cut, good color, and the appropriate style for the shape of our face can make a great difference in how we perceive ourselves - and apparently… how others perceive us.

Using those parameters for good hair will typically involve a good - no… great, hair stylist. Unfortunately - finding one often means visiting several and experimenting a bit. But… it's just hair and anything that happens to it (outside of catastrophe) will 'grow out', be it length, layers, or colors; so be brave!

I was often directed to books of styles and asked to choose one - my stylist would then accommodate my request by cutting, curling, or coloring my hair to match the picture I provided. The one MAJOR problem with this method is that my face never matched the photo. Had I cut a few of those styles out and tried to visualize them on my face, on my body - I might have saved months of regrowth time and hundreds, if not thousands of dollars - over time. Today at least, we can use Photoshop to try this method of style selection, or…

We could let the professional use their best judgment after they consider our hair texture, patterns, and face shape; not to mention the amount of time/money/energy it may take to sustain the style! Finding a great hairstylist may take time and money. The dude I've been using for 13 years now is *not* cheap and from time to time I have allowed other people to cut - thinking they could just follow 'his' lines - but no! It's never the same and I finally conceded that I'd rather drink less Starbucks and have him do the cutting. The tradeoff is totally worth it! Some things in life are just priceless so do yourself a favor and …

Find a great hairdresser.

#48 Get a pedicure

From the top of your head to the tip of your toes, life is better when things are put together. No, that's not really the kind of poetry I referenced a few days ago. I'm talking about making your toes - and your heels - pretty. Even the funkiest feet are prettier with clean, trimmed nails and soft, smooth heels. This includes - YOU, gentlemen.

Admittedly, I was well into adulthood before I had my first pedicure but quickly understood it was such a simple pleasure that I added $25 to my monthly budget from anywhere I could in order to treat myself. I love to go barefoot and so - no visual needed - my feet were in constant need of TLC and I was slow to respond personally. The fact that there are people in the world willing to take on that task blows my mind but I try never to look a gift-horse in the mouth (sorry - for all my non-American or much younger readers, I'm not sure of a good substitute for that idiom). I graciously accept the loving care that anyone is willing to commit to my feet.

Our feet are important! They carry us where we want to go. They hold us in position. They are abused, squished, tormented, and only sometimes - temperature regulated. They deserve any extra attention they can get!! Additionally, when 'professionals' are regularly assessing a body part, they are more apt to discover early warning signs of potential problems (i.e., bunions, corns, fungus). Pedicures most often include a brief foot massage - improving circulation. And, if absolutely nothing else - taking 30 min. - give or take - out of your daily routine to completely relax has its own specific health benefits.

Of course, there are some people who don't want their feet touched... I simply cannot understand denying yourself that pleasure as it can be almost orgasmic with the right massage - but o.k., I respect that a few will protest this suggestion. Winter, spring, summer, and fall... once a month just because ...

Get a pedicure.

#49 Splurge on an outfit

If you're on a tight budget, a mom, a dad, tightly focused on the future, or following a similar trajectory, there is a good chance that you fail to treat yourself once in a while. And, while I am the champion of practicality and budget focused financial achievement, there is a time that splurging on an outfit that helps you feel strong, beautiful (or handsome), and confident - is totally warranted.

Do it for your next job interview, or the next wedding you attend. Imagine the sensation of standing a little straighter or smiling a little brighter because you feel empowered by attire that is flattering, well-constructed, and in fashion.

It doesn't matter your budget. At one time, buying a pair of sandals that weren't rubber was an upgrade for me and I felt confident in my stride. I splurged on a classic black dress by a well-known designer at another point in my life and it was my 'uniform' whenever I had a cocktail event to attend for years (It's still a classic and dresses up or down with jewelry accessories).

While classic purchases are the more practical consideration, an occasional splurge on something you may never wear again can be an uplifting accomplice for a very special occasion. When I finally earned my B.A. in midlife, I treated myself to a bright red patent leather belt and matching shoes. They were the perfect complement to my black and white outfit and I just never had another occasion to for that combination. The accessory combination was more pricey than that designer dress I've worn dozens of times but my confidence that day was out the door and the belt was the icing on the cake.

This is not to say that what we wear is how we construct our personality or the basis of our identity but psychologically speaking, what we wear affects our mood. When we wear quality clothing that fits well, we feel better so treat yourself and …

Splurge on an outfit.

#50 Make dinner for your neighbor

What a special treat it is to come home in the evening and not have to worry about making a meal! Demonstrate a gesture of kindness by doubling a recipe tonight and taking the extra to a neighbor so they won't have to cook tomorrow!

We are generally good about supporting the dining needs of our friends and neighbors when they are sick, have a baby, or a death in the family but why not... just because? Not that I think we should be feeding the whole block or that our next-door friends can't take care of themselves but why not treat them to something completely unexpected?

For practically no extra effort and very little expense, duplicating a pan of baked ziti or an oven roasted chicken might just make the day for a family with very little time or a single dad exhausted after a long workday.

If your neighbor is single or elderly, invite them over to share the meal or offer to stay and provide company while they eat what you delivered. Food is often a neutralizer of gender, age, and differences. It can open people's hearts and consequently, their minds to new experiences, ideas, and conversation. If nothing else, it is an extension of generosity that might just also make or fortify a meaningful, connection. Give it a try. The next time you're making a crock pot or casserole type meal, double the recipe and ...

Make dinner for your neighbor.

#51 Try new recipes

At the age of 12, I found myself responsible for making dinner for my family several times a week. My recipe collection was limited to the three things that I recalled my mother making... Tuna Noodle Casserole, Meatloaf, and Spaghetti with meat sauce. That's it. Sadly, those meals went into a rotation that seemed endless. So much so, that my siblings still resist anything resembling those entrees.

When my children were small, getting them to eat was a challenge sometimes and so I leaned into the pattern of making the dinners I knew wouldn't be met with opposition. They were mostly uninventive, predictable, mundane, and bland. Eating wasn't much fun for the adults in the house.

Until I made an effort to try new recipes.

I'm not talking about exorbitant delicacies from Bon Appetit, but those from Rachel Ray or Ina Garten; maybe even a really simple - follow the picture - recipe from Tasty that proliferates our Facebook and Instagram feeds.

A great way to explore new recipes and flavor combinations is to use a meal delivery service such as Blue Apron, Hello Fresh, Plated or the half dozen others that are now in the market. We've tried several and what they share is variety from the meals I've cooked for decades now. Using a meal service has allowed us to regenerate an interest in cooking again. We've been introduced to foods like Israeli Couscous and Lemon Risotto; using olive oil and lemon zest more than ever before.

The meal service allows you to try different recipes without committing to an entire package of something as they send only enough for that particular meal. If you find that lamb with mint jelly isn't your thing then at least you won't be throwing away an entire jar of it.

We challenged ourselves to introduce a new recipe into our evening routine at least once a week when we weren't using a meal service and the intrigue continued, anticipating the preparation and new flavor combos. Who knew that stimulating our dinner routine was as easy as ...

Trying new recipes.

#52 Deep clean something

Some of you may already do this on a regular basis and it may contribute significantly to your level of happiness and/or good living. I do not. And yet, it IS something that ends in total satisfaction and sense of accomplishment.

I have a friend who deep cleans a room in her house each month. For years, she has committed to moving through a room - top to bottom & inside, out - re-identifying the need for and usefulness of everything it contains. With an eleven-room home, she gives herself the holidays off and then starts from the beginning - giving each room another do over. Organized drawers, filed papers, freshly caulked and painted woodwork, windows, light fixtures, etc. - once a year.

Oddly enough, one of my comforting childhood memories is coming home from school and finding my mother embedded in this process. The house smelled clean, the tidiness felt safe, and I knew she was taking pride in our home - providing an environment where we could flourish.

Personally, I've developed a comfort level with dust bunnies that may not be entirely healthy. I'm honest enough to say that I have yet to master this seemingly simple system, but I strive to make it happen and can at least attest that the gratification of having accomplished one entire room has been amazing!

Some people I've known only deep clean when they move from place to place, others do a Spring cleaning annually, and my good friend found solace in creating a deep clean rotation. No matter the specific procedure or the direct timing, it always feels good once you've...

Deep clean something.

#53 Explore

Exploring can be so many things. It can be wandering through your neighborhood looking for window box or front porch decorating ideas. It can be a walk in the woods identifying trees or through a meadow looking for four-leaf clovers.

My goal, however, is driving along the back roads and exploring the countryside, little towns, or city neighborhoods. My father instilled a love of exploration when I was a small girl. He loved to drive and hence, Sunday's were for piling the fam in the car and taking off to discover what jewels existed along a route we had never taken.

I still love the adventure of not knowing what lies ahead, the discovery of a quaint little museum or an artisan haven. I've accidentally discovered a membership only ski mountain, dozens of hole-in-the-wall greasy spoon restaurant boasting amazing bacon or French fries, a bathing location of George Washington, and an Indian arrowhead museum.

I've wound up on dirt roads that travelled across fields that were more than likely private property, had to drive in reverse for a half mile after hitting a marshy dead end, and come up on moose watering in a pond that perfectly reflected the fall foliage behind it.

I've stood in awe of nature's beauty more times than I can count simply because I took a chance on a road that looked less travelled and I've prayed what I thought were my last prayers as we traveled across a switchback moving us into a Redstone canyon. I drove through a population of jackrabbits in the middle of the night that scared half the wits from me and along Eastern Shore roads that led to a rope ferry.

Of course, it's helpful to know how to read a map and have a companion as you undertake this kind of exploration unless of course, you have flares, extra food, and warm blankets. Cell service is not entirely reliable if you're out in the boondocks.

Finding treasures, locating interesting venues, and getting away from the routine of home lends to authentic joy, peace, and contentment. It's as simple as learning how to ...

Explore

#54 Paint your front door

What is the first thing you notice every time you come home? Does the entrance to your living space welcome you? Even on the dreariest of days, arriving home and entering through a doorway that is inviting and positively staged, can revitalize your energy.

It may be as simple as painting your front door!

When your point of entry "pops", people (including you) are more likely to respond positively. Guests will feel welcomed and newcomers will be entering with a great first impression. Your personality can be displayed quickly and easily by using a quart size can of paint.

Think of a color that represents 'happy' to you and then step outside and imagine it on the rectangle that is your front door. Imagine how it looks with the brick, siding, wood, or stucco that covers your home... is there a color on that 'happy' spectrum that would be a nice compliment to your overall curb appeal? Is there a color that comes to mind that might strengthen your mood at the end of a long day?

Of course, there is a technique involved but with only a couple of pointers to keep in mind, the entire appeal of your home can be enticed. Using an exterior paint with a high gloss finish and a low nap (or foam) roller is most often recommended. Start with a clean door, lightly sanded, and primed. In as little as an hour the look of your home will be updated with your individual personality!

And remember... it's only paint, so go ahead and spruce up your entry by....

Painting your front door!

#55 Eat outside

Whenever the weather turns, I am immediately excited for the opportunity to sit on the deck with a cup of morning coffee or fire up the grill and eat dinner outside. It seems that eating outside brings back memories of favorite childhood moments, or at least mimics those 'feel good' sensations.

More and more we are seeing restaurants claiming sidewalks, clearing patio space, and adding decks to lure us with the tantalizing option of eating outdoors. The Europeans have been doing this for decades and the trend - for public dining at least - is catching on here in the U.S. Outdoor spaces are offering propane heat, blankets, and in some cases fur coats so that we can embrace fresh air while dining and digesting our meals.

I imagine that we were born with the innate instinct to consume food in the outdoors. From the perspective of time, it's only been a blip that we've taken to dining indoors. And while I don't know the anthropological origin... I imagine taking our meals inside was a condition of cold weather and comfort more than anything else (rebuttals welcome). So, it's in our genes to enjoy a meal in fresh air.

It doesn't matter if it is a picnic in the park, a sandwich on a trail, a restaurant patio, or you own private terrace... dining alfresco is not only in style but perhaps intrinsic to our nature and at the very least... enjoyable. Summer is only budding here on the northern hemisphere so as you consider preparing your primary meal, think about gathering your peeps and taking it 'on the deck' to ...

Eat outside

#56 Take a hike

The term 'hike' simply refers to a long walk and yet it instills images of heavy backpacks, rustic camping and ragged trails for many. Personally, the word conjures thoughts of burnt calories and heavy sweating on one hand and serene communing with nature on my other.

Truly, a hike can be a lot of things and it doesn't have to be arduous or exhausting. In as little as 20 minutes on a trail behind your office park or around a community pond, a hike can be short and sweet. It can be a couple of hours along a creek in the country or along an old rail bed through a mountain gorge. And ultimately, it can be a trek spanning states or an expedition up a mountain.

Regardless of how it's done, hiking is good for the mind, body, and spirit. It's an activity that satisfies all of our basic needs for exercise, tranquility, and connection. A stroll through nature's splendor highlights some of life's most basic beauty no matter the environment; an ant mound that showcases the perfection of a natural community, views of countryside that extends for miles, or clear clean water flowing quickly over moss covered boulders.

Allowing yourself to 'attune' to nature may nurture innate instincts that our brain rarely uses. Our internal wiring is still programed to exist in the midst of natural habitats; to embrace the energy released by living organisms. A quiet walk in the midst of nature's glory may be just the piece you've been missing. So, get out there and literally...

Take a Hike.

#57 Meditate

Wikipedia says that meditation has been "practiced since antiquity" - it's the exercise of being still and directing all focus to a single object or thought. If you haven't heard about meditation and its benefits, you've been living in a cage without Wi-Fi!

Research in recent years has demonstrated that meditation may be significant in the reduction of anger, pain, stress, fatigue, depression and more. A well-developed meditation regiment may be just shy of a magic pill for most of what ails our sick and tired, fast paced and distracted society.

Most of the time, I find that people who don't have a regular practice misunderstand the process of quieting the mind. People say, "I can't stay focused" and "My brain is too active" - indicating that those elements must prevent them from having any success. Actually - we all experience those barriers when we begin.

I think of meditation as the art of noticing thoughts just like the lights that pop up on a peripheral vision test while I am focused on the white dot in the middle... I see - and stay trained - on the dot in the center, not allowing the other lights that pop in and out of my field of vision to redirect my attention. It's not *not* having other thoughts that is the goal... it's to *not* pay attention to those other thoughts that we work to accomplish as a beginner. I was once told that after 10 years of dedicated meditation practice, a teacher was excited when as much as 5 whole minutes passed without a recognized thought - 10 years!

Just keep coming back to your point of focus; and coming back; and coming back - without judgment about how well you're doing or if you're doing it wrong. Using an app like Headspace or guided meditations like those of Ron Seigel are great ways to begin. The challenge is to add dedicated time to your day in pursuit of meditation.

It's like anything else though... what you prioritize - you WILL make time for. It's a universal law. So, think about what ails you and do a little research. I'm sure you'll find that relief may be as simple as some still time. Set aside some time, get comfortable, find a focus, and ...

Meditate.

#58 Eat mindfully

Most of us never do this and even those of us who have tried it a time or two don't spend many meals engaged in intention but when you do... is a whole new experience.

Eating mindfully is frequently taught with a raisin. Sometimes it is referred to as an eating meditation -mostly because ALL of your focus is on the process - the entire process - of eating.

Imagine the raisin. Hold the raisin and notice how it feels in your finger; notice the ridges, the color, and the size. Intentionally, place the raisin on your tongue and let it sit there for a minute; noticing its smell, the sensation of it there, and perhaps how you begin to salivate. Move the raisin between your teeth and gently squeeze... notice the texture, the flavor, and how your mouth responds. Notice with each movement of your jaw - how the raisin changes - the change in flavor or texture or size. And finally, swallow the raisin - paying attention to the sensation of it moving across your tongue, to the back of your mouth and then down your throat.

Now do this for an entire meal. Same process with each and every bite.

Yes - it will take a long time to consume your food - and it will be good for you. The first time I had ate something other than a raisin intentionally I immediately noticed how reflexive it was to put a spoonful in my mouth and then immediately shovel the spoon back into my plate of food - prepping the next bite. That's NOT mindful.

I was curious enough to persevere through an entire plate of Kung Pao Chicken, but it was cold by the time I was finished, and an entire hour had elapsed. I had visions of my father telling me to "stop fooling around and just eat!"

Out of all the people I've ever known, very few eat slow enough to truly 'experience' their food and my personal belief is that it is becoming problematic in our culture. We eat so fast, we don't know when we've had enough to satisfy hunger and consequently, we frequently overeat. Mitigating that issue is easily rectified when we ...

Eat mindfully.

#59 Listen carefully

Ahhh… If only we all did this!! What does it really mean to 'listen carefully'? First and foremost - it means NO interrupting! Too many of us have the bad habit of not letting people finish a complete thought before adding our two cents worth. How can we fully interpret the context of what someone is telling us without the entire presentation?

Listening carefully means confirming our understanding of the words, the vernacular, and the reference point of the speaker. It's nice when we are able to successfully infer meaning in a conversation, but you know what is said about too many assumptions….

While it may not be necessary to utilize reflective listening in each exchange - the tools that technique teaches eliminates a lot of assumptive problems. When we mirror the statement of another, we are validating that we've received the message and most importantly - interpreted it correctly.

"Well I'm not doing that again." said Diane

"In not doing that again - do you mean today or never - ever?" asks Pete.

It's important to stop when we listen - to give our attention to the speaker. One of the greatest stories I've heard is of a man who pulled over to the side of the road after dating a woman only a few weeks to hear what she was saying about her father. When asked what he was doing, he responded "you're getting ready to share a big part of your history with me and I'd want to give it my full attention." That's *listening*.

Acknowledge receipt of the message in some fashion, even if it is with a quick "wow", "that's great", or "no kidding". Having no reaction at all fails to communicate back that you received what was said. People want to be heard. Even if you feel defensive or become distracted - finish receiving the speaker's comment and reply to *that* expression before moving on. Verify that they are finished with that thought before anything self-serving is introduced.

Our best friends typically *listen* - which is - in large part - why they get that title. If you want to be a best friend learn to…

Listen carefully.

#60 Play music

In the car, in the kitchen, in the bathroom, outdoors, at work, any genre, any volume, etc., get your groove on and play some music. I know that the younger you are, the more likely it is that you are playing music most of the time so this post is ultimately for the those of you who have fallen out of the habit of listening to music randomly throughout the day.

Our options are almost unlimited these days with music available on our cable stations, our phones, and the internet. It's as easy as a callout to Alexa or Google (maybe the best feature of those devices) to play a song or an album from a favorite occasion or era. Spotify, Pandora, Sirius or XM... they all offer us the ability to access tunes anytime; anywhere.

Music lowers blood pressure, reduces stress, improves immune function, and increases concentration in various forms. We are innately wired to respond emotionally to music. Happy people report listening to music more often than people rating themselves as unhappy. Music inspires us and may help us to recall happy memories.

If you've gotten out of the habit of listening to music throughout *each* day... make that change immediately and find a channel or a genre that moves your spirit in a positive way. Oldies, Rock & Roll, The Blues, or Country... let the melodies move through your space and into your core; experiencing the vibration as deeply as possible.

Happy and upbeat music is literally responsible for increasing well-being so open the drapes, blast Jimmy Buffett, and begin your day by ...

Playing Music.

#61 Light candles

For more than 5000 years, candles have been a part of our lives - first for providing light, then ambiance, and in more recent time - they have offered us a way to make our environment smell better. Additionally, candlelight is attributed to romance, relaxation, and focus.

Candle meditation is beginning to rise in popularity as the flame offers a specific point of focus and is naturally soothing to our brain. Candle yoga is offered in some studios for the same reason. Our faces and bodies look softer (and younger?) in candlelight. The low light conditions of a room lit by candles resembles dusk to our brain - creating a reflex to begin winding down - and our body naturally starts to relax.

Companies have made giant fortunes on the business of providing us with candle options. From the home party company Candlelight that many of us were familiar with as it made its rounds through suburbia in the early 2000's, to the Yankee Candle Co. storefront in malls across America - businesses are marketing to our adoration of soft light and nice smells.

Some of us have even been introduced to the correct 'way' to care for our candles, depending on how many wicks it has and what kind of ingredients it is made of. Craft stores have dedicated entire isles for candle making supplies as the creatives among us take on the challenge of personalizing our little wax lights. And the combination of scents has matured from Rose and Cinnamon to Roasted Nutmeg Butternut Squash and Cucumber Melon Ocean Breeze... tantalizing us with the idea that an ocean breeze could actually be contained in a jar filled with wax.

Nevertheless, there does seem to be validity behind the idea that lighting a candle at home - for a variety of reasons - may add to your sense of well-being. So, if you are seeking relaxation, aromatherapy, or a nice romantic evening I'll offer the simple suggestion of...

Light Candles.

#62 Honey-do lists

I am forever thinking about something that I'd liked fixed around the house whether it is a loose handle, a light fixture that needs updated, or a gutter repair that I only remember when it is pouring rain. Similar to the list I talked about in tip #9, I keep a running Honey-do list of little fix it / move it items.

Murphy's Law states that whenever you have time and/or a helping hand - you can't remember the things you've been planning to tackle. Keeping a running list allows you to write it down WHEN you think about it and offers your partner/husband/wife/friend - a starting point when an available hour or Saturday morning rolls around.

Extra tip: For items that have a due date or a 'need by' date - offer that piece of information in bold or highlighted writing.

I bought a new flush mount light fixture once that got stuck in the closet during a quick clean up. The item 'install new hall light' was on the list forever and seemingly kept getting passed over until finally, in frustration, I asked why that wasn't getting accomplished. My partner didn't realize that I had picked out and purchased the light - a communication error on my part that would have been easily rectified with a little notation on the Honey-do list as to the location of the new fixture.

I am the fixer-upper person in my home but there are some items that require a handyman or another person as a helper, so the list is still relevant. If one of my brothers, my son, or daughter is in the house, I glance at it to see if there is something, I need help doing. Even if it serves only as a task-oriented maintenance list for the inside and outside of my home - I still keep a ...

Honey-do List

#63 Send thank you cards

When you receive a gift please consider bringing back the lost art of sending a 'real' card - not a message on Facebook or an e-card. A paper card inside an envelope with a stamp, mailed, and delivered by the good 'ole United States Postal Service with a note of thanks for the gesture you were given.

Louis Prang, an immigrant from Poland and known as the father of the American Christmas Card, is also credited with what we now think of when we think about 'thank you cards'. Although, the practice of sending notes of appreciation to friends and family dates back to the Egyptian era.

Social etiquette used to dictate the distribution of appreciative notes so much that the proper way to do so was specifically taught in 'finishing schools' worldwide. Emily Post - the mother of modern manners - was insistent its demonstration of good taste. So much so that her family has dedicated an entire chapter in the book *Emily Post's Etiquette, 19th Edition: Manners for Today* to how cards should be inscribed, addressed, and sent.

Yes, there is a time and place for all that formality and yet I think the moms, aunts, and grandma's in the world would be happy with something scribbled on the back of a napkin or paper plate... it's the gesture of expressing appreciation that is most meaningful; especially in this digital age where most of us communicate via email and/or text messaging so frequently.

All said, as we approach graduation and wedding season where gift giving is common... take the traditional approach and handwrite a few sentences of gratitude for someone's presence and/or their presents! A few minutes of your time will honor the gift you received and more so - the giver when you...

Send thank you cards.

#64 Watch an old movie

The term old here is 'relative'... depending on your current age, the movie that comes to mind when I suggest watching an old movie may be Casablanca from 1942 or it may be Saturday Night Fever from 1977. Frankly though... I am specifically referencing something that was filmed before the mid 1950's when color films were the new standard. Black and white films starring Cary Grant, James Stewart, and Humphrey Bogart or the actresses of that era Irene Dunne, Ginger Rogers or Ava Gardner. There is something special about allowing your imagination to create the color of the scene - to imagine that the sky is a light blue or deep azure - depending on the context of the screen.

Does a character soften in your thoughts if she is wearing a light pink blouse instead of a stark white one? Would it matter to you if a sofa was dark grey or brown? How might the tension in the scene change if you imagined bright orange walls? While I am certainly not a film critic or even a student of film direction, there is most definitely something to the lighting techniques and shadow play in those old films that lend to the character of the scene and so black and white movie viewing is an experience worth having. If you can't quite get there, try something from the sixties like The Graduate from 1967 or The Apartment from 1960. Old movies remind us that the shot is everything... that techno effects and postproduction editing, while nice - aren't necessary for a good film.

For me, old movies remind me of rainy Sunday afternoons when Shirley Temple reruns were played back to back or a childhood sick day when mom and I curled up on the couch to watch Esther Williams synchronize her swim strokes to Hollywood music. It's like a stroll through an antique store missing only the musty smell, dust, and occasional cobweb. The next time you don't feel well or are treated with a lazy Sunday afternoon, forget about binge watching The Office or catching up on Hulu's latest hit and try treating yourself to something unfashionable but classic...

Watch an old movie.

#65 Volunteer

If you regularly volunteer for an organization or a person ... Thanks for all you do and move on to the next tip! If you do *not* regularly volunteer - *this* post is for you!

It is often said that when we offer our time and/or talent to a person or a cause, we are engaging in our truest purpose. We believe that when we volunteer, we are experiencing selflessness at its highest point and yet... there are so many individual and personal benefits that perhaps it serves the deepest purpose of self.

You see, when we donate time and talent, we are opening ourselves to experiences that grow our spirit, our strengths, and our hearts. Sometimes, the value is much more significant to the person who helps than to the receiver. Benefits include growth in compassion, strengths, empathy, purpose, and esteem. When we expose ourselves to new ideas, new people, and new experiences we expand our hearts; a benefit that has long lasting impact.

For maximum impact, it's necessary to volunteer in an area that is of interest. A population that inspires you or a project that connects with your passion. Whether it is working with an animal shelter, building homes, or interacting with youth - make sure it is something that motivates continued participation.

Volunteering fosters happiness and leads to longer life expectancy. It deepens our skill sets, strengthens our weaknesses, and improves our overall outlook on life. What's not to love? It is a win-win endeavor for everyone involved. If you're looking for a way to improve your mood or your quality of life, it may be as simple as looking for a space where your time and talent is used as you ...

Volunteer.

#66 Use a caulk gun around the house

Recently, a friend prepping for a big family gathering mentioned that she spent the day 'caulking'. When I inquired further, she indicated that she has made it an annual habit to roam the house looking for woodwork that had settled and/or separated over the years.

While I am quite familiar with a caulk gun when I am constructing something (built some bookcases a few years back), I've never randomly searched for areas in my home that needed that particular attention unless I was doing a thorough paint job - which, definitely doesn't happen annually.

When I built those bookcases I mentioned above, a friend shared the tip that "a little bit of caulk and a little bit of paint, make the carpenter what he ain't.". I've never forgotten and believe me... there was a tube or more on those shelves.

After the discussion with my earlier friend, I've noticed many places around my own home that were quite oblivious before that conversation. Little cracks appear in almost every baseboard and I've noticed a few windowsills that can use some attention.

Remember that post about Honey-do Lists I posted last week? This task is being added without further ado...

Use a caulk gun around the house.

#67 Have an at-home spa day

This may be the ultimate in Self-care activities. Spending an afternoon or an entire day pampering your face, your hair, your skin, and your nails. Back in my youth this meant massaging a gross amount of mayonnaise into my hair and wrapping it in a warm towel; rubbing my heels with Vaseline and covering my feet with cotton socks; and then applying baby oil all over my skin from head to toe. Just to be cute I would use cucumber slices on my eyes on occasion but mostly they got cold compresses. That was the process of beautification as I knew it.

Today, while those methods may work fine, there are dozens of fancier options. From homemade facial scrubs to electric foot baths - having a personal spa day is easier than ever. Get started with a bath, a glass of wine, some soft music, and a few drops of your favorite essential oils. Spend time moisturizing your hair, your face, and your extremities. A sugar scrub for your face, hands, and feet will exfoliate and prep your skin for the lotions that come next. Using honey, buttermilk, coconut oil and/or avocados are a natural way to hydrate the largest organ (your skin) on your body.

Finish up with attending to your finger and toenails - to polish or not is a personal preference. Some light yoga or meditation may be a great way to still your mind while your body regenerates and then perhaps some outdoor time in a garden or a short nap.

In my late twenties I treated myself to a full day of pampering and as I attempted to buy wine the next day - I was asked for ID. As I got back in the car to go home, I slammed a solid fist pump into the air believing that my primping was responsible. Who knows? The more you take care of your skin - the longer it looks good so go ahead and treat yourself to an...

At Home Spa Day.

#68 Phone a friend

This suggestion works nicely if you are playing a television game for a million dollars but it's also important if you are interested in maintaining friendships. With our evolving habit of texting conversations - some of us have all but eliminated vocal interacting. Why not phone a friend?

Think of someone you haven't spoken with in a while. What has prevented you from chatting? I occasionally hear that a friend hasn't called because "I didn't know if you were busy". Frankly - that's why voicemail was invented, wasn't it? If I am busy, I will let the call go to message, but I'll know that you were thinking about me.

I'm miffed when someone says "I've been thinking about you forever..." but I have no way of knowing it because there's been NO communication to that extent. If you are thinking about someone - phone them; say hello and let them know you're thinking about them or leave a message. It's simple really.

I realize that we all have busy lives and it takes time to maintain friendships. I find that most of us don't need extended conversations and deep, meaningful interactions to sustain an existing friendship, but we do need contact - real - live - connection. So, think of someone you haven't heard from in a while and ...

Phone a friend.

#69 Babysit

This may sound like an odd suggestion for increasing happiness but indeed - it may be just the thing you need as children tend to remind us how precious life can be. Even if you have your own children, another child can offer a fresh perspective. Children know how naturally present and in the moment, and they instinctively understand what it means to be authentic; traits that we adults, need reminded of far too often.

If you have children:

Babysitting another child can offer perspective on the value of your own children. It can be another form of the blessing you experience every day and/or it can be a reminder of the potential your own children have. It may remind you why you made the decision to have children in the first place.

If you don't have children but are thinking about it:

Babysitting other children may inspire you in your decision to move forward or it may cement the decision not to commit. Spending time with someone else's child may demonstrate the joy that a child can carry into your life or it may validate the concerns you've had about readiness.

If you've made the decision to never have children:

Babysitting will remind you of life's innocence. It will help you put life stressors into perspective and open your eyes to another way of viewing the environment surrounding you.

If you are an empty nester:

Babysitting your grandchildren and/or another child will have you counting blessings in many directions. There's nothing quite like the spirit of a child to brighten our space, our spirit, and our sense of purpose. And... they seem to find all the things we've hidden or lost!

Aside from all the personal benefits... taking the time to babysit for someone who needs a break may just be the thing that allows them to be a better parent; returning to their own child/ren refreshed and ready to tackle a new day. It's an extension of kindness in a subtle way and yet it really is a personal treat each time we...

Babysit.

#70 Clean out / go through your jewelry or ties.

When was the last time you ventured to weed out your jewelry stash? Do you still have Holiday pins that are now tarnished? How many serpentine necklaces are there that were broken due to their delicacy? Would you be willing to take a bet on how many single earrings are in your jewelry box cemetery? In addition to many of those pieces, I know mine is large enough to contain some of the trinkets and treasures that my children bought at 'Santa Sack' while in elementary school; you know, the adjustable rings and pop bead necklaces they were so proud to present. Something has prevented me from disposing of them until now.

Keeping a few key pieces and of course, the valuable or treasured items is a must, but the rest can go. In some cases, there may be enough to create a different kind of treasure… Pinterest has a plethora of ideas.

Dudes have the same issue at times with ties. My dad's tie collection grew annually and only a few of them were in style or matched his taste. Seemingly, ties are the gift given when we just can't figure out what else works. Cheap ties tend to be wider and thicker than the good ones; meaning that they collect dust faster and end up in the back of the heap - forgotten.

My grandfather kept his ties (much to my grandmother's chagrin) so long that he had a few classics tucked away in the back of his closet when Paisley made a comeback. That's not to say we shouldn't wean down the collection. Again, keeping some of the 'classics' is appropriate, or the one that only gets worn on St. Patrick's Day each year. Maybe there's even vindication for keeping the one he proposed in - if someday there will be a re-creation photo session to celebrate a big anniversary. Other than that - keep only the ones that are clean and in-style.

This is one of those productive tasks that takes minutes but offers great satisfaction each time we open the jewelry box or each time we reach for a tie. Go ahead, put it on your master list…

Clean out / go through your jewelry or ties.

#71 Create a vision board

This suggestion is a leading recommendation of life coaches across the country. It went mainstream when the Law of Attraction merged into Pop Culture. Even Oprah got in the game when she included a Dream Board on her website.

A vision board is a collage encompassing all the things you wish to 'attract' into your life. The premise is that what you 'focus' on - you will create / attract in your reality. It's not meant to act as a metaphoric 'Jeannie in a bottle'... it's meant to inspire you to engage in activities that lead you in the direction of the goals / vision of your life that you've included on your board. What do you want? Go ahead and include the material items you wish to attain. Spell out the words of the attributes you want to grow (i.e., patience, compassion, etc.) What is your dream job? Include a photo of a graduation or a photo of a location where you'd like to vacation. It's a combination of photographs and words that will inspire you to keep going... to keep working.

A vision board uses the concept of 'imagery' to encourage and inspire. There is no right or wrong way to do it. I have encouraged clients to use photographs, cut pics out of magazines, find words that are meaningful, ideas that you want to expand upon. Ultimately, a vision board is a visual representation of where your FOCUS lies. Theoretically, what you focus on is where your energy goes. Why not create a physical representation to remind you what to focus on day by day? It's easy... think about what you want; where you want to go; and what you want to achieve and ...

Create a Vision Board.

#72 Pick up litter

I'm not suggesting that you put on an orange vest, grab a pointed stick, and walk down the side of the interstate. My suggestion is much simpler; more basic; and perhaps more impactful than those crews we see walking alongside the roadways. Although, I am grateful for those individuals who volunteer to clean our environment.

This tip for happiness is subtle. It addresses those random pieces of litter we see and think nothing of. It is the random cup left on a park bench; the napkin that blew away; or the bottle top that went rolling. While I certainly wish that we could all be responsible for our own refuse, I am suggesting that we also individually accept responsibility for properly disposing of a piece of trash that was left behind by another.

If we all engaged in this activity once a day - every day of the year - I am certain that the amount of litter, we see from day to day would be significantly reduced. Besides, the energy we spend bending over one extra time during the day would be good for us.

At the very least, keeping this suggestion in the forefront of your mind will remind you to toss your own trash appropriately. The 'happiness' this suggestion induces may not be immediate and yet I am certain that when there is less clutter, trash, and chaos in our immediate environment, our sense of well-being is increased. So, not only might you be increasing your own internal sense of contentment because you know you are doing something worthwhile, but you may inadvertently be increasing mine because the absence of litter reduces my distress. All because you decided to...

Pick up Litter.

#73 Create a *no phone* zone.

This is perhaps one of the most common pieces of advice I give to my clients when they are seeking closer relationships with people in their home. The cell phone - our hand-held computers - are here to stay and they have most certainly disrupted our ability - to communicate and connect in the same manner that was once taken for granted.

Facebook recently reminded me of a photo with their 'On This Day' feature that all four of my children were home for Mother's Day a few years ago. In that photo, each one of them has a phone in their hand and only one daughter is looking up as I took the photograph. My heart was overfilled with joy that all my peeps were in the next, but my intellect wants to be insulted that their attention wasn't there with me. I'm not alone... it's a complaint that I hear almost daily.

The solution is to create a "no phone zone" in your home. Perhaps it is the family room - in which case this photo would look different - or the kitchen table. When I was growing up, we weren't allowed to get up and answer the telephone if it rang during dinner because it was 'family time' and interruptions weren't accepted.

We blame a lot on cell phones, but I remember asking one of my daughters to "put down that book and talk to me" when she buried her nose in a book for hours on end. Likewise, I recall my mother asking my father "can you put down the paper and listen to me?" And I've heard complaints from clients that beg for partners to "leave the work at work" so that their time at home can be dedicated to one another. When we create a 'no phone zone', what we're really seeking is an opportunity to interact with the people who are sharing the space with us - to be present. Ideally that means it's a 'no newspaper', a 'no book', and a 'no work' space as well.

The human nature in each of us desires attention and interaction; a situation much more attainable these days when we ...

Create a *no phone* zone

#74 Look at the stars

As a little girl I would lie awake at night and look out my bedroom window. On a clear night I could see the Milky Way and name most of the constellations in the night sky; at least the ones there before midnight. It was easier from that small northern Pennsylvania town than it has been near the big cities I've lived close to. The light pollution dilutes many of the stars that were once visible to my youthful eyes.

There was great joy in that activity though and it (or at least the memory of it) remains each time I am able to direct my attention to the night sky filled with the sun's reflection of planets and stars across the galaxy.

When we look up, we cannot dismiss the concept of infinity... we have no choice but to try and absorb the realization of our overall insignificance. We automatically experience wonder and curiosity and imagination. For a brief time - unless we are more scientifically oriented - we may digress into a childlike fascination with the vision.

Take an evening, a clear early summer evening, and sit outside with the intention of identifying as many constellations as you can (a phone app like Star Chart or NASA Sky is great for this activity) and identify where you are in terms of the galaxy. Take time to just look... perhaps you'll see a shooting star - depending on your location - a meteor shower is common in the summer months. If you can get to a beach and look oceanward... or the mountains - away from any light pollution - the effect is better. Take the time to consider your position in the universe as a whole.

What thoughts come to mind when you take a good hard ...

Look at the stars.

#75 Watch a thunderstorm

Are you one of the people who love to watch thunderstorms? Do you like the sound of thunder and the beauty of lightning? This typically warm weather phenomena is a nuisance to some and magic to others. They range from quick and basic to drawn out and downright dangerous.

I love the sound of a thunderstorm approaching – the gentle roll of thunder across the horizon, like the purr of a kitten letting you know it will be bigger at some point. I like the potential of seeing a flash of lightning cross the sky like a fracture of ice crystals across my windshield in the cold winter months. A thunderstorm most often announces its presence, giving us time to find a perch.

I am always amazed at how nature is so tuned in to its arrival that the leaves turn upside down and critters scoot for cover far in advance of our human tendency. I was taught to count the seconds between a lightning strike and a thunderclap – indicating the corresponding number of miles the center of the storm was from my location. I laid in wait, anticipating its arrival but only rewarded with the occasional epicenter unleashing its fury overhead.

Those were the moments that a smart person would move away from the open window or head in for the safety of walls and roof… but those were the moments I was most interested to see as the lightning struck close and the thunder simultaneously boomed its announcement of arrival. Sometimes, there would be more than one demonstration of dominance but more often than not the storm would move away as fast as it blew in and I would find myself counting again… the distance it had travelled from me.

For those few moments, my attention was completely focused on Nature and its beauty; its fury. I was more interested in what was happening outside in the world than in my own little dramatic circle. I was taken outside of my narrow view of the world and offered a glimpse of something larger, and more powerful than I could ever hope to be – put in my place by a random but scientifically viable operation of weather. It's another example of how we can easily and without expense, step outside of ourselves and be present. A simple idea really... just take time to…

Watch a Thunderstorm.

#76 Listen to the sound of water

If you're looking for a different way to relax and/or meditate - try listening to the sound of water flowing. There's no denying that aside from initiating the urge to pee - running water is known to help us relax. Indeed, it's true for so many people that white noise machines routinely include the sound of streams and/or oceans.

Science suggests that our brains relate the sound of water to a NON-threat environment; walks on the beach, picnics by the brook, and sitting by lily filled ponds are all pleasant, pleasure inducing visions or experiences. Others suggest that the sound of water is one of the first elements that we experience in our womb environment - more data that our brain relates the sound of water to safety and security.

I'm not suggesting that being *in* the water is the same as I know many people have negative experiences regarding being in water; not knowing how to swim, bad boating or ocean experiences, etc..... But listening to the sound of water is the prominent point.

If you find yourself with a cranky infant - walking over to the sink and running the water will almost instantly calm the baby. Oceanfront rooms around the world attempt to capitalize on the idea that you can hear the waves simply by opening the window or sitting on the patio/deck. We've added fountains and water features to our pools and landscaping in an effort to bring that calming effect to our outdoor living space and there are any number of tabletop fountains that bring the sound of running water neatly indoors for your listening pleasure.

Focusing on the sound of running water will induce a calming effect within minutes, especially if combined with mindfulness. Use this strategy to bring a tranquil element to your space when stress is present in your life or if you anticipate a stressful situation. In an emergent scenario use this tip... find the closest bathroom, stand at the sink, turn on the faucet, and ...

Listen to the sound of running water.

#77 Explore Google Earth

I've always been a map lover. My dad taught me to read a map when I was young and ever since, I've studied maps for fun. I enjoy knowing how to get from here to there more efficiently, with more scenery, or with a specific stop in-between. It's no surprise then that I have thoroughly enjoyed the experience of being able to tap into Google Earth.

For anyone who doesn't know - Google Earth is Google's effort of bringing the world to our fingertips - at least visually. Almost anywhere the Google car - with all of its virtual cameras - has travelled across the globe - you can see and explore with internet access.

When a family member moved to Europe, I was able to type in the address and virtually explore the street they lived on, the park nearby, and landmarks they were excited to visit. Since I couldn't get there right away, it was a way to feel connected to their new experience.

I've sat with my children and explored the town where I grew up, the schools I've attended, and had a virtual 'drive by' of some of my favorite childhood haunts.

When I'm planning a vacation, I explore the area 'virtually' a little just to get my bearings and bolster the anticipation. When I want to go somewhere that isn't in my budget or when I don't have time available but want to simulate a little vacation experience - I get on Google Earth and 'take a little vacation' by visiting places that seem fun to see. What does it look like from the top of Mount Olympus in Washington state? Google Earth will take you there.

Beware: you can get lost in the wonders of the planet and spend far too much time exploring ... but it's amazing and fun and interesting; some would say downright educational. So, the next time you want to take a little trip but don't have the time or money - grab a cup of coffee, a cold beer, or a glass of wine and sit down to ...

Explore Google Earth.

#78 Ride a bike

When was the last time you rode a bike just for fun?

While biking has been a stable pastime for children since the introduction of a miniature tricycle, it seems as if we Americans ditch the bike for 4 wheels and a motor as soon after the age of sixteen as possible. Certainly, the exception is those adults who use bicycles for sport and exercise or those of us who mosey along side streets while on a beach oriented vacation; perhaps taking advantage of dual pedal power on a tandem machine and some people have converted their primary mode of transportation at least for commuting.

But... when was the last time you just took a leisurely bike ride... just because? Most major cities have made amazing progress in becoming bicycle friendly, offering rideshare stations and dedicated bike lanes. And... while after a visit to Amsterdam where bicyclists have the right of way at all times because there are millions of them - really... they are everywhere and as a pedestrian, you are easily overwhelmed. But, we're not there yet. In fact, the bike lanes in our cities are mostly open... beckoning us to grab a bicycle and get out there.

I rode my bike as a kid and then didn't own one again until my 30's... rode my babies around a bit which, resembled working out too much and so that equipment was donated to a worthy cause. Fast forward 25 years and I've taken up bike riding again. It's different for me because it is purely recreational and fun. It's not a workout (at least not intentionally), which means that I am often riding a Rail Trail (flat) or just cruising around town a bit. I meander a bit - not in a hurry - just enjoying the fresh air, the breeze across my face, and the scenery that I don't take in while driving by at 30+ miles per hour. It's mind time and I have two simple requests for the people who may ride with me. First... don't push - I ride slow. Second... don't talk - I am in-a-zone.

Biking can be simple. Do yourself a favor and find a bike share station, put on a helmet, and ...

Ride a bike

#79 Grow your own food

Whether you opt for a fancy raised bed with organic soil, a clay pot with a trellis, experiment with hydroponics, or design an 'upside down' garden on your patio... growing something you can eat is highly rewarding.

When we grow our own food, we have to step out of ourselves enough to care for something. Unlike my houseplants which get water when they wilt enough to remind me - growing tomatoes on the deck or sowing a zucchini plant in your Azealia bed and tending to it through the fruit (or vegetable) production stage takes some dedicated attention. Water and sunshine mostly; but the right amounts of both. Otherwise, you get a big plant with no fruit or you get a short burst of fruit production and a quickly decaying plant.

There is no shortage of help on the internet to get you started on the method of choice or the proper way to fertilize and nurture your seedlings. There's organic instructions and tons of advice on which chemicals will keep the critters away. There's so much advice in fact, that you just need to pick something and go with it.... Journal your results so you know what to do (or not to do) next year when you try again.

The first time I grew veggies, I threw a packet of cucumber seeds into a raised bed with shrubbery that ran alongside my home. I didn't do much to it, but it must have been beginner's luck because that darn thing took off. It grew in and out, over and around those shrubs and produced so many cucumbers that I couldn't give them away fast enough. There were so many that I was inspired to learn how to make pickles (I must have had some spare time on my hands). I made sweet pickles, dill pickles, and sliced pickles, and spear pickles. I gave away pickles for two years.

Since then I stick to food, I know we will eat an excess of and as the years go by, I find that I am inspired differently from year to year. Sometimes it's only tomatoes and then I try something new. I've come to really enjoy growing fresh herbs and then I dry the excess for home produced herbs that I use most often. That's easy too! Pick something and give it a try...

Grow Your Own Food

#80 Savor a memory

The science of 'savoring' is relatively new. It's a component of Positive Psychology and it has received a fair amount of attention in recent years for its ability to increase feelings of well-being (happiness). The act of savoring is known to most of us. Just sit back and think of the last time you ate something that you exclaimed "was the best thing you've ever had!" or the last time you saw "the most beautiful sight you've ever seen!" ... Chances are you savored that moment.

Now, to engage in this tip, I am suggesting that you choose a pleasant memory. Take yourself back to that time and space - in your mind, your thoughts. Take some time to imagine yourself reliving an experience that brought you peace, delight, or contentment. Breathe in.

With your mind's eye... review the memory and all the specifics - noticing each element in great detail. Notice the colors, the sounds, the smells, and the textures. Remember the good feelings, try and recreate the way it felt in your body; the smile, the butterflies, the movement.

Remind yourself of the emotions experienced during this pleasant experience; joy, gratitude, love, appreciation, hope, or awe for example. Breathe in again, imagining that you are able to simply inhale emotion of it all again and again - whenever you wish. Take your time and feel it completely. As the sensation fades, recall another memory and begin the process again.

This process - savoring - is gaining popularity for improving symptoms of depression and has been indicated in the immediate improvement of stress responses when completely activated. It is frequently associated with mindfulness, but they are different processes.

When you need a little boost or you're in a pinch and need an immediate positive distraction ...

Savor a memory.

#81 Play an instrument

Are you one of the millions of people who started an instrument as a kid (piano, clarinet, trumpet) and then dropped it like a hot potato when getting better meant practicing all the time? Clearly, a few of us developed into passible musicians – able to tap out a tune here and there – and even fewer became accomplished.

Well, it's never too late. In fact, it may be easier than ever to get lessons, especially for the piano as the Internet is full of YouTube instructional videos and there are programs/apps that teach step by step. I imagine there are even digital pianos that have those programs built right into the instrument. A handy headphone port allows for peace and quiet throughout the house while you practice. We aren't talking Steinway baby grands here but that's not what beginners start with anyhow.

Maybe the piano isn't your gig – there's always the violin, the drums, the flute, or the accordion. An old friend of mine began playing the Bagpipes after watching a parade one New Year's Day. I've seen instruments available at yard sales and pawn shops for pennies on the dollar – sometimes a nice one. There was an old wooden clarinet in a box that I won at auction once... the pads had rotted out and the reeds were too brittle to play but an expert brought that sweet thing up to speed quickly and it had the most beautiful sound. I couldn't help but wonder if it had crooned through the big band era with the help of an older man who closed his eyes and swayed as he played.

There are thousands of YouTube videos online that will take you step-by-step no matter the instrument you choose. With a little patience and dedication, you can teach yourself.

The point is to make music... music makes us happier and making it yourself in a way that sounds appealing can be tremendously satisfying! It's something you're never too old to learn. Actually, playing music stimulates a part of the brain that is attributed to intelligence and so it may indeed, keep our minds stimulated and healthy. Decide what you're curious about and set yourself up a bargain instrument, YouTube, and some patience.

Learn to play an Instrument.

#82 Read a 'beach' book

Sometimes we just need a break and that's why we go to the beach and often, when we get there, we read a random book - something easy and relaxing. However, not all of us can get to a beach so my recommendation then, is to let yourself read a 'beach book'. You know - it's one of those - sometimes known as 'junk novels' - a book without critical acclaim, perhaps not even a solid plot. It's one of those easy to read, easy to absorb, and easy to finish books.

Romance Novels are the obvious choice for a lady's poolside read and the variety exists along the continuum of Nicholas Sparks and Danielle Steele (with solid plots) or to the other end with a good ole fashioned Harlequin Romance type of read that shakes out the storyline in the first forty pages and becomes predictable half way through. Not that there isn't a place for reading that style of book - they're light and fluffy... perfect if you want a quick, easy solution for fun-in-the sun (sans electronic) entertainment.

I've never known a man to be interested in romance novels - my thoughts about 'beach books' for men are similar but oriented more toward spies and zombies. My intent, of course is not to be sexist here as I completely acknowledge that those genres are not gender biased by any means and that there is a man (or many), that I simply have yet to meet that truly gets into a Nora Roberts novel.

Summer is the perfect season to take this suggestion. By then, many of us are simply ready for some physical and mental R&R... put down the academic journals, textbooks, the self-help bibles, and the heavy duty winter reading books that make you think about the world in a new way and pick up something less intense, less thought provoking, and less educational for your outdoor relaxation time...

Read a 'beach book'.

#83 Learn a new hobby

I taught myself how to crochet a few years ago while recovering from surgery. It's become a favorite pastime in winter months and now most everyone I know has an afghan, nothing fancy but they were all made with love. Once again, I learned by watching YouTube videos (really, there's just so much to learn out there!).

Think of a hobby that you've always wanted to learn... what stopped you? Perhaps mountain climbing isn't an option for you at this stage of the game, but indoor climbing might be! What about card tricks or magic tricks? The Philadelphia Eagles player Jon Dorenbos taught himself magic as a hobby (and ultimately became a professional) and came in 3rd on America's Got Talent last summer. It was a hobby – football was his career – and he became passionate about getting better.

But you don't have to be great at your hobby. My stepdaughter makes magnificent crocheted items that are sometimes artistic masterpieces. Crocheting is a hobby that she enjoyed into mastery. My crocheting hobby is not an artistic endeavor... it's something to do in the evenings as I listen to music, chat, or watch television.

Try to put perfectionism aside and try your hand at something new; something that interests you, perhaps something that has been a secret desire. You may develop an interest in something that becomes a great little pastime (self-care) or turn it into a professional or profitable endeavor. It's as simple as …

Learning a new hobby.

#84 Join a club

One of the important elements of happiness is to surround oneself with likeminded people. It's critical for our social emotional health. Perhaps one of the best ways to do this is to belong to a club or organization where all participants gather around and participate in a shared interest.

The opportunities are boundless... Some of the more 'old fashioned' options are fraternal organizations that may have been family interests such as the Masons or Eastern Star both of which are tradition-based service organizations. Civic organizations such as the Lion's Club also offer opportunities for involvement in local communities. Charities, foundations, and faith-based groups are also great options for kindred spirits.

In addition to all those choices, the website GroupMe.com matches people to their inclinations. From book clubs and dance groups to sports activities and card players, GroupMe identifies others in your locale that share similar interests. It's a great place to start, especially for people moving into new locations and looking to establish themselves socially and/or people just wanting to reinvent themselves from a social perspective. Additionally, people wanting to 'test' the water or experiment with other social groups have a plethora of options via GroupMe.

We are positively impacted each time we have an opportunity to surround ourselves with others who share the things we appreciate and even more so when those occasions allow us to impact the world around us in a positive way. If you are seeking a way to increase your social interaction and/or impact other people, you might consider...

Joining a Club.

#85 Plant flowers

The gigantic flower industry is proof that there is something about the beauty of a flowering plant which adds an element of pleasure and/or downright feelings of happiness in our life.

Enjoying the beauty of flowers all summer long is easily accomplished by planting them. Where do you spend time on a beautiful summer morning? Where do you relax in the soft heat of a summer night? Plant flowers in that space.

Adding color and texture to your entryway is also a great way to feel good about coming home (aside from that beautiful front door that you've already painted!) Positioning a few pots so that they can be seen from the inside is a nice way to make sure you enjoy the color no matter where at home you spend time. In addition, a large pot of flowers at your door, bursting with a color that you enjoy will brighten your mood as you return home each and every time!

Planting annuals (flowers that need to be planted every year) is a great way to have constant bloom. Flora in the family of petunias can survive a fair amount of neglect - for those of us who profess our thumbs are blue instead of green. Portulaca is a great option for direct sun and intense heat (think rooftop deck). Begonias and Impatiens add bold and beautiful color to shadier areas (although they need a bit more attention to watering).

Even if you are in an apartment without a deck or outdoor entry - take the time to plant a few pots of colorful annuals to sit beside a window. With just a little imagination and an open window, you can share the experience of enjoying an outdoor space.

Be creative! Over the years I've experimented with colors, textures, and varieties. I've selected plants with only white blossoms and added greenery like ivy and vinca. I've gone for full out color and mixed them all together. My preference tends to lean into pinks and purples with a little orange for a fun burst. I love the anticipation of the growth through the season and watching a planter that starts thin and delicate grow fat and overflowing.

Add a little happy to your summer by...

Planting flowers.

#86 Write a letter to yourself

Sometimes, we need a little reminder about life and the very best perspective into our lives is our own!

There's value in writing a letter to your younger self. Think back a few years; 10, 20, or even 30.... Where were your thoughts? Your values? Your goals? What have you learned since then? By sitting down and writing a letter to your younger self, you are taking stock in how far you've come. You're describing a perspective that may not be actively conscious until you take the time to think. Think about the mistakes & lessons, the challenges & successes, and the insights & ah-ha moments that you've had; maybe the ones you wish you had known back then.

When you're finished writing that letter, you'll have a wonderful reminder of how much you know and how you've grown up till now.

A letter to your future self can also be a great option. Think about what is happening right now that will be important to remember! Perhaps you've just begun adulthood and there is a simplicity in your life that you hope to carry through... write yourself a letter reminding your future self to keep it in mind. Sometimes, we allow the stressors of adulting to override the basics we enjoy in the beginning. Life can get complicated and it may be really helpful to have a reminder of the more simple tenets.

When you finish writing that letter, put it in a special place that you're likely to find in a few years.

It only takes a few minutes and it's best completed without too much forethought. Let the words come naturally - allowing your heart to guide the advice or wisdom that is seeking to be imparted. You know yourself best so let the self-compassion flow as you ...

Write a Letter to Yourself.

#87 Surprise someone

Sometimes, a surprise is a really nice thing! When you surprise your mom or dad… your grandma or favorite uncle… When you put away the dishes without asking or when you bring someone home their favorite ice cream, you are acting in an unexpected manner and pleasantly surprising another.

Surprise activates the pleasure center of our brain. The experience of being surprised produces a burst of dopamine in our brain, allowing us to feel good then and there. Each time we recall the intensity of the surprise, a little more dopamine is pushed into our system until it fades away. The more meaningful the surprise - the longer the effect lasts.

Surprise pulls us into the moment. When we feel surprised, our attention is on the here and now versus some other point. Staying focused on the present eliminates frustration from the past or anxiety of the future - at least temporarily.

Surprise breaks up the monotony. We sometimes fall too easily into routines that become boring. Whether it's our daily schedule or the way we engage in our relationships, too much certainty becomes boring. When the pattern is broken or at least, interrupted by little surprises, it allows us to reset and relax; producing feelings of pleasure.

Surprise can motivate learning. When we are surprised, our brains rush to discover 'why?' or 'how?'. We wonder, "how did I miss that?" or "why did that happen?". Learning always strengthens our brain capacity and again, pulls us into the present by forcing us to pay attention. Our curiosity is activated, and confidence may increase - producing more 'happy' chemicals in our brain.

When we give - we often receive. In this case, you'll be pulled into the present moment as well. You'll be focused on something (someone) other than yourself. You'll be creating feelings of pleasure and happiness for another human being. You'll more than likely be the receiver of appreciation - activating pleasure centers in your own brain. It's a win -win situation when you pleasantly…

Surprise someone.

#88 Learn to drive a stick-shift

Of course, some of you may know how to do this but there are millions who do not. It's true that you may never need to know how to shift gears while depressing the clutch but then again, knowledge is power. And, we never know when our obscure talents may be needed.

The car I learned to drive on was a little Mazda that my dad cherished. There are lots of family stories about my early driving... my brother can get a crowd howling when he describes getting whiplash on the way to Little League practice. And then there was the time that I coasted straight into the garage door of my Aunt's home because her driveway was situated on a steep incline.

Don't let those incidents deter you. It got better!

Knowing how to drive a standard transmission vehicle (also referred to as 'stick-shift') can come in handy. It will save you hundreds of dollars on a weekly car rental in Europe where most of the cars are still standard. It may help you in the event of an emergency when you need to drive any car available and the only one is stick. Or when your designated driver forgets his duties and you're the only sober one in the crowd.

It's never a bad idea to develop a skillset – especially one that is disappearing. True, self-driving cars may eventually eliminate the need for any of us to use this skill, but I'm a 'just in case' kind of gal and my recommendation stands...

Learn to drive a stick-shift.

#89 Do a good deed

Think about this phrase 'do a good deed' for a minute. What does it mean to you? Does it mean a kind gesture? What would that look like?

There are more ways to do a good deed than there are words to describe how it may be enacted. From returning a grocery cart for someone to paying for a full grocery order - it can cost nothing or as much as you would like to give. It can take barely any energy or be a full day of hard labor. It might be working with a bona-fide charity or simply some random act that was spontaneous.

It doesn't matter how large or small a good deed is, the act itself is important. Why?

Turns out that when we do something nice for someone, the pleasure centers in our brain are activated - another way that we produce the happy chemical dopamine. Research has repeatedly indicated that people who are consistently benevolent report higher levels of well-being than others.

Perhaps the key element here is 'consistent'. I'd wager that most of us have done something nice for someone at one point or another and we may not consider ourselves 'happy'. Yet, when we extend kindness over and over again, day after day… we are also benefiting.

Kindness begets kindness and so our good deed may in fact, be the one that begins a ripple in the energy of generosity. Some would argue that the extension of kindness is the ultimate journey for our souls; that to aid those less fortunate than ourselves is a social or spiritual rule. In any regard - it will help you feel better about yourself and probably about your circumstances as we can always find someone more in need than we are.

Do yourself - do someone else - a favor today and …

Do a good deed.

#90 Write down a favorite childhood memory.

Close your eyes for a minute and allow yourself to go back in time - back to when you were a child. Allow yourself to remember a moment of laughter, of comfort, or fun. What was happening then? Who was there? What were you thinking and feeling? What about that particular memory stands out?

Go ahead and write down the details - the answer to the above questions - for this memory and then do it again, and again.

Take the time to cherish, even savor, each of those memories as you write them. The act of writing will refresh your memory even more (perhaps stimulating additional details). Remembering pleasant times stimulates those pleasure areas in our brain and while they don't spur the same level of chemicals that the actual even does, there is some dopamine production with the remembering.

Writing down the fun times helps to honor the experiences so that they balance our perspectives more evenly. Our brains are still wired to be noticing everything that is wrong (survival instinct) and so when we take time to reflect on the positives, we appreciate the true balance that typically exists in our overall existence.

If nothing else, writing down these memories captures them for our later reflection or maybe even more importantly, for the people who love us. My children are always intrigued about my childhood and how I spent time before video games and electronics. They find it interesting to imagine how we lived in a time that they've only read about or seen represented on television. The world is continuing to change, so capturing this little slice of history may be impactful to all of our future generations. How fun for all when we sit around and remember that time when Granny…

Write down a favorite childhood memory (or two).

#91 Share knowledge with a child

There's a special kind of feeling when we teach someone and they 'get it'. No matter who you are, you have knowledge about something that you can impart to a child. Extra points for that knowledge that isn't offered in a 'book'; real life experience.

When I think of this suggestion, I think about a Grandpa standing with a fishing pole, teaching his grandson how to load the hook. I think about the scout leader who teaches a youngster how to build a campfire. I think about a neighbor who points out different bugs in the warm summer dirt to a curious next-door friend wanting to dig there.

As any teacher can tell us, many children are simply sponges for information and learn best by getting their hands wrapped around the essence of an experience. When we share ourselves and the things we know how to do, no matter what they are, learning ensues.

In our fast-paced world, too many of us are 'doing' instead of 'teaching' the things we know. Yes, it's easier. If I bake the cookies myself, I know that the ingredients have been measured correctly, the kitchen is cleaned up as I go along, and I've turned my head to sneeze. And yet, the technique or recipe that my mom shared with me cannot possibly be handed down unless I am patient enough to make messes and tolerate a few potential germs.

Each one of us has something we can share even if it is how to think positively or embrace the joy of life. Perhaps those are the dogmas more important than anything one may be able to learn via a book or the internet. Be an example of something and watch understanding wash over an innocent face as you…

Share knowledge with a child.

#92 Get up for the sunrise

Some of you may do this daily as you prepare to begin your workday and yet there are millions of you who don't frequently make time to experience this daily wonder; do you really 'see' it?? Depending on the day of course, the sunrise is either visible, or not. It is either majestic, or not. But it is always dependable and THAT is part of its wonder.

The sun comes up regardless of politics, pains, joys, seasons, etc. and while it may seem like a rather primitive or conspicuous concept, it has value because of its constancy. Like 'Annie' always sings… "the sun will come up tomorrow". It's good to know that no matter how much change happens in our lives, the sun will still come up like it did yesterday and will again tomorrow; whether you actually 'see' it or not.

So, getting up and watching the sun rise may impact your thoughts; reinforcing that there are constants in the world. Standing with your face against the Eastern breeze as the sky turns orange and/or pink offers a perfect opportunity to experience a very specific type of mindfulness. Depending on where you live, it takes somewhere between 2 minutes (at the equator) and 5-6 minutes in northern latitudes for the sun's disk to rise above the horizon. That offers a short - but impactful - opportunity to practice mindful gratitude with a very specific visual.

Yes, gratitude because the sunrise represents yet another opportunity for you to begin anew. It acts as a reminder that some things just are - no matter what - a reminder that is beneficial to us periodically. It represents a certain amount of energy available from the Universe and if you are there - watching it… go ahead and grab it.

It's just a few minutes of your time and although it's early in the morning, I can't think of any other way to jumpstart each morning. Grab your coffee or tea, step outside, and embrace the magic of the moment since you made the decision to…

Get up with the sunrise.

#93 Behave like a child

Well… good behavior only please. One of the most endearing elements of childhood is a child's ability to be present - in the moment - at almost any given time. They are free from the fear of judgment for a few years (until socialization kicks in high gear) and so they live freely.

A child doesn't care about what they're wearing or even if their shoes are on the right feet. They don't care about sitting in the dirt or how much sand ends up in their britches. They play outside in the cold or heat without much bother and when given the chance - they'll use their imagination to discover an entirely new world. They'll make noise and jump around in silly ways. They laugh and cry at will.

They'll say, "I love you" and "no" without hesitation. And there is rarely an ulterior motive. For a few brief years, we all exist without the restrictions and rigidness that growing up births.

Today - or this week at least - find a playground and swing on the swings or sit on the merry-go-round as it spins and laugh yourself silly. Grab an ice cream cone and share it with someone you love - taking turns with the licks. Sit in the grass and look for four-leaf clovers - reveling in delight should you actually find one. Or have a brownie sundae for dinner without any guilt or shame at all.

If you need help thinking of something to delight in like only a child can, spend a few minutes watching a group of children. Notice how present they are. Pay attention to the raw emotion they demonstrate at any given moment. How might your life benefit from a little reminder of what it was like before you learned not to…

Behave like a child.

#94 Skate

I know there are adults out there that routinely either roller or ice skate but as a percentage of the population, I believe the number is quite small. As a kid, my favorite Saturday morning past time - right after cartoons - was a walk down to the skating rink so that I could be there right at noon when they opened. It was the reason I babysat - my allowance wasn't high enough to rent boots, skate, AND have snacks.

Once I was able to drive my wheels - skating took the backseat and eventually, failed to make the ride altogether. I'd like to think it was because as I grew taller, the falls fell harder; but really it was just laziness. It was far easier to drive to a variety of places that I really wanted to go versus moving myself around in circles and breaking a sweat even if we did so to some really groovy music and a huge mirror ball.

Today, inline skaters cruise along boardwalks and streets, roller skating rinks are updated and making a comeback, and ice rinks are a great place to cool off on a hot summer afternoon. Many of us who grew up skating have introduced our kids to the joys we experienced before electronics dominated our time. Skates have transitioned into rather comfortable footwear making tricky footwork even more possible for those tempted to get fancy.

Skating is a great way to burn a few calories, laugh, and perhaps reignite a few of those fun childhood memories. It's an activity that you might try on one of those days when you "can't think of anything to do" or when you're just tired of doing the same old thing. Whether you're at the beach and trying some outdoor time with inline rentals, taking your children to the local Skatetown Rink, or deciding to glide across ice, it's great exercise and family time when you get together to ...

Skate.

#95 Clean out your wallet / purse

Purses hold much more than wallets, but I've seen a few wallets that bulge far beyond their design. For some reason, many of us tend to collect receipts, business cards, reminders, lists, etc.... in our wallets. Some of us carry around store loyalty cards for stores that we haven't visited in years. I recently found a 'stamp card' for a local ice cream shop that had been closed for longer than I can remember. It was tucked behind another frequent buyer card for a grocery store that I rarely frequent. Both cards were removed and destroyed.

When I was a mom with little kids, my purse was a secondary diaper bag. At any point it contained a pacifier and a package of wipes. Those items may have still been in my purse when my youngest was four because I was famous for neglecting the organization of anything personal. Today, cleaning out my wallet or purse is a weekly event and takes seconds.

Why is this important at all? It's a tiny thing - literally taking less than 60 seconds when done frequently - that demonstrates a clear 'personal' priority. Your wallet and/or purse is something you reach for consistently... potentially several times a day. By taking time to organize and prioritize that thing we constantly have in our presence we feel more in control, more in the know, and aware.

All of those things contribute to overall feelings of well-being. Really... it's a collection of little things that lead to feeling the big things. This suggestion is simple and yet so effective... find out what happens when you ...

Clean out your wallet / purse.

#96 Save $5

Who doesn't love a sale?? We used to say that you could mark a price *up* - add a 'sale' sign and my mom wouldn't even notice. She loved the 'idea' of getting a bargain yet often spent money she didn't have on things she didn't need just because 'they were on sale'. Today.... I am suggesting that you try to save *five* dollars as you move through the day - spending what you would ordinarily spend. This isn't a suggestion to buy something you don't want or need for the mere fact it would save you money 'in the long run'.

Why $5? It's a relatively small amount that adds up quickly and over just a little time - it's big money. In fact, it totals $35 a week and over the course of a year - with consistency - it amounts to $1800!! What would you do with that much money? A trip to Europe? (I checked this morning and a RT ticket to Barcelona, Spain from Newark, NJ in October is only $396) What about a cruise? Perhaps you're thinking something more practical... pay off a credit card... buy a new fridge... new carpet perhaps? How about a Christmas fund? Potentially better... how about putting that money in a savings account for emergencies or a longer-term savings goal?

Many of us spend five dollars without blinking an eye. We drive through Starbucks and spend more than that on a Venti Latte or at Dunkin Donuts where at least we can get a couple of glazed to go with the coffee. If you are buying lunch every day (instead of grabbing leftovers from your home fridge), you're spending $7 or more dollars - and perhaps throwing away those dinner remnants. With gas prices at the $3/gal mark, we might be spending five bucks just by driving without considering the most efficient route. Is there a toll road you can bypass? What about using coupons? Extreme savers buy two newspapers to double up on the coupon opportunities, but we can print them from our computers too.

If you can't save $5 - try making it. Use yard sale sites on Facebook or apps like LetGo to sell something that you no longer use. With the snap of a photo, you can transfer ownership of clothes, household goods, tools, etc.... very easily. Whether you use this method or focus on saving, you'll be amazed at how quickly you begin to accumulate funds. All because you stopped to think about ...

Saving $5.

#97 Appreciate nature

So, maybe the 'tree huggers' were on to something. It seems as though literally embracing nature is good for mental health and fosters happiness. There is a certain homeostasis in the outdoors to which our internal barometers react positively. While it's better to get outside on a sunny day to absorb as much of that Vitamin D as possible, studies tell us just communing with the great mother earth in any capacity will bolster our feel-good rating.

It can be a walk in the fog which offers a distinct visual perspective that ignites our sense of mystery and wonder. Perhaps taking a stroll in the rain that excites your auditory system from the sound of the droplets on an umbrella to the great rolls of thunder in the dense sky above. It might even be as simple as sitting in the center of your backyard as you watch the squirrels scamper across a fence or the branches of a nearby tree as you notice how the evergreens have sprouted new spring growth.

There is so much to notice and hence, appreciate about the natural state of our planet and its animal inhabitants. Even though I work diligently to keep them away from my kitchen counters, I easily find myself mesmerized by the workings of an outdoor ant colony and could make their trail the focus of meditation without much effort.

No excuses here. Even city dwellers can step outside and look up. All kinds of birds allow us a window to the appreciation of one of Mother Nature's wonders. The goal is to see, acknowledge, and appreciate the essence of nature and its interwoven magic. Just a few minutes at a time; deliberate and with attention…

Appreciate nature.

#98 Self-help books on the nightstand

Heraclites, a Greek philosopher stated "Change is the only constant in life" – a quote you've probably seen a hundred times as you moved into adulthood. Rarely do I find that people are introspective about personal change.

Unless of course, they are of the 'self-help' mindset and/or focused on their mental health as a habit. I'd love to encourage everyone to adopt a 'self-help' mentality – in part so that we each take personal responsibility for our actions, reactions, relationships, and lives. The broader part though is that we too, are always changing and if we are not doing so in awareness, we get caught off guard.

Keeping a 'self-help' book on your nightstand or in your kindle/e-reader will help you stay present with where you are and what you are thinking. If doesn't have to be heavy duty stuff all the time. It can be a book of inspiring quotes that reminds you of the progress you've already made. It can be a bible that reinforces your faith (yes, I put the bible in a 'self-help' category).

I don't pick self-help books – I let them pick me. In the days that I began my collection, I would peruse the personal development and/or the spirituality section of the bookstore; allowing my eyes to roam across the titles like a gentle wave until something specific caught my attention. Once it did, I would pick up the book and without reading the cover, I would open it haphazardly and read what was there. IF it resonated, even slightly, I considered it. I still use that method, but I buy half as many bound books these days as I've fallen in love with Audible and the ability to listen no matter what I am doing. I often listen to books over music and find that I'm 'reading' more than ever with this option available to me.

I will caveat this idea with the warning that one can 'overload' on information and it's equally important to allow yourself to step back from 'self-improvement' from time to time so that the things you've learned can take root. Personal growth is best accomplished the way we physically grow – in spurts with solidifying periods in between. I found the best way to keep myself motivated along the way is to have…

Self-help books on the nightstand.

#99 Take a bath

A friend of mine has described growing up in a home with ten people and one bathroom - without a shower. The only option for personal hygiene was the tub which, doesn't sound especially pleasant. Once showering was a common household option for body cleanliness, the tub was for kids. And then Calgon enticed us to get back in the tub and the bathtub took on new meaning.

Indeed - taking a bath is good for your health on many levels.

Most importantly, relaxing neck deep in warm water for even a few quiet minutes can help your body dismiss built up stress. The warmth of the water helps to sooth sore or tired muscles. It can moisturize your skin. With a few drops of aromatherapy, it may offer benefits to your sinuses and/or respiratory system.

To make the most out of your bath time, turn the lights down low or turn them off and light a candle. Play some soothing music and grab a glass of wine or a cup of tea. Leave your book, magazine, or electronics in another room so that this time is dedicated to you and your thoughts. Quiet your mind by concentrating on the sensation of your body suspended in the water. Stay in until your fingers crinkle or the water turns tepid.

Understandably, you may not be able to indulge yourself with a 30-minute time out every day of the week but scheduling time with your tub on a regular basis is a great addition to your self-care plan. Surely, one of the most basic pleasures is to ...

Take a bath.

#100 Wipe down your baseboards

I know, this isn't the most glamorous or fun-loving suggestion. It's likely to conjure images of sweat and wrinkly hands and for some of us... fatigue and back pain. It's not exactly a recipe for happiness. It is a recipe for satisfaction though and satisfaction is a major component of well-being.

Our baseboards are mostly invisible - perhaps not literally as I'm sure you can take a look right now... down toward the floor, that area that bridges the joining of wall and floor. We rarely think of them and you probably can't see the whole of them as you look around as furniture and miscellaneous items are surely obstructing part of your view; but they're there and if your house is like many of ours... they're dirty - or at the very least... dusty.

Baseboards are a forgotten element for a vast number of people, and they can get grungy... perhaps even enough so that the accumulated dust gets stirred up and negatively impacts the air quality in the home. Have you noticed frequent sneezing? A runny nose? Or a tickle in your throat? Grab the vacuum and a bucket of hot soapy water. You may find it more efficient to bribe (I mean hire) short young people for this task. There were years where my children thought it was a fun task because they wore big yellow gloves and rocked out to MTV - which I never let them watch otherwise!

I guarantee you'll be pleasantly surprised when you're sitting on the john and glance down at the sparkling clean woodwork. It may be an unpleasant task, but you'll be completely satisfied after making the decision to ...

Wipe down your baseboards.

#101 Pick wildflowers

Do you remember the smile on your mother's face when you presented her with the first Dandelion you ever picked? Do you remember how much fun it was to see the yellow glow of a buttercup under your friend's chin? Have you known the delight of watching a stem of Queen Anne's Lace change colors because you added food coloring to the water it was in? Have you felt the satisfaction of collecting naturally grown flowers from a field or the side of a road?

These are simple joys available to many of us with the simple act of collecting a few wildflowers (or weeds as they might be). It's an example of one of those childhood activities that promotes innocent delight almost immediately. Flowers grow naturally and spontaneously throughout the world and while their natural beauty is enjoyable, there is something even more special about collecting pieces of it to share indoors. I'm certainly not speaking about digging up a natural landscape and transplanting... only picking a few sprigs of color to surprise a loved one, brighten your own home, or to dry and press as an addition to your memory book.

The flower itself is only part of the experience of course... walking through nature's beauty is, in and of itself an activity that promotes happiness; being outdoors, moving, and breathing fresh air is good for us all. Enjoying the scenery of blooming flowers - especially entire meadows or a forest undergrowth can be breathtaking and awe inspiring.

Of course, if you are walking through a nature preserve or another protected property - please be respectful of your surroundings and don't pick - just enjoy. Additionally, a large bouquet of Goldenrod may not be an appropriate presentation to someone with seasonal allergies. However, a few stems of honeysuckle will make your entire home smell good for a few days and a handful of violets will add a lovely purple splash to your windowsill all week.

Take advantage of a nice day and find a quiet place to take a walk, enjoy the scenery and if appropriate...

Pick wildflowers.

#102 Follow a self-care plan

When a battery runs out of juice, the object that it powers cannot operate. When a plant doesn't get watered, it dies. When our automobiles run out of gasoline, they will not move. Quite simply, when something is not cared for, it will not be able to function properly. There is a concrete reason that we adults must place the oxygen masks on our face *first* and then, our children even though it seems to go against our caregiving nature.

You see, for us to function in the world we must have the energy, the stamina, the drive, and the desire … to keep going. It doesn't matter if our role is motherhood, boss, nurse, postal worker, farmer, delivery driver, or trash collector. Unless we have taken care of ourselves, we are unable to properly serve in the capacities to which we have otherwise committed.

Using this simplistic line of reasoning - self-care is not selfish, it is a necessity.

What is self-care? It is anything that charges your batteries, waters your soul, gases your tank, etc. It could be a bubble bath, reading a book in a hammock, a round of golf, a girl's night out, crafting time, veggin' out for a bit or any similar activity that feels nourishing to *you*. It's classic 'me time'.

I've heard it argued that cleaning house and pulling weeds are also 'me time' for those who absolutely love those activities and/or those whose sense of satisfaction are so high afterwards; they bask in the completed results - so okay. It's not the outlet for my energy but that's the key behind self-care; it is personal and unique to each individual. The only requirement is that you establish and…

Follow a self-care plan.

#103 A Day of Photography.

In her book Big Magic, author Elizabeth Gilbert posits that we all have at least 'some' creative energy that is often untapped. Photography is a great way to begin unpacking artistic instinct. So, grab a camera - whether it's your phone or a 35mm that's been collecting dust - and go outdoors.

Take a walk or a drive but with your artistic eye. Go out with the intent to capture color and/or light versus people or things. Part of what makes what we look at interesting and beautiful is the way that it appears in light; distinguishing colors and textures. Change your typical perspective by sitting on the ground or getting up high. As you move through your environment, look past the usual and seek to see more detail. When you notice it… capture it from as many angles as you can.

The digital element of photography these days means we can shoot as many images as we want without regard to expense. It's another gift of technology. By taking the time to examine a scene or an object through the lens of a camera and with attention to shadows at a variety of angles, you may see the same things looking immensely different.

Don't worry about knowing what to do … use your instinct at first and if you find that you have ignited a talent and/or an interest, you can keep learning. Or, you can remain a noob and shoot photos for fun and interest.

Warning: there is a rabbit hole here… once you capture a few images and upload them onto your computer there is a whole world of photo editing that may seize your curiosity and imagination. Play and have fun. This is an opportunity for you to be creative, get outdoors, be present, move your body, and experience your world in a new way. So many benefits from a simple …

Day of Photography.

#104 Remember when...

This recommendation might sound a bit like the idea of savoring that I presented earlier but it's a bit different in its goal. The idea here is to recall random shared memories of minor debacles when you are with another person with whom you have some history. Ideally, you're thinking of a time that you can laugh about now. A time when you had solved a problem, survived a hazard, or preserved through a challenge.

The goal is laughter or at the very least, an appreciation for the lesson learned. It's an opportunity to review a moment in time from another perspective and share a sense of satisfaction of a previous experience.

'Remember when we got that flat tire and...'
'Remember when I left the cake in the oven for an hour...'
'Remember when we took the wrong bus...'

We all have countless recollections of mishaps and momentary errors in judgment that are retrospectively funny or immensely satisfying. Sometimes, just recalling the collection of awkward moments we shared with another strengthens our appreciation of their role in our life. It's another type of walk down memory lane that can have you rolling on the floor laughing or being grateful that it is over now.

Pick up the phone today and share a blast from the past with an old friend or randomly bring it up at the dinner table tonight... "hey honey..."

Remember when...

#105 Change your curtains

I've talked a lot about little things around the house that create a big impact on our mental health and sense of well-being. When our daily environment is in order, we feel more in control. When our personal space is tidy and tailored to our taste, we experience a deeper sense of comfort and belonging - both important elements of true happiness.

One of the little things that can change the entire feel of a room is to change the curtains. Window dressings can be art, contributing to the overall decor in a majestic way.

They can be simple and elegant.
They can be creative and a deeply personal expression of you.
They can be eclectic and colorful.

Some people invest a lot of money in window treatments and feel compelled to keep them for a long time. The only problem with this concept is that style and interest changes as time goes by. After a few years, that significant investment represents a dated design.

If you're not feeling particularly creative, use Pinterest to collect images of things you might like, things you may want to consider as you contemplate a change. As you consider modifications, remember to step out of your comfort zone and take a bit of a risk. Without that, nothing can be different. What would your choice be if you were to …Change your curtains.

#106 Freshen your pillows

Do you have a plan to replace old, worn out pillows? If you're like me, I think about it when I am changing the linens and then I forget or put them at the bottom of my priority list - you know, below pedicures and sushi nights. Admittingly, there have been times in my life when I was forced to double case a pillow to hide the dried drool stains and evidence of age if I was in a pinch. At those moments, new pillows became a priority.

Let's face it, one-third of each day is spent in bed with our heads on a pillow; having the right one is a necessity for a good night's sleep and potentially, for our health. According to some experts, the basic polyfill pillow needs replaced every six months (what??). The more expensive memory foam pillows can last as long as 36 months (double what??). I'm embarrassed to admit that mine are much older.

Indeed, my primary - my favorite - pillow is perhaps 8 years old at this point and I've kept it because I can't seem to find one that I like as much. There are so many different pillow options these days and if money isn't a concern three are plenty to consider. We must choose between content; feathers, down, memory foam, microbead, water, gel or buckwheat. Then there are the different body parts that pillows support; neck, body, and shoulders. There are pillows for health; sleep apnea, allergies, back pain, and migraines. And, not the least of which is important is the degree of firmness - several options in that arena are also available.

The best time to buy pillows is in January when most of the major merchandisers have annual white sales but I for one, am usually not shopping that time of year... more like recovering from December's blown budget. It seems rather sensical that I bite the bullet and search sales for new pillows on those beds that get used daily at least annually... (yes, I'm inclined to buy the cheaper ones).

If I've totally grossed you out now that you are thinking about how old most of the pillows are in your house, the fix is simple... for just $12or so (each) this weekend at the nearest department store, you can...

Freshen your pillows.

#107 Repurpose something

Have you caught on to the repurpose craze? Are you a DIY'er that would rather spend $10 and ten hours of your time to create something new-to-you versus buying something brand new from a store? Repurposing isn't a new idea, or even something that was emphasized when HGTV made it mainstream.

Most of our grandmothers were queens at repurposing. I don't think mine ever threw out a plastic bread bag - those were her baggies. She never trashed a Styrofoam tray once butchers began using them - they were her paint trays. Necessity made repurposing a household habit perhaps as many years ago as there have been people on the planet. And yet, the concept has taken on new life and now, it's not just practicality that serves the idea of repurposing - it's imagination and art.

Thousands of blogs share creative ideas and tutorials. Pinterest is overflowing with photos of possibilities. Resale shops like ReStore run contests to promote the sale and rehabilitation of donated items. Goodwill sells dresser donations as quickly as they are donated. Yard sale buyers aren't antique and flea market dealers anymore. A stroll through craft fairs and art shows demonstrates all kinds of people who have taken repurposing to an entirely new level.

This is one of the great uses of sites like Pinterest; gathering ideas and inspiration for projects that you'd like to entertain. After an hour or so of evoking your creative potential you'll be ready to hit a yard sale or resale shop to find the pieces you'll reinvent. Whether it is a piece of art, a conversation piece, or something more practical like shelving or under-the-bed storage… you'll for sure, experience tremendous satisfaction once you…

Repurpose something.

#108 Activate for a day

How do you find purpose in life? One sure fire way is to become involved in a cause. Working to save the planet, animals, clean water, personal freedoms, borders, etc., will surely boost your sense of purpose. Thousands of animals are saved and replaced each year because of the love and support of people working to save them. Millions of gallons of clean water are provided to people in need because someone is dedicated to that initiative. Millions upon millions of people have marched over the years in support of a cause that they felt loyal toward.

It's possible that activism is more prevalent today than at any other time since the Vietnam War. In part because of our current political climate but also because the need for sustainable support is significant around the globe.

What does it mean to be an activist? It is a "person who campaigns to bring about political or social change" and it can be accomplished in a myriad of ways. Make a poster and walk with it; stand on a busy street corner with it; post it in your window or yard. Spend a day calling the 'powers that be' - the president of a company, or your elected officials. Engage in a letter writing campaign or find out what type of supplies your cause uses and shop for /donate them in person.

These are but a few methods of involving yourself in an activity that serves something you care about. An argument I hear a lot is 'one person can't make a difference' but truly... it only takes ONE person's idea or love of something to get a ball rolling. In fact, most radical change is accomplished when a MINORITY of people get on the same bandwagon and make noise. What do you care about? What cause or group of people stimulate your values or moral beliefs? What are you outraged about? What breaks your heart?

Think what might change if every single one of us got up and became committed to ACT on a cause close to our hearts. If you are not currently contributing any time or talent on behalf of someone other than yourself, I encourage you to...

Activate for a day.

#109 Spend a day nude

The more modest of you may cringe at this idea and yet I am confident that most of you will find it liberating. There are benefits to living some of your life (or occasionally part of your day at least) in the buff.

This suggestion is especially important for those of you who have skin problems. Clothing can exacerbate many of those issues because fabric can be abrasive and tight enough to compromise circulation. Air freely circulates when we don't cover our bodies and perspiration evaporates more effectively.

Connecting skin to skin promotes the release of oxytocin - a chemical in our brain that helps us feel good. It's the love hormone. Just the act of being naked for a prolonged period will entice you to want sex; you'll feel sexier. Your libido will increase.

The more comfortable you become with your body, the better your self-esteem and the more quickly any accumulated / taught shame you may have been taught about your body, will dissipate.

When you allow ALL your skin to capture sunlight, there is a vast increase in vitamin D absorption. Of course, that's a happy vitamin. Higher levels of Vitamin D will contribute to higher feels of well-being.

We all sleep better when we are cooler and so instead of lowering the air temp in your house by cranking up the AC... ditch the jammies and you'll reduce your body temperature naturally.

These are just a few of the benefits of stripping down to your birthday suit for a bit of time. I'm not suggesting that you join a nudist colony, but you may find a week's vacation on a nude beach gives you the experience and benefits we're talking about here. Just one warning... on my first experience at a nude beach I lathered all exposed areas heavily with sunscreen with focus on those places that were not acquainted with sunshine. In all the preparations - I forgot my ears! Blistered earlobes are not any more comfortable than burned butt cheeks so lather freely with a high-level sunscreen!

Spend the day nude.

#110 Go on a date

This advice is particularly focused on those of you in a relationship of some nature although I'll mention single folks too. As a marriage counselor, perhaps the single most common reason that people end up in my office is because they lose connection with one another due to lack of energy directed to their relationship.

Dating is how many of us got to know one another. It is how we built emotional intimacy, how we discovered our interests and commonalities. After a few years, we assume that we have nothing left to say and our conversations center on work, bills, and perhaps kids. Novelty, excitement, and interest begins to wane.

I recently discussed self-care and its importance to our mental and ultimately, physical health. Its message pertains to relationships as well. What is starved - hungers; what is not watered - dies.

What is a good date?

First and foremost, do something you consider fun. If we're not enjoying ourselves, it will be challenging to engage positively.

Consider also to do something active. Engaging body and mind doubles our personal interaction and creates a broader dimension for conversation. From bowling, kayaking, a ropes course, or rock climbing... an active date will offer opportunities for conversation that goes beyond your day to day life.

Don't use this time together to resolve issues. Step back from the struggles or challenges in your life and allow the date to be a mental vacation.

Find time to physically connect. Some people use a date night for an exclusive opportunity to spend time connecting sexually. While this is definitely an important element in any solid relationship - it is not the end all. Sex without an emotional connection is available anywhere. To keep a connection with your partner, it is imperative that both the emotional and physical are combined. It doesn't matter which element comes first as long as both are present. To clarify, physical connection doesn't 'have' to be sex... holding hands while strolling through a festival and staring into one another's eyes for a few minutes can intensify a couple's connection nicely.

Are you single?

Most of the same advice applies. I'm hearing more and more from clients and family how single people are dating less and 'hanging' more. The 'Netflix and chill' mentality has infiltrated the tradition of getting to know one another by getting out and 'doing'. I see people who developed a relationship over movies and sex but are now wondering what they actually have in common outside those parameters.

When you've moved past the 'swipe right' stage, step out and do something fun! Find common interests and activities that you can get passionate about together. There's a lot of truth to the old adage... "the family that plays together, stays together.

Do your relationship a favor and make it a point to...

Go on a date.

"Happiness depends upon ourselves" —
Aristotle

#111 Try a new food

Is there a type of food that you've never tried? Have you had Thai food? Vietnamese? Lebanese? Sushi? Beef Tongue? Tripe? Escargot? Liver? Eggplant?

There's a good chance that a few of you already incorporate one, two, or more of these into your regular diet and there's a better chance that most of you have yet to try at least one or two of these edibles. As a child, I never developed a taste for Eggplant no matter how much tomato sauce smothered it and yet as an adult I was blown away by a Ratatouille recipe I found last summer and thoroughly enjoyed some fried eggplant my daughter made after we brought home a box full from our farm share.

My grandfather raised Black Angus cattle and tried to entice us with beef tongue a time or two... honestly - as children we were completely disgusted with the concept but one of my favorite Mexican restaurants serves tongue tacos and they are amazing!

I've ventured into Sushi in recent years and can't quite get to the Sashimi level but most other parts of the menu - the cooked items - are new favorites and really - anything with Wasabi... Yum. (Try mixing a little into ranch dressing for a new kick).

Lots of foods that we turned our noses up to in our younger years may have a new lease in your diet, but you have to give them another chance. I flat out refused to eat Asparagus as a teenager, but it is a staple on my grocery list these days.

New foods shake up our taste buds and make meals more interesting. Trying something out of the ordinary addresses our sense of adventure and may meet part of our need for variety. If you're going to go out to dinner - go someplace new. If nothing else, go someplace that is offering something you won't eat at home (making Escargot may be more involved than a typical weeknight allows for).

Even if you can't get motivated to change this dramatically and find yourself at your neighborhood Applebee's for the second time this week... at least order something different from the menu!! The point is to shake it up a bit and ...

Try a new food.

#112 Plant a tree

I can imagine how many of you have already planted a tree in your own yard and I am suggesting that you go ahead and plant another. This one is for no particular reason other than to do something great for the planet. One mature tree can produce enough oxygen for two people to breathe for a solid year.

This year, the maple trees dropped their seeds furiously onto a warm rain-soaked ground and I have maple sprouts - everywhere! Seriously... everywhere. I dug up a couple and planted them in spare pots with the intention to care for them with my other seasonal flowers. The ultimate goal of course, is to grow this seedling until its mature enough to be transplanted into its forever spot.

I'm not suggesting that you undertake a maple seedling, but rather pick out a small tree that works with your landscape and give it a home. If you are an urban dweller, perhaps you can donate a tree via One Tree Planted - an organization that engages in reforestation of forested lands; one tree - one dollar. At the very least, your dollar contributes to the production of oxygen for the planet.

If you have the ability to plant a tree on your property, take a photo. For reference, ask one of your family members to stand next to it - grab a patio chair - or park your car close by. As the years go by, you can snap another photo and notice its growth. There is a deep sense of satisfaction watching a tree mature over time - particularly one that you planted by hand.

Next time you stroll around the yard pay attention to possible areas where you might...

Plant a tree.

#113 Be adventurous

Are you willing to take risks? Try new things? Test new ideas? Enjoy new experiences? If so… congrats, you are adventurous, and I suspect your happiness level reflects as much.

Adventure is about curiosity. Happiness research indicates that when we are curious in our daily life, it may elevate our happy base line. This is great news for people who tend to be glass half empty type of people. Many of us operate from a state of fear and it keeps us locked into familiar positions. When we are curious… i.e., adventurous… we step out of that comfort zone and - in many cases - are pleasantly surprised.

Adventure is personal. For some, it may be bungee jumping. For others, it may be getting on an airplane. It's the unknown, the uncertain, maybe even the mysterious which, of course is different for us all based on experience.

Taking risks is difficult for some. Start close to your comfort level. Increase by degrees and pay attention to your body which, is uniquely designed to warn you when you are approaching the boundary of risk tolerance. Push lightly - a little at a time - and before you know it, the benefits of being adventurous will be felt.

Adventure helps us grow. When we experiment a little (or a lot), we will have successes and successes grow confidence. Yes, some of those trials will not be as successful as we hope but trying again is being adventurous and each time we try, we open the door to success and the elation that comes with it. There's a great surge of dopamine that travels with the words "I did it!".

Stop for a minute and think of something that would feel just a little outside of your comfort zone, or a place you've never gone, or a thing you've always wanted to do and make plans to…

Be adventurous.

124

#114 Share a secret

Rational thought needs to be utilized here as we don't want to share a secret that belongs to 'someone else'. The idea is to share one of *your* secrets... one of the things we've been keeping hidden for fear that someone will judge us harshly. Perhaps something that causes shame for us.

Letting the proverbial 'cat out of the bag' to the wrong person may not go well. If you are hesitant to share your secret with someone you know there are a couple of options...

Talk with clergy. Either your own pastor or another. Everyone in this position I've ever been acquainted with has an open-door policy and will talk with anyone, regardless of faith.

Talk to someone on a 'helpline'. There are National Helplines for almost any topic one can think of. Generally, the people there are trained to listen well and can direct you onward if you need additional support.

Talk with a Therapist. A psychotherapist that is... someone trained and licensed in mental health. Some therapists do not accept health insurance so ask before you schedule the appointment.

All of those professionals are guided by ethical guidelines and confidentiality unless you indicate you are going to hurt yourself or a child. They are secret keepers, dumpsters, vaults, etc...., dumping grounds for the things that we don't want to hold on to any longer.

Once you relieve yourself of the secret, chances are you will feel lighter almost immediately. A secret only has power when it exists inside. Once we share it - its power is reduced, and we can seek resolution for any additional stress or negative emotions that arise. Sometimes, we just need a little perspective about the issue at hand and once gained, the energy of the secret is greatly diminished.

I once had a client who confessed a deep and, in her mind, shameful secret during a counseling session. Unloading it from her head into the space in my office and hearing how normal it may have been, gave her tremendous relief and in her words "changed my life". While not every shared secret will change lives, it will allow you to live more authentically. Think about it and then...

Share a secret.

#115 Go to an auction

An auction can be great fun. It's bargain shopping at its finest. Generally speaking, you get there a little early and browse through the items to see if there is anything that you want. Once you decide you'll bid on something, check it out. Usually, when you buy something at auction - you buy it 'as is'. Consider a top range budget for your item but always, always start as low as possible. In a lot of local auctions that means $1.00.

Perhaps the most important note about bidding on items at an auction is to honor your top price limit. From time to time you may find yourself in a bidding war with someone else who has decided to take home the one thing you wanted. Since you don't know their limit - honor yours. It's super frustrating to get home and realize you completely overpaid for something just because you wanted to 'win'. A little internet research prior to the bidding for your item is helpful.

My favorite auctions are estate sales on premises. An auctioneer moves around the property selling boxes of items collected from the home. You bid on the entire box of 'smalls' even though you may only want one thing in the box. You take it all if you win. Many of my yard sales were for the 'other things' that I inadvertently obtained by bidding on a box lot. It may be everything that came out from under the kitchen sink - a box filled with cleaning supplies and I start the bidding at $1. Most people are not there for the cleaning supplies and so I win the box… grab a bargain… and end up with random items that may or may not end up in the trash.

Auction houses also sell box lots. They tend to be more organized and related, meaning that there are less 'random' elements. If you are bidding on a box because there is a vase you like… chances are the whole box is related to flowers or decorating. Prices may go higher at auction houses as well because resale dealers ten to get merchandise there. If there are antiques, you can be sure people with retail space are there supplying their inventory.

It's an experience though and can be an adventure that reaps rewards. Hop online and find out when and where an estate sale is being conducted near you and…

Go to an auction.

#116 Nurture a houseplant

Do you have a green thumb? I know some people who have such a prolific way with plants that their home resembles a greenhouse. Growing plants is simple science and with the internet at our fingertips - information on how to keep anything alive is right at our fingertips.

The presence of houseplants in our home increases the amount of oxygen available for us to breathe. Plants use the carbon-dioxide we exhale and create oxygen for us to use. Additionally, they produce a bit of humidity, making the air we breathe soothing on our airways.

Plants clean air of toxins and make a home 'homier'. In research studies, people in hospitals healed faster when plants were part of their environment. In another, workers in office environments that included plants demonstrated higher levels of concentration and proficiency. Plants, it seems, are good for our health in more ways than one.

Time magazine published an article in the Spring of 2019 detailing the 15 most common houseplants and easy-care tips. Watering too much or too little is really the key and keeping track of which plant takes how much and how often.

Look through the list and pick a few that require similar care. I've made the mistake of having some that need water weekly and others that need to dry out completely in between watering's. I would walk around and water them all at the same time not paying attention to what they really needed. There was a bit of self-selection... those that didn't get what they needed - or too much of it... died off.

Instead of investing a lot of money on large mature plants, start small and enjoy the satisfaction of watching them grow. If a plant starts to drop leaves, use the internet to determine an appropriate course of action. Experiment a little with water and sunlight based on the conditions in your own home. Some of the plants listed in the Time article will send off 'baby' plants (as in the Spider plant) when mature; offering you the opportunity to have grandbaby plants.

Go ahead and get your hands dirty; grab a pot, fill it with dirt, and ...Nurture a houseplant.

#117 Sit in a park

Generally, parks are green spaces created with our pleasure in mind. Pleasure because they offer an open space (open is relative here) where we can go for an outdoor experience. Of course, that often means some kind of activity and yet all those benches that we see in parks aren't only for rest in between activity. Perhaps you prefer to plunge right down in the grass, allowing yourself to feel the ground specifically beneath you. The goal is to find a spot in the park and to sit alone and quietly there; contemplating or observing everything in your sight.

Parks are a great place to find a few quiet moments - perhaps not quiet from the perspective of sound - but from our individual lives. There in the park, we can slip away from responsibility, from demands of work and family, and utilize the energy of the outdoor environment to rejuvenate.

As you sit there - in the park - take time to be mindful. Notice the grass, the sky, the people, the sounds, the temperature, and the textures. Pay attention to details... color differences, movement, and decibels.

One of my most favorite memories is finding the jewel of Paley Park in New York City. Walking east along 53rd street, just past MOMA, there's a small break in the storefronts - almost unnoticeable - and yet with a glance you are immediately lured into an open square canopied by trees and flanked by a wall of water falling into a pond. The sounds of Manhattan cease and your senses are filled with nature. The temperature falls instantly by ten degrees as the air is cooled and pushed by the water cascading 20 feet across the entire back of the park. Without hesitation, I pulled up a chair and allowed that space to evaporate the metropolitan energy from my mind; replacing it with a lightness and freshness that can only be induced by Mother Nature.

Understandably, most readers won't be running to Paley Park anytime soon (highly recommended if you find yourself in NYC) and yet there are dozens of options near you at any given time as our culture is rather park-minded overall. A local town square, a community green space, a state game land, or a national treasure all offer opportunities to get grounded if we just take a moment and ...

Sit on a park bench.

#118 Go to a festival

In the summer months, there seems to be a festival for just about anything you might find interesting. If you live in the Chicago Metropolitan area, there are typically more than 40 festivals in the month of July alone! While many of them appear to celebrate or focus on food such as the Roscoe Village Burger Fest or the Tacos y Tamales Festival, others focus on drink (Chicago Craft Beer Festival & the Chicago Whiskey & Wine Beach Festival). Many of them are themed around the arts or music as well. Each weekend there are several to choose from and the choice may be difficult.

Large cities offer a plethora of opportunities for festival fun, but small towns get in the mood as well. As a child, my sister and I looked forward to the Fireman's Carnival each summer. It was a traveling group that made the rounds through all of the small towns in our county and surrounding area. We rode the Ferris wheel and stood in line for the Tilt-a-Whirl no matter the summer temperature knowing we could get ices before going home. The memories made that week each year are some of my favorite childhood reflections.

With an internet connection finding a festival to attend is easy. Most large communities have Facebook pages or independent websites touting the 'things to do' each weekend. More generic sites dedicated to promoting Festivals in general also exist… Festivals.com allows you to enter a zip code to discover what's happening in that locale and it is one of many likeminded sites. It's a great resource when you find yourself in an unfamiliar city and want to get a taste (perhaps literally) of the local scene.

Check it out, look at your calendar and make plans to ...

Go to a festival.

#119 Do something unexpected

Are you predictable?

Is there someone in your life that finishes your sentences? Do people make decisions for you based on historical data? Are you in a stagnant place; doing the same thing day in and day out? When life becomes too certain or too predictable, it can become boring. While we all need certainty to some extent, too much of it is not a good thing. Stability is a great thing, but it needs to occasionally be sprinkled with variety with the understanding that tolerance for the unexpected is totally personal.

For those of us who covet certainty, it's a good idea to take some control of the variety we need and the best way to do this is to get up and do something unexpected. Make sure you're in the driver's seat when it comes to experiencing any change up in routine. I'm not suggesting any wild or crazy things necessarily. Although, if you've always been skittish about heights and suddenly express an urge to go bungee jumping, that may make sense. However, leaving a job that sustains your livelihood without another way to meet your obligations probably won't be in your best interest overall.

In order to step out of your comfort zone and do the unexpected - you must assume some amount of risk. For this reason, it is suggested that you start small - especially if you are just now stepping out. The term 'go big or go home' is novel and sounds brave but could be financially or emotionally expensive and perhaps not a good way to get your feet wet with the experience of variety. Be responsible and take calculated risks or the whole 'certainty' issue becomes more cemented.

Doing the unexpected builds confidence both in yourself and in you for those around you. It requires courage and bravery to step out into the unknown. Even if you are certain of the results, doing something that no one would anticipate can be a recipe for surprise and entertainment; both of which contribute significantly to feelings of happiness.

Do yourself a favor and keep life interesting by making a commitment to …

Do something unexpected.

#120 Go to a fair

Is there anything more American than a County or State Fair? A county or state fair is designed for the exhibition of animals and events associated with agriculture. This is where you'll find the Grand Champion Bull and the best tasting jar of bread and butter pickles. These local fairs are a breeding ground for the future of at least one part of our food supply chain. In addition, they are platforms for students and adults across the nation to show off their hard work in textiles, with animals, food, and plants, as well as heritage and crafting projects.

If you are looking for a new hybrid Azalea, chances are you'll find one at a State Fair. Would you like to motivate your children to take up sewing? A stroll through the textile area will offer a glimpse into the creations of other children in her age group. Do you want to know how to get the best egg production from your Long Island Red rooster? Talk with people who won ribbons in that category. If you're interested, even the vendors are touting their newest and shiniest machinery, gadgets, and electronics to make your endeavors higher producing, more efficient, and/or less costly.

As if all that isn't enough to entice you, some of the best local food can be found at County Fairs. There is typically a 'food barn' where local women have set up a pop-up restaurant of sorts - home cooking at its finest (at least in some locals), usually to support the community 4-H programs that are represented there. Comfort food like Grandma's Chicken & Dumplings or Uncle Pete's Fire Chili (perhaps a Blue-Ribbon Winner) are most likely on the menu.

Of course, there are rides and games to make the environment charged with excitement and anticipation but maybe the icing on the cake is the evening entertainment which, varies of course by location and Fair size. There will likely be tractor pull competitions, demolition derbies, or big-ticket concerts most evenings of the fair. Additionally, it's a common platform for Country music artists early in their career, giving us an early introduction to some great musicians. Typically, a fair runs a week, give or take a couple of days.

Go to a Fair

#121 Rearrange your furniture

As strange as it sounds, one of my fondest memories as a child was coming home from school to find that my mother had rearranged the furniture yet again. It was a habit of hers and I'm convinced that she had a personal goal of discovering an unlimited number of placement combinations.

Perhaps it was something unexpected that brought delight and pleasure to my young and spontaneous mind. Maybe it was the anticipation of change, something new and novel. Maybe it's just as simple as giving an 'old' thing new energy. Sometimes, if the only thing we can find to have control of is moving furniture, then it creates an opportunity to empower.

Rearranging your furniture also allows you to engage your inner 'Creative'. It takes imagination to consider how things may appear in another configuration. It employs our capacity to think in spatial terms; recognizing angles, depth, and size.

When we move into a space we are sometimes in a hurry, not thinking about the best layout and furniture ends up staying in its original location. Other times we replace furniture that may not fit as precisely as its predecessor. And of course, there is the consideration of Feng Shui, the Chinese practice of organizing items in our home in such a way as to create good 'qi' - meaning good 'energy'. Depending on what elements (wealth, health, love) you want to attract or support in your life, you'll want to place certain pieces of furniture in specific areas of your room. Additionally, getting rid of everything that you don't love is imperative - even if Great Aunt Ellen gave it to you.

Take a look at the area you are sitting in now... allow yourself to imagine the space a little differently and then...

Rearrange your furniture.

#122 Start your day with motivation

How do you start your day? Do you grab a cup of coffee and turn on the news? Pick up a newspaper? While it's helpful to check traffic and weather to get your commute organized, it can be a real bummer reading or listening to the day's headlines. When you get ready for your day do you pick through your closet and reject most of the pieces you grab? Are you frequently complaining about a bad hair day? Are you reeling with negative self-talk about your weight, your wrinkles, or your schedule?

If any of the above is true, is it any wonder that your day starts on a low note? Shifting that routine just a little may in fact completely turn around a dull perspective and give you a much more positive beginning each day.

Instead of listening to the news and all of its negativity, begin your day with something uplifting. Once again, we are living in a time when any information we want is at our fingertips via the internet making motivational messages only a few keystrokes away.

This is not a new concept... YouTube channels such as BeInspired and TED Talks are libraries for morning motivation. Searching motivational speakers will return inspiring lectures from Oprah Winfrey, Tony Robbins, Les Brown, Brené Brown, Brian Tracy, Marianne Williamson, and hundreds more. Almost any topic you find interesting is covered from finance and professional development to spirituality and personal growth. What area of your life do you want to grow? Grab your tablet, your smartphone, or tune your smart TV to a speech geared to energize your mental energy and listen to something inspiring instead of the morning news while you eat breakfast or prepare for the day.

The way we view life is greatly determined by the lens we begin our day with. Technology makes it easier than ever to make that choice for ourselves. Make your day better by making the decision to...

Start your day with motivation.

#123 Begin weight training

Truth is, building muscle is good for you. We know working out and aerobic exercise helps us to burn calories, burning at least as many calories as we consume is the way we keep our weight stabilized. The more muscles we have, the more calories we will burn and consequently, we can either eat a little more or loose a little weight.

For women, weight training is beneficial. Muscles burn more calories than fat and so our metabolism increases. Strength training helps us gain strength without building large muscles or bulking up. It also helps us to build bones, which staves off osteoporosis. Stronger bones and muscles means more stability and flexibility, reducing potential for injuries. Additionally, our posture is better, and we significantly reduce our tendency for back pain with a stronger core. All of these result in better mood and quality of life.

Squats, pushups, lunges, and planks are great muscle building exercises. The key is to do sets and build up slowly. Alternating sets and repetitions are one of the primary suggestions of trainers. If you're unsure where to begin, a trainer is a smart way to get your challenge started. Their expertise is invaluable when it comes to what do for what kind of result. Once you get established in a routine, there are plenty of apps, videos, and TV channels that will help you stay motivated and progressing.

Regardless of your age, there is a workout designed to keep your muscles strong and healthy. All you have to do is …

Start weight training.

#124 Keep an open mind

What does it really mean to keep an open mind? By definition, one source states it is "a willingness to try new things or to hear and consider new ideas." A long discussion on Quora concedes that it is mostly about considering possibilities over probabilities for all things because we are constantly discovering that some 'facts' were only our available perspective.

Being open minded means that we are amenable to discovering that what we once considered absolute may not actually be so. Remember when someone thought it was proper to bleed people with leeches? (yikes!) Or, when most of the world's population believed the world was flat? (apparently, some still do!) Indeed, our thoughts and beliefs are always being challenged and without the ability to consider possibilities - no matter how probable - we will forever stay locked in a rigid belief system.

Why would you want to be open minded? Well, it appears that open minded people are actually happier. They tend to be more creative, more inventive, and score higher on academic exams. They are overall more vulnerable, admit to mistakes more readily, and learn faster. Open minded people say, "I can" and "let's try" more than someone with fixed beliefs. Open minded people experience more variety in their lives.

Science and humanity are always teaching us that the only constant is change so it would make sense that believing in possibilities would open more mental and emotional doors. Wrapping our heads around the idea that no matter how probable in this moment something seems, it may actually be possible. A concept worth considering if we...

Keep an open mind.

#125 Sharpen your knives

Trying to cut through the skin of a tomato, let alone most other things, with a dull knife is frustrating enough to rile any temper. When tomato season arrives and your mouth begins to water just thinking about that first tomato sandwich, it's imperative that one has a sharp knife. In fact, a sharp knife in the kitchen is perhaps, one of the most essential utensils. It's one of those things that we don't even know we need until we experience the frustration of not being able to cut our food.

There are thousands of knives on the market, many touting their perceptual ability to sustain a sharp edge. Individual knives can go for hundreds of dollars each, but I think the average household has pretty basic cutlery. In my (average) experience, it's not so much the knife but the ability to sharpen them that counts. Thankfully, these days we don't have to resort to a whetstone or a honing rod.

Electric knife sharpeners are easy to use and relatively inexpensive. Keeping one in a kitchen cabinet where it is easily accessible means that if you can't quite get through that tomato, with just another minute or two you can run your knife across a couple of wheels and get back to slicing. There's something quite satisfying about being able to go from dull to razor sharp with just a few slides across the sharpener and then the simple success of cutting through your food with ease.

Happiness from the simple things is sometimes quite easy and only a reach away. You can start by making the effort to …

Sharpen your knives.

#126 Clean out your filing system

Anytime is a good time to be proactive about the important papers that you've either filed away or piled up. If you're internet savvy, there's really no reason to keep statements these days. Just about any financial statement you may need is available online at any given point - at least for the last three years or so. If you are still receiving paper statements, check them for accuracy and promptly file them or shred it.

Shredding any statement, piece of paper, or bill that has your financial information on it is paramount in our culture today if you aren't burning it. We all know destroying these sensitive pieces of paper is a key consideration to protect our identity and shredding is the most proficient way of accomplishing this task. It destroys the paper more efficiently than any other disposal method other than burning.

In general, the rule of thumb is to think of how difficult the document would be to replace. If it's not readily available online or if it can't be sent via email after a brief phone conversation than a filed copy may be in order. Most other things can be discarded, at least after your accountant has taken a look at it.

A good list of important documents to file versus what to throw away is by the Colorado State University Extension office. Do a Google search for the .pdf and print it for reference.

We no longer need cases of statements or four drawers of filing cabinet space to keep track of our lives. A well-organized filing system needs only to contain hard to duplicate documents, policies, and certificates - in alphabetical order, of course. It's just a little thing that makes your life overall... easier and more orderly so wait for a rainy day and then get to work...

Cleaning out your filing system.

#127 Say "I'm sorry"

This is a suggestion that, for many of us, is a no-brainer. Some of us know when we have committed an infraction in word or deed and we readily and easily apologize. Others, perhaps not so much. Why is it important to say, "I'm sorry"?

An apology demonstrates respect and empathy for the person who was 'wronged'. If we've hurt someone - unintentionally or otherwise - it's important to acknowledge that our actions may have generated unwanted or unpleasant feelings in the person who felt injured. It indicates that we have an awareness of how our behavior impacted another and that we are willing to take responsibility for our behavior.

Perhaps the most important element is that of taking responsibility; of owning the impact our actions have had. An apology only has an impact when the offensive behavior isn't repeated. As the famous saying goes... "the first time is a mistake, the second is a choice." When we own our part in an infraction, pay attention to how it came about, and repent - making a promise not to repeat the offense - it becomes forgivable.

Being sincere is the second most important element in an apology; expressed without anger or blame. When we accompany it with a desire to repair the damage, with humility, and compassion for the feelings of all involved, the regret is more easily accepted.

An apology that includes the word "but" is null and void before it really ever gets started. "I'm sorry but..." becomes meaningless because most of us will only remember the words that came after. If we use any language that implies blame, defense will rise in the receiver and they'll be unable to register the apology. If there is a problem to resolve, work on it after responsibility for hurt has been demonstrated and amends have begun.

Think carefully about someone in your life that may still be hurting from your action or lack thereof... consider taking a few minutes to construct an apology and then...

Say "I'm sorry".

#128 Clean out the linen closet

Why is it that the linen closet is likely at the bottom of our priority list? Maybe because it rarely gets seen by guests and it often collects those items that don't tend to make sense anywhere else. Mine stores much more than just linens and the only truly organized ones that I've seen are those from empty nesters. Does that mean that having kids in the house prevents an organized linen closet that isn't a junk magnet? Or perhaps it means that kids universally can't seem to stack towels and sheets in a straightforward manner. In either case, there's a chance that yours needs a little attention.

If I look closely, I believe there is still a SpongeBob pillowcase deep in the bowels of my upstairs linen closet leftover from my son's bedding ensemble more than 20 years ago. I believe there are water bottles that haven't been used in a decade but made sense to keep at one point. These are typical items hiding in the crevices of sheet stacks that are better delegated as drop cloths these days. Some of those I kept only because they made for good Halloween costumes.

Check the top shelves too... that's where the peach shower curtain from 2003 I thought I'd keep as a backup is hiding along with the bathmats that got replaced a few years later. I'm pretty sure the backing on that mat is now fully dry rotted and will disintegrate as soon as I take it off the shelf. They both have to go. As a rule of thumb - if you haven't used it in three years - get rid of it. If it's torn, tattered, or tired, get rid of it. If it's stained or dingy - get rid of it.

As a side note... most animal shelters will take your tattered towels, sheets, and blankets. Please consider donating them when you...

Clean out the linen closet.

#129 Mindful kissing

If you have a significant other or even a special friend, this suggestion can ignite a spark so, reader beware. Mindful kissing is a special kind of kissing... it's kissing on purpose, with intention, for no other reason than to experience - truly experience - the kiss.

This type of kissing begins with intention. It is a desire to fully engage and participate in the experience of a kiss with particular notice to each and every sensation;

Notice the closeness of your partner.

Notice the smell of your partner, their skin, their breath, their body perfume.

Notice the texture of the lips you are kissing; their temperature.

Slowly inhale and exhale with the focus on the sensations you are experiencing in the kiss itself.

When your focus moves to another part of your body, or somewhere in your mind - bring it back to the kiss.

Notice your saliva production and its exchange.

Notice the desire of your tongue and its movement.

Notice the taste that is exchanged in your kiss.

Notice the interaction between lips, tongues, and mouths.

Notice the as your breath changes; notice your partner's breath.

Allow the kiss to take time. Be patient while you explore and navigate your partner's kiss. Be sure to keep your focus there without the distraction of other sensations. Try spending 5 minutes mindfully kissing - only kissing - and if you enjoy the interactions, increase the time with each engagement.

If you want to jumpstart a little energy in your relationship, this is a great way to get the engines rolling again. It's free, easy, and innate for us all...

Mindful kissing.

#130 Strive for authenticity

One of the most elementary components of those living in a state of peace, contentment, and happiness is their ability to sustain authenticity in their day to day lives. These people know 'who' they are, and they don't compromise their values or beliefs to keep the peace or avoid confrontation. Wait, what? Am I suggesting that you refuse to compromise? Isn't that the cornerstone of relationship success? The answer is "yes" if the compromise is about likes and dislikes; we'll eat Mexican today and Chinese next week or we'll watch Golf today and HGTV tomorrow. It's a big fat "NO" however, if we are faced with compromising our values and core beliefs.

In order to get good at this, we need to have clear focus about what we believe and/or what feels 'right' for us as an individual. If you don't want to take the risk of driving with someone who refuses to wear a seat belt - don't. If you feel strongly about drugs, alcohol, or sex... own your stance and stand your ground. Work to disregard any judgment that seeks to undermine your position with negativity or ridicule. Most often, those convictions are ignited from the core of 'who we are' and when we honor them, we are our most authentic selves.

Our bodies are amazing barometers of our state of authenticity and it's helpful to learn how to read the measurements they provide. When a friend is being racist and that behavior is in deep contrast to your value system, how do you feel? Where do you feel it? Are you nauseous? Is your heart racing? Do you get headaches? Step away from the friend and notice if the symptoms dissipate? If so, your body is blatantly telling you your friends' behavior is contradictory to your core. Either remove yourself from the condition or equalize it by sharing your perspective. To stay and do nothing would be disingenuous to you.

On major topics many of us do a fair job of staying true to ourselves and yet there are little things that are sometimes disguised as keeping peace or just making things easier that corrode our sense of authenticity over time. 'Going along with the crowd', 'not speaking up', and 'giving up' are some of the reasons we fail to honor our core selves. Once or twice may not make a big impact on our system but I find that when it is consistent, our sense of 'self' is greatly diminished.

"Why didn't you go back to school?"
"Because my husband wouldn't have liked me taking so much time from our family."

"Why don't you golf anymore?"
"Because my wife wants me to sleep in with her on weekends."

When you are present in your life and checking in with yourself on a regular basis, noticing these moments of inauthenticity are easier. Learning to communicate about them so that you are consistent with meeting the needs of your core is helpful as well. Being in tune with your body, honoring your heart, and using your voice are critical skills as you ...
Strive for Authenticity

#131 Wear a bold color

Take a good hard look in your closet. What colors do you see? Is the majority of your closet black, navy, grey, and white? Do you have a little pastel mixed in? Out of all the items, how many pieces are Bold?

Many of us don't wear bold on purpose as it may highlight features we prefer to downplay. Others may simply not want to draw attention to themselves, although I rarely find this is a conscious decision. Others still, may believe that a more modest, sterile combination is preferred in a business environment. Truth is, when we make these choices, we could be seeking to be background players, unseen by the masses, and blending into the crowd more often than not. We unconsciously choose clothing that will not draw attention to us.

Ironically however, it's those times that we stand out appropriately that we tend to get the most compliments, the most accolades, and the most romantic interest. One of the ways that we can stand out without speaking, moving, or over performing, is to wear a color that is complementary to our skin tone but bold in contrast.

First, you must know if you have warm or cool skin tones... look at the veins in your hands. What color are they? If they are blue or purple, you have a *cool* tone. If they appear greenish, you have a *warm* tone. Cool tones run in the turquoise, purple, and pink pallets while warm tones are reds, oranges, greens, and yellows.

I'm not suggesting that you don a St. Patrick's Day green suit so that you are bold from head to toe but a deep green blouse or tie may make a great statement to your business ensemble. Carrying a bright red bag and wearing matching shoes creates a dynamic look with an otherwise boring grey suit. A casual jeans and sweater evening can be taken to another level with a deep turquoise cardigan. Pick a few colors from your tone range and seek to add those colors in the add-on part of your wardrobe. Perhaps including a bold dress or polo shirt for those times when it's important to be remembered.

Wear a bold color.

#132 Find a long-lost friend

When you think about your childhood, is there a person - a friend - that you've lost touch with? Someone that you'd like to connect with again, if only to know how their life turned out?

Once again, the internet makes finding old friends rather easy if you know a full name. Websites such as Google, Facebook, & LinkedIn are great places to start. Women can be more difficult if they've married and changed their last name. Likewise, common names such as John Williams or Sara Johnson can be challenging without additional information. The website Classmates.com and those similar charge a small fee but organize names by high schools and graduation years. Some of these sites offer a small period of time where you can use the resources free.

As you think of finding the friend you've been thinking of, consider what your expectation is once you find them. Those of us who were besties in high school may not share similar interests once 20 years has passed. Will you be disappointed if that person who knew all your secrets no longer enjoys the things you do? Will you feel let down if they aren't receptive to your inquiry? What if they want to establish a relationship yet you discover you've only looking to satisfy a curiosity?

One of the great benefits of connecting with an old buddy is that they share a piece of history with you. Whether it's a series of adventures in the neighborhood on bicycle, prank phone calls to radio D.J.'s, or late night whispers about the cutest guy in math class... this person from your past knows a part of you that people in your life today may not have any knowledge of. It can be comforting and downright healing to connect with pieces of memory that remind you of good times past and the energy, dreams, and spirit of youth.

Who is it that comes to mind as you think about what it would be like to ...

Find a long-lost friend.

#133 Say "no"

Are you a people pleaser? Are you challenged to say "no" when people ask you to do something? Are you afraid to let people down or disappointment them?

For those of us that are people pleasers, it is particularly challenging to experience the effect of disappointing people. We tend to over commit ourselves in an effort to meet the things we believe are expectations from others. We crowd our calendars, we stretch our limits, and we spend too much time frazzled as we strive to complete our overextended agendas.

Often, we know we are pushing too far... moving past comfortable as our mind screams "NO!" to our unhearing vocal cords that are deaf to our heart's whispers. Before we know it, the word "ok" escapes even though our internal warning systems are vibrating through our physical system. It's vital that we allow our internal voice to become audible and speak the words that our brain is trying to vocalize.

Honoring our own time limits and personal space is one of the most elementary components of self-care. Before we can take care of others and meet all of their needs, we must make sure to charge our own batteries; stay mentally and physically strong enough to meet the demands of our own life. When we put others needs before ours consistently, we rob ourselves of the ability to stay 'charged'.

There isn't any reason to be brash or offensive as we reject the desires or expectation of others. Most people will understand if we've maxed out the hours in our days. Learn to say, "I'd love to, but I can't right now" or "I need to finish a few things before I can take on something else." or ... you could just...

Say "no".

#134 Re-read your favorite book

What is your favorite fiction book? When did you read it? Why is it your favorite? Would you enjoy reading it again?

In my late teen years, I read *The Thornbirds* and to this day, I remember being enthralled by the generational story. Later, I read and loved Michener's *'Chesapeake'* and again, I remember the ending as clearly as if I had just finished it because it was so vividly depicted. And then there were the Fern Michaels trilogies that told of cousins in various parts of the country; stories that, to this day, are remembered and thought of as if they could be real people in real time in Texas, Las Vegas, or Kentucky.

Why is it that we watch favorite movies over and over, or television series but rarely read a book a second time through? Summer is a great time to visit the library and check out that book that you remember loving from a long time ago. Did you ever pick up Sidney Sheldon's 'Master of the Game'?... it's another of those memorable fiction stories that stuck in my mind because of the intense graphic visual that came to my mind as I read the words.

This suggestion is one of those things that we don't think of often, a thought that is easy and quick... take some time for simple enjoyment this summer and ...

Re-read your favorite book.

#135 Give the gift of your favorite book

The last suggestion was to re-read your favorite book and if you take me up on that suggestion…. Great! I hope you enjoy. Afterwards - or in the event that you don't want to re-read it - write a note about why the book stands out in your mind, tuck it inside and give it to a friend (without giving away the ending).

You might share why you are giving this particular book to that particular person. Is there something about the story that reminds you of her/him, or the relationship you have with them? Is there something else that you think resonates within the story? Sharing things we love is good for our spirit. When we give away something we enjoy, we share a bit of ourselves as we hand over the material item.

This gesture is a small example of how we might foster social connections. Sharing is an integral part of connecting with others. Research tells us that when we share, the pleasure centers of our brain are activated - the same areas that turn on when we eat food that we enjoy or have sex. Because we take time to step outside of ourselves - out of our selfish perspective - we may also improve elements of depression or anxiety. Perhaps the best benefit of all is that we promote kindness which, is known to be one of those things that create forward ripples; kindness begets kindness. Not to mention that the gesture promotes reading. You may never know what goodness happens after you…

Give the gift of your favorite book.

#136 Chat with a random stranger

We live in a world that while connected via radio waves and fiber optic cables, is often disconnected from an interpersonal perspective. We walk around with cell phones and headphones, attending to email, social media, and news headlines rather than the space in which we stand. Most of us can find ourselves standing next to a stranger at some point during the day with barely a glance to recognize their presence there; the ghostly whisper of our mothers "don't talk to strangers" mantra reverberating ever so slightly through our memory.

If we take time to bring ourselves into the present moment while we run our errands, grab our lunch, or wait for transportation, we can simultaneously take time to appreciate the people in our periphery. Why not go one step further and connect with one of the other human beings close by? A simple comment of "that color looks great on you" or "I love your haircut" may be just the thing that person needs to counterbalance a negative from earlier in the day. The few seconds you take to actually connect to someone benefits you too.

Social connection is linked to happiness, personal thriving, and longevity. It seems that even the simple act of acknowledging that we are not isolated - even if we don't know or aren't friends with people - can improve our state of mind. If we look up and acknowledge others in our environment for even a brief interaction, our brains interpret connectivity. The truth is, we aren't isolated anywhere but in our minds. At any given point, most of us can walk out our door, down the sidewalk and connect with a human being in some kind of way - IF we choose.

The premise is simple and most likely etched in your memory somewhere because children do this naturally. (Another example of something innate that we 'unlearn'.) Children - completely unknown to one another - will engage on a playground within minutes of being there. In no time at all, they are introducing themselves and cooperating to extend their enjoyment.

Make a pledge to yourself to disarm those adult hesitations, break away from your distractions, and be present the next time you find yourself in a line, a group, or a crowd and make the effort to ...

Talk to a random stranger.

#137 Buy coffee for the person behind you.

I'm sure you've heard of, perhaps even acutely aware of the 'random act of kindness' movement (#RAK). You may even have performed one recently. What I'd like to suggest is that the next time you get in line to buy coffee, a latte, or a frappé - consider paying for the drink that the person behind you has ordered, assuming you are in a drive through line.

We know that 'kindness begets kindness'. When people are the receiver of a random act of kindness, they are more likely to perform one, but it has to start somewhere. Why not be the one to initiate?

When you are kind, pleasure centers in your brain are activated. Your dopamine levels increase, and you feel happier. When we are surprised, (by receiving a random act of kindness) we also have surges in dopamine, again feeling happier. It's a win - win situation.

When I make this suggestion I sometimes hear objections of how difficult it is to find an extra $5 but really… it's only $5 and it might mean that your coffee tomorrow is forgone but knowing that you've impacted the life of another in a positive way will override any deficiency.

It's a simple suggestion, spending a few dollars on someone you don't even know to promote happiness for you both. Why don't you consider, the next time you are sitting in line at a drive through… promoting happiness by taking the time to …

Buy a coffee for the person behind you.

#138 Give something you cherish to someone you cherish

Earlier, I suggested sharing a book you love with someone so that they can experience the pleasure you had when you read the book. The following suggestion is an even more intimate offering of your heart... to share something you covet or adore with a special someone in your life. In this case, it would be a material thing... something meaningful.

Many of us think about this suggestion only in respect to 'after we're gone'. We may put codicils in our will bequeathing important treasures to people we love so that they 'have something of us' after we die. What fun is there in that?? We don't get to see their reaction and experience the joy of giving firsthand if we wait until the end of our life. There are probably dozens of items in your home that you care deeply about but that would also be meaningful to someone you love.

Try thinking of *one* thing to pass along to a special person in your life that would have meaning for both of you. Grandma's pearls? A platter you've used for every holiday? A framed photograph of someone dear who has passed away? A ring you no longer wear? It can be anything that has sentimental value that you wish to share with a loved one.

The presentation of this item is part of the recommendation. Don't make it a special occasion gift, i.e., birthday, graduation, etc.... make it a 'just because' gift. It would be great if it was a private exchange... meant for and shared by just the two of you. The goal is to really 'experience' the pleasure of giving with the person you are giving to - not to make it a group or public demonstration. Take some time to consider the gift, the sentiment, and the recipient and then...

Give something you cherish to someone you cherish.

#139 Find shapes in the clouds

This may be the epitome of a childhood folly. It's the thing we did as children with mom that was mostly spontaneous, free of charge, and used complete imagination. We could do it anywhere as long as it was daylight and the sky was filled with clouds.

It's a game where there is no right or wrong and everyone is a winner. It's completely subjective and potentially more fun than charades as our imagination and creativity take root to see faces, animals, and inanimate objects in the vapor swirl collections that dance above our heads. Often, before we can describe our vision in detail an upper level wind moves across the sky to change the configuration completely, forcing us to quickly recalculate the interpretation.

Einstein postulated that "imagination is more important than knowledge because knowledge is limited but imagination encircles the world." Indeed, stimulating imagination at all ages fosters creativity which, when used, is a leading characteristic of happy people. As you step outside on the next sunny day where puffy, pillowy clouds dot the sky, take a few minutes to ignite your imagination and...

Find shapes in the clouds.

#140 Finger paint

I write a lot about creativity, imagination, and the simple art of fun as contributing significantly to one's sense of happiness. One of the ways to incorporate all three elements is to don an apron, grab some paper, and dig into a pile of finger paints.

Finger painting works at increasing well-being because it incorporates the additional sense of touch. Incorporating tactile senses allows more parts of our brain to be engaged in the activity at hand. Not only are we stimulated by color, creativity, and imagination, we are spurred also by the sensation of the paint and our hands on the paper - sliding across the page with color trailing behind.

You're never too old to get your hands full of color but if you feel better, or more justified... grab a kid, niece, nephew, or grandchild and make some magic. You don't have to get any special supplies... just follow the following recipe and make your own!

Martha Stewart Homemade Finger Paint

Stir 4 tablespoons of sugar and 1/2 cup cornstarch together. Add 2 cups of cold water and heat over medium heat until the mixture is thick (the mixture will further thicken as it cools).

Divide into four or more containers and add food coloring as desired.

Plain paper works, but photo paper is best. As a last resort, just for the fun of it, you can use plastic wrap or wax paper. These last two won't offer a solution to keep your creations permanently but they make clean up a breeze.

Take some time to enjoy the experience. Make sure to be present - stay focused on the chance to imagine and create. Use colors - or combinations thereof - to express feelings, whatever they may be as you...

Finger paint.

#141 Go to an art museum

Very few of us are actually patrons of art. It seems as though if we aren't creators or investors, our interest in art is fleeting or sporadic at best. If we live in a major metropolitan environment, it is likely that we were introduced to great art via a school trip where we were perhaps more interested in the time away from history and calculus than in the masterpieces displayed in the gallery.

I went to a gallery once on Rodeo Drive just for kicks but fell in love with the work they were featuring that week. I pretended to be able to afford the $10,000 price tag so that I could learn more about the artist's technique. I think there's a part of my psyche that wants to cover my walls in abstract creations full of color and light but my pocketbook doesn't match my intrigue.

And that's the value of Art Museums... they are buildings full of walls that display a variety of talent; from old masters to new savants. On those days when you need a little inspiration or a pick-me-up, a museum offers refuge in the form of a bench in front of some form of art. It's a place to step outside of yourself, to imagine another human being with a brush, pallet knife, or chisel in their hand - creating their own vision that became the piece you view. Somehow, it puts one's own life in perspective via an unusual channel.

Many museums are free to enter or only charge a small fee. Frequently they offer reduced entry fees for special professional affiliations (i.e., military, teachers, etc.) and most often for just a little more, will offer annual membership. It's satisfying to know that your entrance payment keeps these national treasures safe, clean, and in good repair - our history depicted in paint, pen, and stone. Whether it's curiosity, solace, or inspiration you seek - it's possible you'll find it if you...

Go to an Art Museum.

#142 Ban electronics from one room in your home.

This suggestion will improve your family and interpersonal life... guaranteed! Easily for the last ten years, electronics of all types have infiltrated the most elementary moments in our lives and disrupted our ability to feel connected even in our own living rooms.

As a psychotherapist, I am frequently hearing how disconnected people feel from others in their home because someone they love - and desire attention from - is consumed with activity on their phone. It doesn't matter if it is gaming, social media, or news... the fact that it is accessible from the palm of our hand seems to create a temptation for constant access no matter where we are or what is happening. How many of us try to watch television AND play on or watch something else simultaneously on our phone?

In order to experience one of the primary benefits of being a family - we have to actually talk to one another, engage in eye contact, and offer our exclusive attention to one another. It's the oldest method of establishing belonging that is known. Any distraction can negatively impact this process; leaving people floundering for a sense of communion.

There's a quick and easy fix for this problem! Ban electronics (phones, iPad, laptops, etc....) from one room in your home - ideally, the room you most often 'gather' in. It's a simple rule that isn't really any different than taking your shoes off at the front door... something implemented and enforced will eventually become habit and second nature. Before you know it, everyone in the room will be engaged in a shared conversation, focused on the movie, or concentrating on the game and experiencing a strong sense of belonging once you...

Ban electronics from one room in your home.

154

#143 Let something go

What kind of excess baggage are you holding on to? What are you trying to manage and/or control that isn't within your realm of change? What do you continue to think about that has been over and done for a while now?

Pick one of the things you thought about as you read the above questions and write it down. Write down as many details of this thing you want to let go of as you can think of. The goal here is to imagine or remember it clearly - but from a distance; with limited emotion as if it is a story that belongs to someone else.

Once the story is complete, take the paper in your hands and crumble it up, tear it into pieces, or burn it (safely of course). Embed the action of destroying this story into your mind - taking time to be very present and mindful of the paper's destruction. Imagine that the story is evaporating, fading into fog, and becoming blurred.

As you dispose of the paper (or ash) - do so with great intention and acknowledgement that the story is now gone. As you move the paper into a trash receptacle and drop it... see your open - empty - hand. Fingers open, holding nothing.

Visualizing this process of elimination, destruction, and emptying of the things we 'hold onto' is a powerful way to let go of unwanted thoughts, memories, and pains. Once the activity is completed, you can replace the unwanted memory with the memory of eliminating it. Your mind will 'remember' that you've destroyed this undesirable thought. It may be necessary to remind yourself that you've gone through this process and make the connection by observing your open hands.

This technique can be very powerful for those times when you make the decision that it is time to...

Let something go.

#144 Make ice cream

I know it's super easy to reach into your freezer or stop by your local ice cream store but there's something about making your own ice cream on a hot summer evening that evokes pleasure in a way that the other options cannot.

Sometimes, it's the experience of 'doing it yourself' that adds to the fun and satisfaction we enjoy during and after an activity. The sense of accomplishment increases our confidence and overall esteem but perhaps more importantly, we become empowered.

Of course, an ice cream 'maker' is one of the easiest ways to complete this task - most of them come with recipe books for unending motivation but for a simple vanilla flavor, making ice cream at home is super easy with a few basic supplies. You need large zip lock plastic bags, coarse salt, and some arm muscle.

I am recommending the recipe from The Stay at Home Chef blog because it worked well and tasted great! It took a little longer than the suggested 5 minutes to get the consistency that I preferred but it only meant a better arm workout (shaking is super important). What wouldn't taste good if it is mostly heavy cream, sugar, and half & half?? We don't want to calculate the calories in this recipe of course - just grab a spoonful and enjoy.

The next time you need a little inspiration to liven up a hot summer day, remember to pull out this recipe and ...

Make homemade ice cream.

HOMEMADE ICE CREAM

From The Stay at Home Chef blog

1 cup heavy cream
1 cup half and half
½ cup sugar
1 teaspoon vanilla extract
2 gallon sized resealable plastic bags
2 cups ice cubes
½ cup salt
Instructions
Pour cream, half and half, sugar, and vanilla extract into a gallon sized resealable plastic bag. Seal well. Squish it around to combine until sugar is dissolved.

Place ice cubes and salt into another gallon sized resealable plastic bag.

Place the bag with the ice cream mixture into the bag with the ice. Seal the larger bag.

Shake until mixture freezes, about 5 to 7 minutes.

#145 Plan a vacation to somewhere you've never been.

Are you someone who goes to the same beach town each year? Do you have a timeshare that you visit every vacation? Do you have a mountain cabin, lake house, or beach bungalow that is your home away from home? Does that mean that you rarely see other parts of the country or of the world?? Perhaps it's time for you to explore a little and schedule a vacation to somewhere you've never been.

What type of landscape attracts you? What city have you always dreamed of visiting? Is there a place of solitude that has been tugging at your interest? If you weren't tied to your family's choice, where would you go? Are you bored to tears at the lake, looking for more nightlife than the crickets and fireflies offer or are you fed up with the traffic and city lights?

Take a look at your calendar and a good hard look at a map... what part of the world is calling you? Maybe it's just around the corner and is easily attainable. For destinations halfway around the world, it may take a bit more planning and saving but with dedication to the goal - still attainable. If you can't decide then write down the top five and draw from a jar or close your eyes and point. If all else fails, try the old-fashioned dart throw. After a destination is decided upon, investigate and plan. Take a look at all your options and put together a budget.

Allow the anticipation to build as you imagine yourself in a new vacation spot. It will be new and exciting... perhaps a bit strange if you've been used to a particular location but discovering new things is responsible for pleasure more often than not. A fresh location to experience rest and relaxation may be just the thing you need this year so go ahead and...

Plan a vacation to somewhere you've never been.

#146 Drive a road you've never driven

How many times have you wondered where a road leads? Perhaps it's a road you pass every day on your way to work, or one close by home that you've never had the need to drive. If you've lived in the same place for a very long time it's plausible that you know all the local routes and yet personally, there are still spots I've not discovered after 25 years of living in the same location.

It seems as if we rarely take time to wander. We are so often in a hurry to get from point A to point B that we fail to discover variations in our routes. We develop habits that apply to our driving so much that even that becomes a rote behavior. Consequently, we deny ourselves opportunities to experience our home regions completely.

I recently found a great little farm stand that is new to me after driving a 'new' road that was always a 'wonder where that leads' street. There are times I 'think' I know where a road leads but discovered other things there that I didn't know existed. There's a road by my home that is one way to get to a nearby town, but I typically go there a different way. Recently I took the 'near my home' route and found two trailheads to a walking trail that I've always been curious about.

There's an experience of delight with each resounding "oh… that's where that is…" sentiment when you…

Drive a road you've never driven.

#147 Release guilt

This is one of those tips that is far deeper than can be addressed in a mere few paragraphs, but I'll introduce the idea of releasing the guilt that doesn't belong to you as something that will increase your overall sense of well-being.

By definition, guilt is the result "of having committed a specific or implied offense" and/or "making someone feel guilty". While I could talk for several minutes about the semantic of "making someone feel"... guilt is an appropriate emotion when we *intentionally* offend someone or commit an offense.

It's fair to feel bad when someone we care about is hurting and if an accidental behavior on my part generated the emotional harm then I am deeply sorry but do not hold 'guilt' once I apologize. Accidents happen. When we accept responsibility for the damaged feelings of another and the damaged feelings are because 'of something we purposefully did' then guilt is what keeps us in check but far too many of us accept guilt when it is not *ours* to own.

Too many people fail to communicate expectations and then charge us with having committed an offense - imparting feelings of guilt. If we don't know we are supposed to meet a standard - or expectation - and we offend someone, we need not 'own' feelings of guilt. We need to learn to release feelings of guilt when they are erroneously associated with behaviors that are unintentional, with unexpressed expectations, untruths, or unreasonable demands.

Use visualization techniques to release guilt... imagine writing it on a chalkboard and then erasing it. Imagine writing it on a paper and then tearing it to shreds. Imagine it is contained in a ball and throw it in the ocean. Imagine it as a word in your hand and watch it evaporate or disintegrate. No matter what image you conjure or what technique you employ, the secret to improving your overall sense of happiness is to...

Release guilt.

#148 Have a yard sale

I may be preaching to the choir here as I know yard sales are very popular weekend activities and some people have them annually. I know others who have never had a yard sale as they don't "have the energy" or want to "take the time" and yet with just a little bit of energy, it can be rewarding on several levels.

Obviously, the first step is to declutter. I keep a box in the bottom of my closet for clothing that needs to be recycled and another in my basement for 'things' that I no longer use or need. When I look in a cabinet and realize that it's been a year or more since I've touched something, I pull it out and put it in the box. Sometimes an item ends up there simply because I'm tired of looking at it after a few years.

I think this is where people get caught up when it comes to having yard sales. Yes... some people lay things out nicely, folded, organized, and individually priced but - it's not necessary. People will come, and if they are interested in an item, they will ask and/or make you an offer. The only time it's particularly necessary to price an item is when it is expensive... a collectible, or valuable. Certainly, have an idea of what those items are worth, so you won't be taken advantage of although clearly, people go to yard sales for bargains.

I've decluttered my house with items that are no longer useful or valuable to me and haggling over prices is a risk that the item remains as I am closing shop. My goal is to get rid of it so... go for the money. Try and adopt the attitude that 'something is better than nothing'. That 'thing' wasn't a dollar in your basement so let it be a dollar in your pocket. Make deals and get rid of it. Toward the end of the time period - sell it in box lots or 'everything for $1.00'. A friend of mine used to have 'quarter hour' - at the end of her yard sales, anything left was $.25... she had people lined up at noon to get bargains.

Vow to take whatever is left over to Goodwill, Habitat, or another charity. It doesn't go back in the house. I box up any leftover items and put them directly into my car for delivery to the closest donation center. The only exceptions are those valuable items that then get posted on yard sale Facebook sites or apps like Let Go.

Have a Yard Sale.

#149 Clean your sock drawer

You may wonder how this particular tip helps you lead an easier, happier, or more productive life and yet I know a ton of people who have a sock pile... a stack of single socks that lie in waiting for the match. Some lay so long that the elasticity of them degrades and any attempt at stretching results in that unwanted crinkle sound depicting sock death.

Cleaning your sock drawer reunites all those singles. Re-pairing them increases the ever-eroding options you have each morning as you dress your feet. How many of us wait until the drawer is empty of pairs before we take some time to organize? I'm convinced that the fad popular with kids these days of wearing non-matching socks is because it is easier than finding matches and/or cleaning out the sock drawer. For those of you not wanting to adopt the fad... maybe it's time.

If your house is like mine, there will be socks that don't match. I used to keep them for a year or so and then at the end of a year I assumed they were buried inside my washing machine or tucked in a sheet I never use so I threw them out or found a way to repurpose them.

It really takes just takes a few minutes to lay them all out and make matches of the ones that have been separated from their mate. Matching the few pair that exist there will allow you to feel more organized, a little accomplished, and aware of what's really there. Consider taking a couple of minutes as you dress tomorrow to ...

Clean your sock drawer.

#150 Organize your 'Tupperware'

I am using 'Tupperware' to represent all food storage containers which, I think is a generational thing, but you know what I mean. Like yesterday's post, this suggestion is more about a tiny thing that will make you feel better each time you open the cabinet than some grand design to promote happiness. Ironically however, you may find a sense of 'feeling good' overcome you because your level of annoyance will be reduced each time you open the cabinet where you keep food storage containers.

There's an entire industry aimed at helping us keep these plastic or glass dishes with their accompanying lids under control. It's interesting because one would think it's much easier than most of us make it and I'm not sure where it goes so wrong. It's true though, unless you live alone or you have anal tendencies, it seems to be a major challenge to keep any consistent organization to the food saving containers we accumulate over time.

Maybe it's because this is the place, we grant our hoarding desires a pass. We may tend to keep every container that is reusable - adding it to our already sufficient supply. Eventually they accumulate to the point that they overrun any good intention. And... what happens to the lids? Do they meet up with the socks that disappear? Ideally, we keep the lids and bowls together but then we run out of room quickly and so the nesting of bowls takes place and maybe, the lids get disgruntled because some of them disappear for good.

So, the challenge is to get in there again. First rule - discard any container that does not have a matching (and well fitting) lid. Next, consider how often you will use said container. If it's a keeper, set it aside - if not, recycle or repurpose it and get it OUT of the cabinet. Once you have all the keepers together, make the choice to nest them and stack the lids or store them with the lids attached; either is perfectly acceptable.

Organization helps us to feel a sense of order - to feel in control of our lives. It's great that we keep general appearances in good shape but superfluous if each time we open a cabinet or drawer, the chaos screams hello. This is one small step you can easily take to keep disorder - and mayhem - at bay. Next time you put away the dishes, take a few minutes and... Organize your 'Tupperware'.

#151 Make a 'Before I Die' list

What kind of things are on your bucket list? Who do you want to settle things with? What do you want to learn before you die? No matter how much time you have in front of you, it's possible you have a long list of things you want to do before your time on this Earth runs out. Put it in writing.

I recommend that the list be divided into categories such as travel, people, learning, achievements, and good will as well as any other header that you deem appropriate. It doesn't matter how outrageous it seems today as we never know what our future holds. Disregard - in the moment at least - the money needed to achieve any list item; this is just a 'master' list; a dream list.

I suggest that one of the lists is 'little' things - regardless of topic - so that while you plan for the bigger, perhaps more expensive things, you are still accomplishing items from your list and generating a sense of satisfaction. I know someone that simply wants to "keep a houseplant alive" on her list.

Because we never know what tomorrow may bring, go back to each topic and prioritize the items there. If you want to travel to London, Quebec, and Fiji before you die, which one is most important? Second? Third? Which topic is most important to you? Is learning more important to you now than travel? Does good will tug at your heartstrings more than accomplishment? Since you'll feel good about mastering the things that are important to you, you'll need to identify them.

For many, this may be the hard part. Our thoughts are always running away in short fantasy about how we'll live our lives and then we get caught up in the day-to-day living things, claiming that there aren't enough hours in a day. Life needs balance and it is important to foster a sense of anticipation, excitement, and achievement. In order to feel those things, we have to step up and 'just do it'. So... think about what's important to you, what brings you joy, and what is happening when you feel satisfied. Then, with pen in hand...

Make a 'Before I Die' list.

#152 Snuggle

Who doesn't love to snuggle? From the time we are born, one of the ways that we experience connection and belonging is to get our body up close and connected to another person. Snuggling is *not* sex... it's sharing personal space with another warm body - human or animal friend. It's connecting - heartbeat to heartbeat - with another being to remind us that we are not alone in the world, that we are more than just ourselves. It's part of what keeps us grounded and produces sensations of 'existential significance' - a feeling of having a purpose.

Spending as little as *five* minutes a day cuddling with another being will stimulate an increase in the three primary emotional health hormones: Oxytocin, Dopamine, & Serotonin. Between the three of them, benefits include prevention of depression, loneliness, anxiety, and high blood pressure. They improve your immune system, lower your heart rate, and stimulate your metabolism. All together, they relax you and induce smiling.

If you wake up next to someone each day - try to commit to 5 min either in the morning or the evening to cuddle together (without anticipation of sex) and no conversation. This is just time for the two of you to experience the life force of one another, to feel connected, and to be present with one another. If you sleep alone most of the time, then take 5 min a day to snuggle with a child (yours or someone in your care) or an animal friend. Cats and dogs are great snugglers (well... some cats.) and the living energy that exists in them can still mingle with yours for the existential benefit of realizing that you are not here alone.

In addition to all the 'connection' elements associated with snuggling and their benefits, the ability for us to be still and present for 5 minutes a day has its own associated perks. In that small allotted time, nothing else matters and we are able to feel centered in our space. For those few moments, the pressures of the world are quiet. Breathe in the stillness and allow it to settle in your soul. Allow yourself to take the time to...

Snuggle.

#153 Pick fruit & make jam

Pick your own fruit orchards have become popular in most states for years now and almost any taste you may have can be satisfied straight from the vine.

Whether you pick apples, apricots or peaches from the tree or perhaps berries from a vine, it's plausible that you bring home more than you can eat. I stopped by a peach orchard once and bought a bushel of peaches only to find out that they were buy one get one free and two were carried to my car! Even if we all had eaten peaches for breakfast, lunch, and dinner we could not have made it through two bushels. The only option was to learn how to make jam. It's happened with strawberries, blackberries, and cherries more than one year in a row.

Making jam is way easier than one may think! It doesn't have to be the toil and trouble that our mothers encountered; pouring wax over the top of bubbling fruit. The manufacturer of Ball jars offers a Traditional Peach Jam recipe you can easily find online. It uses a 'water bath' to seal the jars, a simple process of boiling.

There's also a procedure that some would believe more simple; freezer jam. It differs from traditional processes because there is no boiling. Instead of keeping jam in the cupboard, you fill containers and keep it in the freezer. The absence of so much 'cooking' allows the fruit to retain more of its sweet, fresh flavor. It's like having sliced fruit on your toast. As above, a freezer jam recipe is readily available online.

This can be a great family activity or a great way to fill a Sunday afternoon. It's a fantastic way to savor a little bit of summer throughout the year and perhaps save a few dollars along the way. From picking the fruit, eating a bit, finding a recipe, and creating the jam - you'll have fun experimenting. The best benefit of course, is savoring the sweetness of a warm summer day that was captured in the jar when you made the decision to ...

Pick fruit and make jam.

#154 Dry your sheets outside

For much of the population, having a machine available to dry our clothes is something that we take for granted. Few of us hang our clothes on 'the line' to dry in the sun and breeze. If you have had this experience, you know that there is a sweet scent of fresh air that permeates the material so that when we come nose to fabric there is no question as to the smell of sunshine.

I know most of us don't keep a clothesline permanently installed these days but having a line that can be temporarily strung and used once in a while offers us the opportunity to bring a little of the outdoors - inside. Sheets are easy to dry this way because they can be draped over the line - no clothespins needed.

Crawling into bed with sun dried sheets is an experience we should all have at least a few times in our life. It takes clean sheets to an entirely new level and may offer the sense that you are sleeping under the stars - at least as far as your nose is concerned. You may be used to the pleasant aroma of your brand of dryer sheets and yet I'm certain that you'll fall in love with the fragrance of the sun after you...

Dry your sheets outside.

#155 Sit by a waterfall

One of the best ways to cool down on a humid hot day is any location in close proximity to a waterfall. Often, there are shade trees to soften the intensity of the sun and as the water moves over rock and falls, it stirs the air and simultaneously cools.

Even if you live in a major metropolitan region, there are water features available in the form of fountains that serve much the same function as a natural waterfall; water - colder than air temperature - moving the air and cooling it. There may be less natural shade in that environment but it's a close second. In the event that you live a more suburban life, there is a good chance that a waterfall exists within a drivable distance. A basic Google search for waterfalls near Philadelphia returned an article listing 11 that were an easy drive away. Pack a picnic, put the kids in the car, and escape the heat with a little hike leading up to a cool lunch location.

The sound of falling water is a known soother. Rain, creeks, and waterfalls are options on a variety of white noise machines advertised to calm our nerves and induce relaxation. It acts as a buffer to city noise or the chatter in our brain. It connects us to nature in the most elementary way.

Eliminating the stress and misery that comes with bracing the summer heat will certainly improve one's disposition and overall sense of well-being. Getting outdoors and into air that moves - a little at least - compounds the benefit. Adding the element of water is akin to icing the best cake. It improves stress reduction techniques that are proven to increase happiness.

Escape the heat - reduce the stress - and make your way to the nearest location that allows you to...

Sit by a Waterfall

#156 Love yourself

In the pursuit of happiness and overall well-being, self-love is practically a requirement. Our ability to look in the mirror and find peace with the reflection may be the ultimate experience of living a fulfilled life.

If it were easy, the mental health profession wouldn't exist and so this suggestion is made with the knowledge that while some are on the path and some are comfortable and confident, there are more who avoid the concept, the practice, and perhaps even the idea of self-love.

Maybe the first step is understanding that each of us is born perfect... has here ever been a baby born without perfect love and full of preciousness? We really are 'born that way'. And then... our environment, and our experiences therein, teach us to think otherwise - true or not. And then we discover that we'll never be perfect - a revelation that many of us find difficult to accept. Somehow, we come to believe that we've failed, or that we simply 'aren't good enough'.

This may be the first lie that we tell ourselves. Perhaps the first lie that we believe. And, it keeps us from self-acceptance - from self-love.

Philosophers and poets haven't spoken about the importance of self-love for thousands of years by coincidence... it turns out to be a necessity of good relationships and of a good life. The ability to practice self-compassion and self-acceptance - components of self-love - are timeless. They apply to humans regardless of age, gender, race, religion, or socioeconomic status.

If you're not consistently on the path toward established self-love, then it important for you to take a couple of simple steps. First, practice self-compassion... speak kindly of yourself, forgive yourself, and let go of perfection. Secondly, practice self-care... take time for yourself, take care of your body, and raise your consciousness. Look in the mirror each day and speak to yourself as if you were your own best friend; say "I love you". Don't worry if it feels uncomfortable to start. It gets easier as you learn to …

Love yourself.

#157 Reflect honestly

I've encountered a lot of people who prioritize truth telling yet lie to themselves. If we are attempting to live our best possible life, it's important to self-reflect with complete honesty. We avoid the truth because it may induce feelings of shame, guilt, or embarrassment; none of which feel good. We conjure stories about our lives that help us cope with living them - sometimes regardless of whether or not it's a reflection of what is real. We create subjective narratives for emotional survival.

One way to access our life honestly is to step back from it and view it as if it is a stage play with players you don't know or perhaps a television show with characters that are not emotionally attached to you. If your life was a television show - would you watch it? Would you be screaming at the screen trying to tell one of the characters something? Would you be disgusted and turn it off? How would you rewrite the script?

Sometimes taking this perspective means seeing things we don't want to see. It means we may need to make a change that we don't feel prepared for or equipped to make. It means accepting that what we wanted, may not happen or what we believed, is actually false.

If you believe you have been avoiding a compelling truth in your life, garner a support system (another family member, a trusted friend, or a counseling professional) and begin the unraveling of what is true. Sometimes it's a simple effort; at others, it's more complicated because one lie often begets another and they become convoluted and woven into reality. It may take time and patience to see yourself in well focused light.

As a professional, I often find myself in the position of helping people in this manner and one of the distinctions is aiding clients in understanding the difference between 'who' they are and 'what' they do... one is personality and the other, behavior. Clarity may take time, but the benefit is authenticity.

Authenticity is not possible without truth. When we are hiding from what is real, we are unable to demonstrate our most authentic self; to feel our absolute best. There is great freedom in living only from a place of truth. It's the origin of true happiness and possible only when we ... Reflect honestly.

#158 Use aromatherapy

For more than 5000 years, scent - the aroma of oils and plants - have been used as therapies for healing everything from clearing out sinuses, helping us sleep, improving circulation, and calming our mind. It's considered an alternative or 'holistic' treatment to complement medical treatment.

The oils used in Aromatherapy stimulate the olfactory system in our body - the one connected to our nose. When we inhale the oil molecules, they affect the limbic region in our brain which impacts our emotions, our memory, our hormones and our heart rate. When the diluted oils are massaged into our skin, it may improve circulation and improve the absorption rate.

Common plant oils like Basil and Pepper help with body aches and migraines. Eucalyptus is great when we have colds to help us breathe better. Lemon oil, Thyme, and Lavender are known to improve our mood, reduce stress, and enhance sleep.

Some of these oils can be toxic if used inappropriately. They can promote an allergic reaction or interact negatively with one another, so it is imperative that a trained professional guide the use and application of essential oils. An aromatherapist will use a medical history, your current health history as well as diet and lifestyle to develop a strategic plan for medicinal uses.

If you just want your home to smell good and trigger a tranquil feeling, try a diffuser with a diluted scent that you find pleasant (lavender is commonly used for tranquility). There is a large variety of diffusers from reeds, ultrasonic, and mist contraptions that allow the oil molecules to permeate the air. A quick search will return more options than you'll need.

Once you do a little research and visit a pro, you'll find that your mental and physical well-being can be improved with a decision to…

Use aromatherapy.

·

#159 Take a mental health day off

When was the last time you took a day off for no reason other than to stay home and binge watch T.V., go on a hike, or picnic by a waterfall? All too often we save our vacation days for purposeful tasks or family vacations where the only thing that is different - is the scenery. Sometimes, we just need to have a mental health day.

All too often I find that people accumulate sick days in anticipation of having a major illness. I've known people to sell back more than six months of time that was accrued. While that was a nice 'bonus', most of us would have been better off taking one or two of those for no other reason than we wanted to have a champagne lunch with a friend.

Everything is easier when we take a break. When we exhaust ourselves physically, we take a break. When we sit too long, we take a break, and when we've worked our fannies off - we deserve a break. Even taking a half day can make a difference. Leaving work at noon - grabbing a pedicure without waiting and getting into the house before anyone else, can shift an entire perspective from raunchy to rested.

The little break you take with a mental health day can help you get a new perspective, or at the very least it can give you the metaphorical deep breath you need from work and the people there. It allows you to step back from stress, controversy, or uncertainty. If we are seeking clarity or solutions, it may be the break that offers it to us.

Look at your work schedule as soon as you can and identify a time when you can …

Take a mental health day off.

#160 Take a hike

Many of us walk on a daily basis but few of us get out in nature and literally 'take a hike' as often as we might find enjoyable. What exactly is the difference between a 'walk' and a 'hike'? A hike is generally differentiated by distance; meaning a long way. Theoretically, a long walk could encompass the concept of 'hike' but generally it is also referenced as happening in the country or wilderness. Indeed, most of us conjure images of mountains, rivers, trails, and backpacks when we talk about 'taking a hike'.

The benefits of 'hiking' are similar to many of the other tips that I've referenced in so much as the overall benefit is an increase in general well-being. Perhaps most prominent is the advantage that the exercise has on our body and spirit. Hiking develops muscle, strengthens our bones, and is overall heart healthy. The time we have to commune with nature is also beneficial as it helps us stay grounded.

Escaping suburbia or metropolitan chaos for the peace and quiet of tree studded hillsides allows our mind to settle and tune into the solitude. People who hike have lower rates of depression and anxiety. The choir of natural life creates masterful sonnets designed to touch our soul. For some, it's a downright spiritual experience.

Walking for long distances is not without risks and so it is necessary to take a smart approach. If you are just getting started - go easy. Train your body to move consistently. Drink plenty of water, wear good shoes, and be prepared for the unexpected. Start locally and move your way up to more advanced trails. If the Appalachian Trail is on your 'Before You Die' list, you'll need to be conditioned. Get off the couch and...

Take a Hike.

#161 Stop Internalizing

When was the last time you thought "what did I do"? Perhaps someone close to you snapped a sassy response and your thoughts went immediately to "why are they mad at me?" Maybe you didn't get a dinner invitation to a neighbor's get-together and your internal voice is wondering why they don't like you. Or, you see a friend across the parking lot, but they keep walking without waving hello.

These are the kinds of scenarios that promote 'internalizing' - assuming that another person's behavior has something to do with *you*. My mother often said, "what makes you think you're so important that everything is about you?" It's a common misperception and one that is dysfunctional to the extent that it interferes with our ability to see things clearly. All too often, the behavior of another has absolutely nothing to do with us!

Learn to validate your thoughts and feelings. Look for concrete evidence - preferably direct from the source - that confirms your suspicions. If you get the sense that someone is mad at you... ask them. If you imagine that you've being shunned from a party because someone is upset with you... ask them "have I offended, you?"

Our responsibility is to work with the information we have but only the information that is accurate. In order to determine accuracy, we have to validate. We can only 'know for sure' what we see and hear since we are not mind readers. Even when we 'think' we know what someone is thinking - if you find yourself internalizing - validate!! There's a pretty good chance that you are *not* the center of another's discontent. Once you realize this you can ...

Stop Internalizing.

#162 Plan your funeral

Whoa... I know this is a morbid topic but keep reading. This is important stuff and may not make you directly happier, but it will definitely benefit the people you love who are left behind. It doesn't matter how old you are and while we all hope to live into a ripe old age - some of us may not. We will all die at some point and it's just not fair for us to leave all these decisions to people who will be riddled with emotions. Take some time today to think about how you would like to be sent into the spirit world.

It's rather easy these days with organizations like Five Wishes. You can either order the booklet or sit down online and answer a few questions. Then, between a funeral director and the completed document from Five Wishes - your loved ones won't have to be making any major decisions and can celebrate your life by going through photos and creating a memory board.

Five Wishes serves as a 'living will' also in some states so if you want the plug pulled when there is no brain activity you can say so there. If you want Van Halen or Bach's Fifth Symphony playing as you take your last breath - you can say so. If you want to be clean shaven or have the hairs plucked from your chin - you can designate that too! Do you want to be cremated? Or have your remains placed in a Mausoleum? Do you want pallbearers? Do you have an interest in writing your own Obituary?

Since we don't get to choose when or necessarily how we are going to die, planning the funeral is about as close to being in control as we'll get. Essentially, family disagreements are prevented when you've designed your exit. I once had a client who had a new outfit hanging in her closet specifically to wear at her own viewing. She left very clear and specific instructions for a hairstyle, complete with a photo for artistic direction.

Some may say it's silly but in a time that may be completely outside of our control - this little bit of planning allows us comfort in knowing that some part of it will be directed as we wish. If you haven't given it any consideration, stop for a bit and think what feels authentic to you. Then sit down with Five Wishes or a piece of paper and ...Plan Your Funeral.

#163 Meal prep

Hundreds, if not thousands of blogs in recent years have been dedicated to different ways of meal prepping. This is not one of them. I'm writing about it because when we have taken the time to do a little meal prep our lives become a little easier, happier, and ultimately... more productive. Yes, it takes a little time and commitment but if that's how you spend a rainy day then on a nice evening when all you want to do is sit on the deck and enjoy a summer evening - your meal will be almost effortless.

Perhaps the most important element and the first step in doing a little meal prep is deciding what you'd like to eat this week and get the grocery shopping done. Thinking ahead means that those decisions won't have to be made day by day, which is sometimes the most challenging thinking after a long day of work. Grab your family members and make it a joint venture or... kick everyone out of the kitchen to other tasks, turn on some jam music, pour some wine and go to town!

If you know that you'll be grilling in the evenings, then plan your 'side' dishes in advance. Boil a big batch of potatoes so that you can throw together a potato salad, smashed potatoes, or potato casserole (make that ahead of time and freeze). If you'll be having corn on the cob, cook a few extra on the evening that you want to eat them fresh and then shave the kernels off the cob for a corn side dish later in the week.

Don't forget the endless opportunities to set aside pasta dishes, casseroles, and soups or stews! Most of them freeze really well and if you pull it out in the morning, it's ready to bake when you get home - no thought or real effort involved! You'll be able to come home, change, and spend 5 minutes making dinner rather than the 30 or 45 minutes it might have taken to get dinner on the table.

What's clear in the study of happiness is that when we use our time efficiently, we feel more organized. People who are more organized are less stressed. People who are less stressed - are happier. So, it stands to reason that you'll be happier overall if you step away from binge watching HGTV or ESPN on the next rainy day and make an effort to ...

Meal Prep

176

#164 Own your story

Take a look around - a good look. Notice where you are, who is with you, and what is good about your life. It may not be everything, but chances are, something in your life right now IS right. Maybe it's your job or your relationship, your home or your kids. Maybe it's your best friend or your bank account. It might not be any of those things but just a complete sense of peace upon your heart. Now, think about the road that brought you here - to this very place - right this minute.

The path you've been walking may have been riddled with boulder sized problems. Some of it may have been underwater and you thought you might drown before you got to the other side. Some of it was easy-peasy... a long straight away without any curves or steep areas that wore you out. No matter the terrain - each and every step you took brought you here. To this place.

Many of the people I talk to resent the journey, are ashamed of their journey, or avoid thinking of the energy that got them this far. I contest that it is critical to stop from time to time and look back at all the challenges. I believe it is important to honor the struggles, the mistakes, and the embarrassments so that we can stand tall today knowing that we made it through each of the storms that tried to take us down. No matter what they were, taking responsibility for them and acknowledging that they taught you something is an important part of personal growth and shame release.

Maybe one of the most difficult aspects of gratitude is looking back at those difficult times and finding the energy to be grateful that they happened. The reality is that walking that way - brought you here. Each turn you took - even if it was a wrong one - led you to where you are right now. As we considered a moment ago - there IS something great, positive, and wonderful about the here and now. Express gratitude for the road, the storms, the uphill struggle and every last detail of what they taught you. That's the way to emotional freedom... to...

Own your story.

.

#165 Spend a day in service

What does it mean to you to 'spend a day in service'? Martin Luther King called for Americans to spend a day in service by "providing solutions to our nation's most pressing solutions". For most of us that means volunteering. But what if we spent a 'day in service' to our significant other, to our parents, to our best friend, or a neighbor?

How might our relationships benefit if we spent a day in service to them? What would that look like?

It's as simple as one thought... "what can I do to make your day better?" It's a question that doesn't necessarily mean 'waiting on someone' or 'spoiling' them. It's more focused on the literal definition of "performing duties or services". It may mean completing that project that's been on the back burner forever. It may mean practicing batting or pitching for hours on end. Or going through years of photo albums to help organize them. It's essentially making an effort to engage in any and all activities that helps the person you are serving. It's complete focus on a to-do list - improving the environment of the person you're serving.

Quite simply... when you give your time and talent, you receive satisfaction, gratification, and appreciation ten-fold. It improves your self-esteem, your confidence, and your overall life satisfaction. Depression rates fall when people spend time giving of themselves. One common characteristic of people who have lived long lives is that they volunteered regularly.

I've written about volunteering and community service. I'm aware of the countless loving hours many of us spend in service to organizations, religious communities, and social causes that are meaningful and yet this suggestion takes a different spin on those activities. Pick a day - any day that would otherwise be ordinary (i.e., not a birthday or anniversary) and commit to helping someone you have a relationship with in any way that they might find helpful. I'm sure the relationship will be enhanced significantly because you took the time to ...

Spend a day in service.

#166 Take a nap

I know that perhaps more than half of us don't need any suggestion or help to act upon this happiness tip - we've mastered it … hands down. Part of the population already knows that taking a nap midpoint throughout the day can be highly beneficial and improve our health.

One of the most important benefits of a nap is its ability to help us reduce stress. Sleep deprivation can increase the amount of cortisol in our bodies. When we sleep, our bodies release growth hormone which neutralizes cortisol. Let's face it - our lives get busier and busier leaving us less time to sleep and when we do… it's often difficult to quiet our minds. When we are tired, it is hard to process information, control our emotions, and stay focused. Everything is worse when we are exhausted.

A 90 min. cat nap is what professionals recommend. The ratios of sleep during this short cycle, mimic a night sleep and is therefore, more refreshing. At least it is for those of us who have typical schedules and sleep between 11 pm and 7 am. Additionally, as long as your nap is three hours before you turn in for the evening - your night's sleep should not be affected.

Taking naps will also increase your happiness. Getting more sleep makes us more productive - another element known to increase happiness. We'll be less stressed, feeling a higher sense of well-being, and feel healthier. All of which gives us something to be happy about.

If you are in a traditional 9 - 5 job, this suggestion may be very difficult for you to arrange. Yet, perhaps it's possible for you to rearrange your hours in such a way that at least some part of the strategy is an option. If you work evenings, are a college student, a homemaker, self-employed, or work from home, it may be possible to enact this nap initiative. Many European countries honor the tradition of a 'Siesta' and indeed, stress related health issues are not as prevalent in those cultures. Maybe we can learn by their example.

If you are inspired to reduce stress, increase happiness, and generate a better overall life - it may be as simple as setting aside time each day to … Take a nap.

#167 Visit a drive-in theater

As with most baby boomers, the drive-in theater was a staple of my childhood. Seemingly by the 1990s they dwindled in number and today there are only 336 drive-in movie screens in operation in the U.S. Before it disappears completely, I thought it vital to suggest bringing a little of this evaporating American tradition into your family's life. Find a theater close to you, pack some snacks, some bugspray, a few pillows and blankets, put the kids in their P.J.'s, and spend an evening enjoying the nostalgic experience watching a first run movie.

There's so much to love about going to a drive-in... It's a fantastic family experience. It's an opportunity to fill your lungs with fresh evening air, do a little stargazing, and enjoy a movie. It's time away from obligations and responsibilities. It's a chance to mentally escape and be entertained. And, it may induce great childhood memories of a more simplistic era.

Drive-ins are great for restless movie watchers; kids who can't sit still, as well as those who want to eat, drink, smoke, and fart their way through the feature. Whether or not you bring lawn chairs to relax in, recline in the bed of a truck, cuddle in the back of a van, or snuggle in the front seat... watching movies at the drive-in is perhaps the most comfortable way for the whole family to experience an outdoor cinema.

Be sure to check for a theater near you and then make plans to visit when you know the weather will cooperate. Gather the family - nieces and nephews if you must - and ...

Visit a drive-in theater.

#168 Play a board game

I know people who get together for the sheer purpose of playing board games on a weekly basis and what they have in common is an ability to have fun! Sure, some people are uber competitive but overall, playing an adult level board game (as opposed to Candyland or Monopoly Jr.) is a favorite pastime for many.

As a kid, the neighborhood girls had a running Monopoly game going all summer long. So much so that I'm not a huge fan of the game these days but my family members get it out at every large overnight gathering. Somehow they've turned it into a drinking game now that everyone is over twenty-one. There's usually a lot of high-fiving and deep groans as property and money change hands. Fun.

These days, The Settlers of Catan is a family favorite along with Ticket to Ride - both playable with just three players. They use a fair amount of strategy, but luck plays into card draws and dice rolls... disrupting even the best strategy. For two players, I know people who have a lot of fun with Code Names and the couple of times I've played, it was challenging in a thoughtful kind of way.

The first Backgammon board dates back to Persia over 5000 years ago and ever since every culture has a history of board games. It seems to satisfy the human need to socialize, strategize, and intellectualize. It teases our desire to be winners and keeps us coming back for a second chance and/or to defend our position as champion; apparently basic elements of the human experience.

What is your go to when you ...

Play a board game??

#169 Learn a card trick

Think back to your childhood for just a moment and recall the delight you felt when someone demonstrated something unbelievable. When our minds are 'tricked' into thinking one thing when another actually happened via magic or fancy... it is fun. We are often in awe of magic performers and a simple card trick can induce that same kind of feeling.

There is a certain amount of wonder that happens when we can't figure out the 'how' behind something. How does someone know what card we picked? Or what the next card in a pile will be? We are captivated and charmed as these illusions confuse us even though they generally amount to basic mathematics. We are entertained by things we can't explain and during adulthood, when most things make sense... it's a break to experience the fun side of 'not knowing'.

Card tricks are great because there are some very simple ones anyone can learn and no matter how silly or cheesy they are, the children in your life will be filled with delight by your ability to 'trick' them. Once again, I direct you to YouTube where there are numerous videos that will help you will learn simple tricks that are sure to tickle the fancy of your youngest fans.

Who doesn't love a little suspense and fun once in a while? A deck of cards is easy to carry around and you'll be the best aunt, uncle, grandma, or Pop in the family if you can perform and ultimately... share the skill after you've taken some time to...

Learn a card trick.

#170 Hug someone

Why do hugs feel so good? Have you ever wondered? Of course, as in many other things… hugging causes the body to emit oxytocin - the feel-good chemical. In addition to producing feelings of calm and relaxation… it lowers blood pressure and stress on your heart. Hugging is good for your stress level and your physical health.

Hugs help us feel safe. In addition to oxytocin, levels of serotonin and dopamine also increase when we are firmly hugged. Both of these body chemicals promote a sense of well-being; of belonging. When we experience a sense of safety and belonging, our entire world feels better. Our perspectives are balanced.

Hugs educate us about giving and receiving. They promote equilibrium in our day to day life. When we hug people there is an energy exchange. Some people believe that the interaction seeks to equalize the vibrations in the union… taking from one and giving to another. After a firm hug, we may automatically feel more harmonious and peaceful.

When you have a little extra energy, why not share a little? The hug you give someone may be just the life they need to push through the rest of their day. If you notice a person with low energy and you feel comfortable - offer a hug. You'll likely make a difference in that individuals' day and all because you made a decision to …

Hug someone.

#171 Get new eyeglasses

Eyeglasses are expensive - or at least the lenses are and so they are one of those things that we don't update as much as perhaps would be good for us. I've talked to a number of people through the years that only get 'new' glasses when their prescription changes. Yet they'll buy new shoes or new purses for the sole reason that they've grown tired of the ones. Eyeglasses are perhaps more important because they sit on your nose most of the time you are awake during each day.

Some people use their glasses as a fashion statement. For those of you who remember Sally Jessy Raphael, you'll remember her iconic red glass frames; they were her trademark. Drew Carey is another who is easily recognized because of his eyeglasses. Have you thought about making a statement with yours??

If you're old enough and been wearing glasses long enough, you've more than likely collected enough photographs to clearly see a transition of your own style through the years. What's important to look for is whether or not you've been stuck in the same 'style'. Perhaps it is time to try something new and or just bring your spec look into the 21st century.

When choosing new glasses, you can get daring or different and yet still follow the basic rules that go along with choosing frames. Consider the shape of your face. Someone with a heart shaped face will want a different style than someone with an oval. Also pay attention to skin tone. If you have olive skin, you'll want to pick very different colors than if you have a pasty white complexion. Perhaps the most important consideration is your personality. What style combo best fits your persona? If you've always been conservative, maybe it's time to pick something a bit more edgy. If you've always been edgy, try something classic.

The point is to switch it up a bit and …

Get new eyeglasses

#172 Be curious

Have you heard the phrase "curiosity killed the cat?" I actually grew up hearing that quite often and never paid much heed to it, but I find that many people are hesitant to be curious. The phrase is credited to an English comedy play from 1598 and I can't help but wonder if it propagated with the simple intent of keeping wandering children or nosy neighbors in line.

Today we know that curiosity is one of the fundamental attributes of happy people. When we wonder, we are apt to try new things and when we try new things, there is more novelty in our lives. Novelty keeps things new and fresh - boredom is rare in curios people. People who are curious are constantly learning, exploring, or trying new things; expanding knowledge and boundaries.

When we are curious about people or perspectives, we ask more questions. People who are curious tend to have more friends and deeper relationships. They have developed an ability to delve deeper into the conversations that build emotional intimacy, even in platonic relationships. As their perspective expands, they are able to have more empathy; a trait which leads to more consistent reports of well-being.

Your talent and desire for curiosity may determine your capacity for personal growth. Researchers have identified a correlation between the two. If we don't ever wonder who we are, why we are, or how to change - then growth simply won't happen.

Many of the ideas I've written about to make your life happier and more productive have been identified as a result of people being curious… "I wonder what would happen if I…." and then a sense of satisfaction, comfort, and/or peace sets in and you feel happy. Trial and error… not everything we are curious about will be something that we really wanted to know.

In most things, your life will be enriched if you find the energy to…

Be Curious.

#173 Sew something

Can you sew on a button? Are you a dressmaker? Or perhaps your ability lies with making curtains which mostly requires sewing a straight line. Most of us have been introduced to a sewing machine at some point - at least in our school years depending how old you are. By the 1980s, children in the U.S. were exposed to wood shop and Home economics regardless of gender. Introductions to the tools in both arenas were made. Yet, for many people - that was the first and last time they held a needle and thread.

I'm not sure there's great value these days in sewing clothing unless you are hard to fit. Fabric is expensive and clothes are cheap (relatively speaking) so it doesn't make sense to make your own blue jeans. However, if you are tall and it's difficult to find things long enough - knowing how to put together a skirt or a pair of slacks is really beneficial. Knowing how to hem or take a tuck in a dress is great if your shape isn't perfectly hourglass.

Perhaps the greatest benefit is in knowing how to create products for your home. Curtains are super expensive and crazy simple to sew. Knowing how to run a few straight seams across a length of fabric means you can have almost any kind of curtain you desire. I've seen people make valances and drapes from the most unusual fabric source... old bedspreads, flower sacks, and even tee shirts. Pinterest is full of creative ideas and once again, YouTube will have a video showing you how to manifest the notion.

With a few simple swipes of the sewing machine and a couple of hand stitches, you can have new throw pillows on your sofa or bed. Even pajama bottoms are quick and easy... for years everyone in my family had matching ones each Christmas.

Similar to knowing the basics with a hammer and saw... this is a basic skill that comes in handy more than you'll realize. Dust off your sewing machine or pick up a needle and thread, grab some practice fabric, turn on YouTube and ...

Sew something.

#174 Focus on self-awareness

Some might think that 'ignorance is bliss' or that 'denial is safe' yet living in a state of either can lead to rather dysfunctional coping and/or relating. Even though it may seem rather counterintuitive, being 'aware' is the emotionally healthier option.

If I could teach people all over the world any one skill, it would be an ability to become self-aware. It's not necessarily an easy task! Sometimes, awareness allows us to see things we didn't really want to notice. That's where avoidance and denial come into play - they protect us from seeing what feels bad. Who wants to feel awful about themselves?

The only reason we don't' want to 'see' these things is because on some level - we are judging them. Think about it. If you get a tattoo that you love but your mom hates - no problem. You like it so there's 'no judgment'. If you get one during a drunken stupor even though you've vowed never to 'ink' yourself, you may have a judgment about it. It's likely that you'll cope with your own disappointment by creating a story that makes it 'ok' for you. The preferable scenario is that you simply accept both the drunken stupor and the impulse to get a tattoo without any negative feeling.

Regret is a waste of your emotional energy. For most of us, we do what we do in each moment because it makes sense based on what we know/feel - at that point in time!! And then, like Maya Angelou said, "when you know better, you do better".

Even though it may be difficult, seeing yourself clearly - how you think, why you think and feel the way you do, why you engage and react in the manner that is common for you – it's important information. Nothing changes unless you know it exists. Behavior is only dysfunctional to the extent that it impacts your ability to have the life or relationships that you desire. So, if it works for you... it's ok. However, if you are missing a piece of that link, then a good hard look at *you* is in order. And since we are always changing in response to our relationships and our environment... it's an ongoing process.

If your goal is to live with authenticity, then it's imperative that you develop a lifelong goal to ...

Focus on self-awareness.

#175 Go fishing

For some, fishing is an active sport that is frequently practiced. For many more of us, it has yet to be enjoyed. There may be an 'art' to fishing but this suggestion is more aligned for those of you who wish to have the experience versus a refined talent. But you never know... the talent may be lying dormant.

It's easy to get overwhelmed if you walk into a sporting goods store and know nothing about fishing. There are a variety of 'types' of fishing; freshwater, deep sea, fly, surf, shore, ice, boat, rock... each one sporting technique and equipment. But for most of us, keeping it simple and basic is a good starting point.

The first step is to obtain a fishing license. It's necessary in most cases. Many of the places that sell bait also sell licenses for those over the minimum age requirement. I was always a bit squeamish about putting worms on a hook but soon discovered that there is a tool for that (looking very much like tweezers). If you are fortunate enough to actually catch fish, there are size requirements (length) for most species. Catch and release is where my interest lies even though I do love to eat fresh fish... cleaning them is an entirely different story and so I'll leave that to the people with stronger convictions than me.

You might ask, 'why bother to go through all that effort if you're not eating the catch?' Clearly, the challenge is enticing to some; it's the thrill of the chase (or catch). Strengthening a technique or skill is always good. But there's more... the development of patience. Fishing takes patience. It fosters stillness. It promotes tolerance. It induces calm. It improves self-reliance. It heightens Vitamin D production, cardiovascular health, and may improve overall body strength (assuming you're catching big fish). It encourages family bonding which, boosts immune functioning. It may incorporate laughter, implant fond memories, and encourage travel... more tenets of good living.

Sound worthwhile? It is certainly, worth a try so, grab a friend or family member, do a little research, and ...

Go fishing!

#176 Go to a salt room

You may ask "what?" as you conjure images of a nice big Porterhouse steak hot off the grill with a shaker of pink Himalayan salt... but no - that's not the intent, goal, or process behind a 'salt room'.

Salt rooms offer Halotherapy which, is a process of sitting in a room filled with fine particles of salt. In doing so, you inhale micro particles (similar to breathing ocean air) and it settles on your skin as it does after an ocean swim. Salt is known to reduce inflammation both when inhaled and on your body. [Mosquito bites heal much faster after ocean swimming.]

During your stay at the Salt Room, you'll be sitting comfortably in a chair or on a yoga mat and the session is often coupled with a guided meditation, shifting your relaxation into high gear. Taking this 'quiet' time for yourself is a fantastic addition to your self-care regimen.

Halotherapy has indicated benefits for a number of respiratory and skin ailments; in-particular allergies and eczema. It's safe for people of all ages and there are no reported negative side effects. So far, there is only anecdotal evidence for the benefits of Salt therapy but the testimonies from people who have experienced their benefit is difficult to ignore.

Prior to a year ago, I'd never heard of halotherapy and I'm now aware of two rooms within reasonable driving distance of my home. There's a high probability of one near you. At the very least, a number of spas have introduced some form of salt therapy in their offerings. The combined benefit of meditation would direct me toward a full functioning location and so I encourage you to take a step out - try something new - and ...

Go to a Salt Room.

#177 Ride in a hot air balloon

Is this one of those things on your "before I die list"? Have you done it? Maybe the question is 'why'? Why would someone leave earth in an open-air contraption without any intent of going from point A to point B? Shortly after the USA was born as a country, the first hot air balloon was launched in Europe. By the end of the 18th century, balloonists were crossing the English Channel and traveling for thrills sake. It took almost 200 more years for ballooning to make significant impacts in terms of height and distance. Even though they've been recorded at speeds close to 250 mph., they do not allow for convenient transportation. So why bother?

Ballooning is a fantastic hobby for thousands of people and a career for few. It's considered a sport and there is an industry built around its competitions. Yet the real business lies in offering a thrill to those of us who rarely leave the ground outside of a commercial airliner. As you lift off the ground, there is little sound outside of the flame providing the 'hot air' that is generating the lift. The scenery - often just after sunrise or later in the day at dusk - is accentuated by the sun and allowing you a bird's eye (or drone) view of the countryside.

If you are like me - there's a certain fear of flying involved when you stand in an open basket many hundreds of feet above ground level. After researching for this post, I'm more convinced of the safety elements inherent to ballooning. The pilot of a hot air balloon is trained along with the pilot of your jetliner... their aircraft is just a bit different. Indeed, it is reported to be even more safe than flying in an actual airplane.

This suggestion relates to making your life more enjoyable, thereby increasing a sense of overall well-being. In fact, when we face fears, add variety, and accept some level of risk in our lives - we ARE happier. Perhaps this activity will help you step outside your comfort zone, allow you to cross something off your bucket list, help you surprise someone, or spend quality time with a loved one... again, all elements associated with an increase in overall happiness.

If you are looking for an activity for a 'special occasion' or something to add to your Christmas list, why not ...

Ride in a hot air balloon.

#178 Swing on a swing

Robert Louis Stevenson wrote a poem called "Up in a Swing" and published it in A Child's Garden of Versus in 1885. It was one of the first poems I recall memorizing and I cannot hop on a swing - even today - without thinking of that poem.

Most playground swings will fit adult sized behinds and there is a certain charm to partaking in the childhood delight of moving through the air. Close your eyes and imagine for a moment the sensation you remember from the last time you played on a swing. Do you remember how you learned to 'push' your legs to gain height? Do you recall jumping off the swing? Seeing who could jump further or from the highest point?

Swings may be one of the first opportunities that humans had to experience movement off the ground. The freedom we feel as the swing moves through the air, pushing it against our face and lifting us up and across the ground may have been the inspiration for bigger and more industrious flight.

In those few moments that you allow yourself the childish delight of swinging, you allow your mind to take a break. It will automatically settle into auto mode and recall the body movements you learned in childhood to lift and push the swing across the ground. It will automatically flashback to youthful memories of play and simplicity; perhaps offering you a much-needed mental break.

A mental break is often just the thing we need to interrupt a stress response and/or regroup our energy. This is another suggestion that will get you outdoors in the fresh air - good for your body and spirit. It will induce pleasant memories and perhaps laughter - increasing serotonin levels. It will reduce cortisol levels - good for your mind and body.

If you find yourself passing a playground, remind yourself to take a few minutes to give yourself a short mental break and ...

Swing on a swing.

#179 Sleep on the beach

It's an amazing experience to sleep on the beach overnight, allowing the thunder of consistent wave action to lull you into a deep slumber. If you haven't allowed yourself the pleasure, I highly recommend it.

These days it's almost impossible to pitch a tent in the dunes as they are protected along almost every coastline in the USA but... there are dozens if not hundreds of public and private campgrounds that border ocean beaches. With a little advance research, you can pick a spot as close to the wave action as possible. In some areas, tying a hammock between a couple of trees may even give you a sunrise view over the top of any dunes. As an avid camper, the only drawback I've ever noticed about beach side camping is the amount of sand I end up bringing home.

Perhaps the best spot in the Mid-Atlantic is Assateague State Park. It's a bit of a pain to get to and the flies can be atrocious at times, but you just can't beat the location! California has tons of locations as well as Florida. (I guess the more coastline you have, the better the opportunities!) The Travel Channel did a piece and after seeing the options, my bucket list just got a bit longer.

Now, this suggestion is to actually get down in the sand... form it to your body and sleep there - preferably under the stars but I'm aware that might be simply too much to ask of some people. So... with a bigger budget you can go all fancied out and rent a beachside bungalow in almost any beach community. Certainly, around the globe there are thousands of options and perhaps the only reason that people go to places like the Seychelles islands where the beach and luxury go hand and hand; where almost every sleeping option is either over sand or surf.

No matter how you do it or when, there's a magical element of being able to drift off to the sound of ocean currents embracing the beach. Treat yourself with the experience as often as you can...

Sleep on a beach.

#180 Play a card game

In my mother's generation, it seemed that everyone - really, everyone - played cards. If it wasn't Bridge or Poker, it was Spades and Canasta. People often had a deck of cards in their purse or glove compartment and it was a great way to whittle away time or get together with friends. Now we have smartphones and video games. Consequently, I've noticed that a lot of young people don't know how to play even the basic card games like Rummy.

Card games are a great way to bring people together for conversation, entertainment, and a little competition. Many of them are quite strategic and like some board games, generate great worldwide contests. Yes, there's a bit of luck involved insomuch as the draw or deal of your cards but 'how' you play them... that takes some finesse.

Grab a friend, family member, or grandchild and dust off a deck of cards. Perhaps one of you can teach the other even if you have to search the internet for the rules to your favorite game. Remember the games Spit or Euchre? Bicycle - the dominant and market king of all card companies - even has an app that allows you to pull up the rules for almost any game you can think of! Remember 'I doubt it' and 'Hearts'? The rules are there too!

It's one of those simple things that keeps us humble, connected, and present. The comradery you experience will help increase endorphins that increase feelings of happiness. Using strategy will help keep your mind clear and sharp. Learning and or laughter will also improve your overall mood so make an effort to step out of your routine, clear your schedule, invite some friends over, and do something fun the old-fashioned way...

Play a card game.

#181 Carve something

This suggestion is entirely recommended for the creative side of you. It's something that is probably off your radar and yet it's fun, challenging, and possible for even the most basic beginner.

To start you need a small knife; preferably a handy-dandy pocketknife with a selection of blades but a small paring knife will also suffice in these early stages. The only other requirement is a bar of Ivory soap or a piece of Balsa wood; either choice is soft and easy to carve with little pressure.

This creative option is often taught to children in scouting programs which, may be the last time any of us made an effort to try this activity. Yet, today your dexterity is far more developed and with a little patience your imagination can transform the soap or wood into an entirely different shape and/or a functional item.

I can imagine a few of you wondering "why?" - thinking that I am stretching this 'creativity' piece a little far and yet I'll reiterate that just 'trying' new things is good for your soul. It's great for building your imagination, your confidence, and your curiosity. It's a wonderful way to foster creativity and wonder.

Soap carvings make great gifts! Even if you carve small hearts and put them in a box with a little essential oil... what a nice gift for a guest bathroom! Carving little figurines, small toys, or an ink stamps from balsa wood can also make great gifts. This is also one of those little thought of talents that can really come in handy when you need something unique and custom - as in an ink stamp or a unique name.

Try a Google search of 'beginner wood carver'. Hop on YouTube to watch a demo. Both will get you the basics and begin to satisfy, challenge, or develop a number of little personality characteristics that get stimulated with creative energy! Find an easy project and challenge yourself to ...

Carve something.

#182 Wallpaper a room

They say if you live long enough, everything comes back around. I've seen several trends reappear; shoulder pads, high-waisted pants, and wallpaper! If you've ever tried to remove wallpaper from plaster walls that were never sized, you'll remember it was nearly impossible. I've known some people who thought it was far easier to put up new drywall than try and get that wallpaper off.

However - the wallpaper today is new and improved! Or perhaps the products that we prep the wall and then ultimately remove paper with are tremendously better than their aged parents. Some 'wallpaper' today is similar to contact paper and is removable as such - perfect for those in rental units who want some style to their temporary digs.

If you're an HGTV fan, you've recently seen many of the designers use wallpaper as decor for 'statement' walls in dining, family, and bedrooms. Often, it is bold and reminiscent of mid-century modern design. Wallpaper is a great way to add personality to a home. In addition, it can cover up flawed walls and can even cover paneling with the right base treatment.

It's not hard to do once you've had a little practice. *TIP - start on a large wall with no windows or doors.* It takes a little practice cutting out windows, doors, outlets, and going around corners (especially if you have a vertical pattern you need to keep straight). If you are great at wrapping presents or if you have a background in origami, you'll probably excel at it. Otherwise, it may be better to hire a pro - especially if the wallpaper is an expensive one. It can be on the temperamental side.

You can order wallpaper online, but I like to sit and look through wallpaper books and turn the pages. Also, take the books home to have a real-world example for decision making. Most companies will also let you order a 'sample' so you can tape it on your wall like a paint sample to see if you want to live with it longer. *TIP: If you're buying random rolls of wallpaper and you find some on sale somewhere - make sure they are from the same color lot (on label)* ... I've hung a whole room only to find out that one roll is different, and the background color didn't match at all! Go ahead, try bringing your home into the era of modern decor and ... Wallpaper a room.

#183 Do one thing you've been putting off

This tip will satisfy all three objectives in terms of making your life 1. Easier, 2. Happier, and 3. More Productive.

When we procrastinate, our inner voices often become critical. Criticism is a negative modifier to happiness. Procrastination complicates our life often because it clogs the flow of productivity - contributing to negative self-talk - fostering dissatisfaction overall.

If you've activated some of the earlier tips about organization and productivity, then you may have a master to-do list. What item on that list has been there the longest? What is preventing you from accomplishing that task? What would happen if it were no longer on your list? If you still can't find the motivation to tackle that task, consider the reason it is there in the first place. Perhaps it's important to reconsider the task in its entirety.

I used to have a separate file for each bill that I paid throughout the year in case I needed to access it at a later point in time. I detested the task of filing and the pile would often grow to an unmanageable height - creating another layer of complexity to the concept of task completion. Eventually I realized that in all the years I'd been spending those hours carefully organizing - I'd never had a reason to go back and pull something from those files.

Today, I simply have a box dated for each year and all the papers go into the box - fully unorganized - completely random and IF... I ever need to find something I will spend the hours necessary to find what I need. I've saved 20 or more hours with this new - chaotic - but time efficient - system. The best part about this 'system' is that I don't have a pile of papers waiting to be sorted - that pile haunted me every year!

Take a look at your master 'to-do' list and identify the item(s) there that you're procrastinating about most. Decide if the item needs to stay on your list or if there is a different solution. For the items that remain, make a decision today to...

Do *one* thing you've been putting off.

#184 Celebrate a milestone

When I started the task of compiling 365 thoughts/ideas/tips of how to live better, I didn't really give much consideration to the significance of the challenge to write every day for an entire year. Shortly after moving forward, I realized it was going to take some appreciable thought and perseverance. This book is a significant milestone achieved by that effort.

There are so many milestones in our lives that we leave unacknowledged or downplay... what about that first time you finish a 5K? Or the time that you were offered a salary you had reached for? What about the savings goal you worked hard to accomplish? Those things are beyond the new promotion, the new house, marriage, middle age, and retirement but definitely worth celebrating!

When you acknowledge and celebrate even your small accomplishments, you honor the work you put forth. You're taking a moment to recognize the part of you that benefits from praise and appreciation. It's an audible "I did it" and an unceremonious "yay for me" that is deserved. It's important to learn how to validate oneself - not in the pursuit of conceit or zealous pride - just an appreciative sense of accomplishment.

So today, I invite you to self-congratulate - if even for a moment - for something significant that you've accomplished recently. What major goal have you surpassed? What challenge have you conquered for the first time? What golden ring have you grabbed? Think carefully, pour a glass of wine, pop open a beer (unless you are celebrating a recovery milestone!), or grab a chocolate chip cookie and...

Celebrate a milestone!

#185 Organize your manuals

Do you have a drawer of manuals? Is it overflowing? Outdated? I know in my house I have historically stuffed booklets in there as I obtain items and then only pay attention when the drawer is too full to take any more. I am often amazed at how many coffee pots I've purchased since the last time the drawer was cleaned! (I go through them faster than tires on my car!)

My dad taught me the importance of keeping manuals and while it's a little less imperative now that everything and anything is on the internet - one of the habits I have is stapling a receipt or at least noting the date of acquisition on the instruction/operation manual. Recording the date of purchase is important for warranty information. Having the original manual is also a nicety for the person who buys the item secondhand from you. It demonstrates that you 'take care' of our belongings and that you are responsible (that's what Dad said).

Looking through a collection of appliance/apparatus manuals can be entertaining as well... the last time I made this effort we found information for a Karaoke machine I had bought the children more than ten years ago... it offered an opportunity to walk down memory lane for a while and giggle at the memories of bellowing teenage voices - the Britney Spears 'wanna-be's'.

It's a simple chore that really only takes a few minutes... a much shorter time than we imagine. Whether it's a tool sitting in the garage, an appliance that you use every day, or a toy that's been forgotten the manual may be lying dormant in that drawer. Right now, while it's fresh on your mind, either tackle the task or scribble on your to-do list...

Organize your manuals.

#186 Learn sign language

When I was in high school, I played the part of Annie Sullivan in our school play production of The Miracle Worker. She was the woman who taught Helen Keller as a child, how to communicate with the world. As a result of that experience, I learned the sign language alphabet and at that time, became rather proficient at spelling out words. Since I was the only one in my environment who had the skill - it didn't do me much good. At least until my sisters learned it and then - we had fun discussing things secretly in crowded rooms.

I didn't have much motivation to broaden my knowledge until I was babysitting my deaf nephew one evening. He kept trying to get out of bed and even though he was trying to signal something to me, I was being quite stern. He wasn't old enough to write things down and I was tired. Eventually, his persistence wore me down and I indicated that he could get up and do whatever it was he wanted so badly. The poor kid ran as fast as he could into the bathroom, and I felt like a rotten Aunt. It was motivation.

Eventually I was able to learn American Sign Language (ASL)- the most common type of 'signing' in the Deaf community. I was known to be theatrical and so it was a good fit because a lot of the communication is via inference of facial expressions and body movement. By then, my nephew was much older and although I didn't see him often, it was nice to be able to 'converse' and I could comprehend most of what he was conveying to me. Over time and without practice, my 'signing' became majorly rusty and barely discernible.

Sign language isn't just for deaf people. There are lots of occasions where interpreters are needed. The American Disabilities Act requires public and certain private organizations to provide assistance so that the hearing impaired can receive the same information that hearing individuals have access to. How many times have you found yourself in a situation where you couldn't (or shouldn't) speak but needed to send a message across the room? I know many of us use texting for this purpose! People who know sign language enjoy an alternative mode of transporting messages.

ASL is widely becoming accepted as a 'second language' in the public education space. It is an option now in many foreign language departments across the USA. Some organizations offer classes and many of the people who act as interpreters in churches and synagogues also teach small groups locally. Generally, it's easy to find an inexpensive and convenient forum to learn.

Earlier this year one of the suggestions I made was to both learn something new and to take a class. This suggestion encompasses both! I hope you'll consider the overall benefits of creating new neural pathways, setting and reaching a goal, as well as having a little fun as you look for a class and make the decision to …

Learn sign language.

#187 Clean your underwear drawer

This is one of those 'areas' that is typically at the bottom of most to-do lists. We automatically get dressed each day without much thought as to the condition of our undies unless we are expecting to be seduced later in the day. And... the less seduction in your life... the worse condition your personals are likely to be in.

I wasn't aware of this phenomenon until as a young widow, someone suggested going shopping to replace my undies collection. I was not yet in a state of mind where that need was recognized but had to agree that the state of my scanties was appalling. Having been married a few years and as a new mom... the condition of my undergarments was definitely not prioritized. There were far too many stretched out, worn out, or faded undies that qualified as only 'period or post pregnancy' panties (you know what I mean ladies?) Some went into 'that' pile and many others were simply tossed.

Our favorite tee-shirt bras, boy shorts, and lace thongs tend to stretch and fade over time, losing their overall attractiveness. We often fail to notice. Men have this issue as well with respect to boxers or briefs that get stretched and stained to the point that they are downright repulsive. I understand there's a strategy to letting the jewels get some air but when they are flapping in the wind also... what's the point?

You'll feel better about yourself when you start with attractive, clean, and well-fitting skivvies. Even white cotton that meets that criteria is more pleasurable to both wear and look at than the alternative I'm describing. Long ago a friend taught me the trick of buying a couple of basic colored bras and then I could choose any combination of colors in my panties and it would look like a 'set'.... One doesn't have to have hefty finances to underlayer nicely.

As you get dressed today, or ready for bed... open the drawer that contains these items and quickly assess the additional lifespan of each piece. It only takes a few minutes and you'll have addressed a personal care item with the simple gesture of ...

Cleaning your underwear drawer.

#188 Dance

If you were ever a Grey's Anatomy fan, you'll remember that Meredith Grey liked to 'dance it out'. It was her way of being emotionally expressive. The truth is, dance is fantastic for emotions - it's great for your body - and it may help you live longer. Indeed, there was a woman on the television show America's Got Talent that took Ballroom dance classes when she was in her sixties and after more than 10 years of honing that skill... she is dancing on national television with the grace of a swan at the age of 71.

When we dance, we burn calories. We release endorphins. We stretch muscles. We build strength. We build aerobic capacity. Our balance, agility, flexibility, and coordination are improved. Our social interactions can be enhanced, and our overall sense of wellbeing elevated.

Dance can take so many different avenues that there's an option for just about everyone. You can disco in the comfort of your living room; take ballroom dancing lessons, spend Saturday afternoon Country line dancing at a local venue. You can enroll in ballet, tap, or modern dance classes at a local studio or community college. Dance by yourself, with someone you know, or with a complete stranger. There really aren't limits except those you apply to yourself.

Think about your motivation to dance... what is your goal? Fitness? Flexibility? Social connection? Would you prefer a partner? Private Lessons? Potential for competition? Do you want a workout or simple fun? Are you seeking to develop strength, coordination, or flexibility? The answer may dictate the style of dance you may enjoy and the intensity you dive in with.

At the very least, allow yourself to take the opportunities when they arise, to move to music that you enjoy. Whether it's a series of hip wiggles or spins around the kitchen... when you hear tunes that motivate you to 'get your groove on' - let the spirit move you and...

Dance.

#189 Record your dreams

Sleep experts tell us that everyone dreams. Do you remember yours? Psychoanalyst Jeffrey Sumber suggests that dreams are the communication avenue utilized by our subconscious and our conscious selves. He posits that dreams are quite meaningful and will often help us process complicated or confusing emotions in a state that is safe and private.

I know this postulation give many of us pause as we recall some of the more bizarre dreams that when remembered - seem to come out of left field. Dream analysis isn't a fixed science even though many representations are made as such. While it may be common for people who dream about drowning to be overwhelmed in some area of their lives, it is an inferred meaning - not a 'fact'.

If you are seeking information about your dreams, the first step is to keep a dream journal on your nightstand. Why there? Many of us forget our dreams within moments of waking unless we wake in the middle of or right after a dream. If we don't take steps to implant the memory of the dream, it disappears because our brain doesn't' consider it necessary information. (Similar to noticing the people next to you at dinner but unable to describe them hours later.) Immediately upon waking… breathe deeply and recall your last known imagery and then write down as many details as you can recall. Generally, as we write we will remember more.

Pay particular attention to 'feelings' in a dream. If you are engaging in an activity - consider what meaning you give that activity. Who is with you? What is their roll in your life? As it relates to the meaning of your dream - *you* are the expert. You're the only one who can ultimately decode the messages as they are being sent to you -via imagery - from your subconscious to your consciousness.

After you've recorded elements from a number of different dreams - look for commonalities. Identify the events during your conscious day that may correlate to elements in your dreams.

In this manner, you'll begin to decode messages or processing strategy that your subconscious mind is working with. It's fascinating to discover another layer of your psyche and promotes an even deeper level of self-awareness --- always a great thing. If you're curious, get a notebook and begin by… Recording your dreams.

#190 Convert your light bulbs to LED

If you haven't been introduced to LED lighting in recent years, you probably haven't left the house or turned on the television. We've been inundated with information about the energy savings available by using LED as well as products that utilize the technology for at least a decade now. Yet, I've noticed that incandescent lighting is still the preferred choice for many simply by noticing what's available in the grocery/home store isles.

The Department of Energy states that "Residential LED's - especially *energy star* rated products - use at least 75% less energy, and last 25 times longer than incandescent lighting." They are more cost effective over time than any other method of producing light. Even though a LED bulb costs more initially, you won't be buying another light bulb for years!

Overall, incandescent lighting is being phased out in most consumer products. This suggestion is meant to encourage you to phase them out in additional home lighting. It's true that it can be expensive for an entire overhaul in one sweep. Instead, replace two bulbs each time you go to the grocery store! Begin with the lamps/lights that you use most often; those kitchen lights, the bathroom and Den.

You might also consider using 'smart' bulbs. This is new technology that integrates with smart home systems like Alexa, Siri, and Cortana. They dim on demand, change color as bedtime approaches to increase melatonin production, and can even notify you of voicemail. Of course, it's controlled via a smartphone app which, means it is at your fingertips whether you are at home or not. These bulbs are reported to last 20 years or more! (I imagine the technology will change before the lightbulb wears out.)

For now, at least, you can immediately start saving money and energy with the simple task of ...

Converting your light bulbs to LED.

#191 Change the knobs on your kitchen cabinets

Want a quick pick-me-up? An updated look? It can be as easy as changing the knobs on your kitchen cabinets. Designers agree that a 'dating' element of design can be easily identified by the metal finish of knobs throughout a home. With a drill and screwdriver, the current decade can be introduced to your homes' cabinetry.

It may be as simple as changing from knobs to handles.

Or changing everything to a metal/look that is current or popular.

Or mixing it up a bit – adopting a more eclectic look.

Depending on the size of your kitchen, changing knobs can be pricey. A new knob can run from $.99 to over $5.00 depending on the quality and look you're going for. Specialty knobs can run as high as $10.00 from places like Restoration Hardware or Pottery Barn. But they don't have to... a can of spray paint can make a huge difference.

A modern, fresh environment feels good. When we experience a sense of being relevant, it settles that FOMO sensation; it helps us connect to the universal need of belonging. We are less timid about socializing at home – any sense of 'not being good enough' dissipates.

Whether it's a can of spray paint or a shopping spree for unique novelty knobs, the look of your kitchen can change significantly with the quick and easy effort of ...

Changing the knobs on your kitchen cabinets.

#192 Refresh the photos in your frames

We frame favorite photographs of people we love or of great memories so that we can keep the moment alive and in front of us. While the snapshots of the kids in preschool are adorable, there's a good chance that they have had a number of memorable moments since.

Grab a piece of paper and make a list of the frame sizes around your home. Many of them are typically 4x6 (the standard print size) or 5x7. Some of us may have special occasion photos that are the larger 8x10. Once you have a list, spend some time going through your phone or your online photo storage app (Google photos, Facebook, Shutterfly, etc....) and pick out a few to print. Most of the time, all you have to do is copy the photo so that they are all on the device you intend to transfer from.

Once you know which photos you want, use a printing service such as Shutterfly or Snapfish. Of course, most box stores (Target, Walmart) and drug store chains also offer printing services. Simply download the photo to their online app, select the size and finish, and then pick them up when you are ready! It's that easy.

Changing photographs is another activity that can help keep your memory strong. By stimulating our recall abilities, we engage memory in a way that keeps it moving... kind of like greasing a cog. Additionally, your brain has become accustomed to the photos currently in place - after a while they become almost invisible to your senses. Changing the pictures will stimulate your brain as it notices something new as you move from room to room.

Replacing the photos in existing frames also protects against excess clutter as the years go by. Continuing to add frames and photos can become overwhelming as time passes. As you go about this project, you may wish to update your frames as well but it's not necessary to replace them. A fresh coat of paint, some embellishments or simply moving them into a different room may be all you need for the overall look to be updated.

You can always add this to your master to-do list for consideration the next time you need a 'rainy day' activity. You'll have fun and enjoy lots of memories when you...

Refresh the photos in your frames.

#193 Review your will

We hear this legal advice all the time and yet I am amazed how few heed the recommendation. When did you originally write your current will? [Stop reading right now if you don't have one and make THAT your priority today.]

The first time we make a will, it contains basic tenets because we're young and have little to distribute. As we grow older, accumulate material items and wealth, have children, and lose older relatives, the way we think about 'who gets what', will change. The people we want to carry out our wishes may also change as relationships morph over time. This is all in addition to and separate from what needs to be addressed when there are dependent children who need to be considered.

Today, in conjunction with the traditional considerations, we need to think about some things that have never been issues such as your digital legacy. Many of us have photographs in online accounts... Facebook, LinkedIn, and other social identities. What do you want to have happen to that data? Your Executor needs to have a list of your electronic passwords and some direction of what to do with that information. Facebook offers a "Legacy" account. Do you want that information deleted or protected as historical data?

Experts agree that our wills need to be revisited every five years; more if our circumstances change (buying house, having children, etc.). It's important to understand what happens if you do NOT designate your wishes. Dying Intestate (without a will) will activate a line of distribution that is automatic when someone fails to make their preference; spouse first, then children. Without a spouse (married partner) or a child, the line of disbursement moves to parents, legal siblings, and eventually - if none of those relationships exist - aunts and uncles. There may be a friend or charity that would benefit from your estate more than great Aunt Mary and so a will is a necessity.

If you haven't recently considered your afterlife wishes, take some time to think about what is important to you and then...

Review you will.

#194 Go camping (or glamping)

I didn't exactly grow up camping the way so many people have but it didn't take long for me to fall in love with getting away and sleeping outdoors, once I did. There's just something very natural about sleeping outside. Perhaps it calls to our ancestral memories when outdoor living was the only option. When we can spend time outdoors (or with the essence of being outside) without the frustration of insects, bad weather, or discomfort - it's a wonderful experience that resonates deeply for most of us.

Camping accommodations are about as diverse as there are places to camp. When you're young and broke, tent camping is a great place to start. Small, easy to set up tents are inexpensive as are tent camping sites - especially at National Parks. There are pop-up campers, hard shell campers, fifth wheel traveling homes, cottages, cabins, yurts, and various contraptions that have been turned into camping rentals (i.e., treehouses, cabooses, etc.). Likewise, prices run from just a few dollars a night to potentially hundreds if you're Glamping in an elaborate tree house with all of the comfort amenities.

Glamping is a relatively new twist to the idea of camping - taking all of the reasons people don't camp - and erasing them. Glamping is perhaps the very best way to experience a change of scenery away from home while embracing a bit of the best camping elements. Glamping gives you a chance to do all of the things that are great about camping; cooking on an open fire, eating outside, stepping out of your sleeping area and taking a hike, embracing copious amounts of fresh air, etc. Glamping is where camping and modern comforts (bed & flushing toilets) - collide.

The idea of Glamping has become so popular that Airbnb lists dozens of owners who are now making money by offering 'accommodations' that take camping to a whole new level. RV's - Tents with beds, and treehouses are only a few of the offerings available now on these online overnight reservation services. Imagine the owner of a farm in western New York who puts up a large tent out on the edge of his tree line, lays in a throw rug, a queen sized mattress with high end linens, a few high powered battery operated lamps, lots of throw pillows, prepares a fire ready to light, and then leaves a tray with s'more fixings for you to enjoy at some point in the evening.

Oh... and don't forget the chemical toilet that's available so you won't have to succumb to any 'out house' experiences. That farmer... smart guy!

Certainly, throwing down a sleeping bag next to a babbling brook after sundown is great all by itself. The overall experience is enhanced when you watch raccoons steal a bag of hot dog buns left on the picnic table as you roast marshmallows over a fire. There is a beauty to that simplicity as well.

Of course, the perfect time to camp is when there are warm days and cool nights. When the leaves change colors and there is a crispness to the air, you can almost hear the mountains call. There are so many advantages to getting away from the daily stressors of your life and communing with nature - even if you do it in comfort! Your stress level will reduce, your exposure to Vitamin D will rise, your connection to family and/or friends will strengthen and your opportunity to 'get grounded' improves dramatically when you...

Go camping (or Glamping).

#195 Roast marshmallows

Roasting marshmallows is a tradition for many. Some people like their marshmallows lightly roasted - the color of toasted bread and soft, almost completely melted on the inside. It's accomplished by finding a part of the fire that is mostly molten coals with a low blue flame, if any. A slight rotisserie action will assure coverage across the entire circumference. It will bubble just slightly and color slowly. If your marshmallow matches this description and you wait just a few minutes after pulling it back from the fire - it will be slightly crispy on the outside as the sugar begins to crystalize - making it absolute perfection.

Others seem to find enjoyment by placing their marshmallow directly into the flame until it becomes a torch. Quickly, it turns black and will consume the sugar entirely if it is not blown out. The underbelly of these are still firm and can often be toasted again if only the blistered 'skin' was removed. It's a great way to extend the life of your marshmallow if - you can tolerate the 'burned' flavor. There are a few who are fearful of burning and lack patience to thoroughly roast so they 'warm' their mallow to the point of being soft enough to quickly dissolve.

A campfire is perhaps, the most favorited location to pass a bag of fresh marshmallows but it's not the only way to experience the joy of the sugary treat. In recent years we've seen an explosion of homeowners with backyard fire pits or chimineas on patios and decks - offering year-round alternatives to traditional campfires. There's always the convenience of a gas grill or the flame of your own gas stove. Pop a marshmallow on a large meat fork, turn the burner on high and rotate. As a novelty, a few companies now manufacture 'roasting kits' using a small sterno can as flame fuel. Hey, whatever works!

No matter how you do it, the simple act of popping a perfectly roasted marshmallow into your mouth or smashing it between graham crackers with a block of chocolate (s'more) will instantly remind you of one of the most fun aspects of childhood simply by...

Roasting marshmallows.

#196 Memorize a poem

Aside from "Roses are red…" and "Miss Mary Mac…" have you ever memorized a poem? Can you recall it now? Memorizing is good for your brain and poems are often good to practice because there is typically a cadence that makes it a little easier. It may be good for your spirit as well… the material we memorize sits a little further in our brains and becomes deep knowledge.

Unsure of your ability to memorize? Think of all the song lyrics you know… you've memorized them without intent just by listening to the song over and over. Really, anything we do over and over can be implanted in our memory banks. Think of the church service you cantor without much forethought, or the pledge of your fraternal organization. Repetition is a key to memorizing.

My mother had a plaque above the kitchen sink that I often read as I washed dishes and I remember it now… decades later; The Irish Blessing:

> *May the road rise to meet you,*
> *May the wind be ever at your back.*
> *May the sunshine warm upon your face,*
> *And the rains fall soft upon your fields.*
> *And until we meet again,*
> *May God hold you in the palm of his hand.*

I encourage you to pick a poem that resonates with you, print it out, and tape it in a location that you can easily read it a couple times a day (computer desk, kitchen or bathroom mirror). Before long, you will have memorized the poem in its entirety.

Memorizing a poem that you enjoy helps to build upon appreciation of artistic expression in general. The 'artistry' in the poem exposes you to language that may not be a part of your typical vernacular; expanding your vocabulary. It has the potential to expand your verbal and emotional intelligence which, are attributes associated with higher rates of well-being.

Take a short tour of the link above, visit the library, or think of a poet you've enjoyed in the past, pick out a verse, print it out, and …

Memorize a poem.

#197 Create a piece of wall art

Creating your own piece of wall art isn't nearly as difficult as you may think! Depending on how industrious you feel, it can be as little as a few minutes with some simple supplies or you can go all out, using power tools and scrap wood.

Starting small and easy is generally a good idea. Some masking tape, a couple of canvases, and complimentary paint colors is all you need for this first abstract look.

I used this technique for the bathroom walls in my daughter's hall bath a number of years ago. It encompassed a pack of coordinating scrapbook paper, an inexpensive canvas, and some Modge Podge. Any shape works but a 'leaf' or 'pointed oval' makes a pretty great flower. You can make this for less than $20.

Using circles is also a great idea. There are lots of options here... Paper on canvas, wood on canvas, wood on wood, even plastic. You can use a variety of items here or simply spray paint wood circles and clue them to a painted board or repurposed canvas you pick up at a thrift shop.

Getting more labor intensive, a variety of wood projects are also low cost. Scrap wood can be purchased at surplus shops for next to nothing and joined to create a panel ready to hang. A painted word purchased on Etsy or at a craft show adds a pop of color and personal interest.

It may be as simple as sending the kids outside to pick up a few sticks that nature provided the last time it was windy! Cutting them to fit inside a shallow box you've built and painted creates a really interesting focal point for a room anchored in natural elements. It brings the outside, inside.

These are only a few options to decorate on a limited budget. It's a great way to change up your home decor without breaking the bank or investing so much that you feel compelled to keep something even though your tastes have changed. Hopefully, this gets your wheels turning about how to fill some empty space on a wall in your home and ...

Create a piece of wall art!

#198 Clean out your car

If it's true that a clean house is a predictor of your health and happiness, then it must follow that the cleanliness of the inside of our automobile is also somewhat of a predictor... especially for those of us who spend a ton of time driving.

Reader's Digest suggests there's much more to cleaning the interior of our car than simply dusting and vacuuming and an order in which to do those things. To start - as in your home - you should vacuum first! But from top to bottom; starting with the dashboard, then the seats, and finally the carpet. Vacuuming creates dust so don't wipe things down until the vacuuming is finished. When you wipe things down, don't stop at the obvious... be sure to wipe the inside of the door - the door jamb - it's the part that everyone first sees and ultimately determines how tightly your door closes.

A true cleaning means getting into the glove compartment (does anyone keep gloves in there?), the center console, and the seat pockets. I'm lazy when it comes to those areas and when I do make the effort, I typically find little treasures that make me cringe, not to mention items I'd forgotten I had. Generally, I'm a few dollars richer for the loose change that has collected there.

The next step is to be sure to remove all the items that one should never keep in a car. Valuables are the obvious choice but there are other items that can be negatively affected by significant changes in temperature (heat & cold); plastic, for example. Eliminate any water bottles that have been exposed to intense hot temperatures possible when a car bakes in the sun. Same advice goes for anything electronic; computers, cell phones, and tablets can overheat when exposed to extreme temperature, rendering them temporarily inoperable. Electronics are also frequent targets of thieves, making your car a tempting target.

Inevitably, getting into a nice clean car that smells fresh ignites that 'new car' sensation - always a good feeling. Cleanliness is like a blank slate and allows your mind to focus on tasks at hand; clutter is distracting. Cleanliness helps us avoid the perils of allergens; the inside of your car is a small space so keeping the air dust free is beneficial. Take a look at your schedule and find some time to ...Clean out your car.

#199 Organize a food drive

Perhaps one of the best feelings ever is the sensation that settles in when we do something selfless and benefits someone else. It seems there is some type of disaster annually that strips communities and its residents of resources. Food pantries exist for this very reason yet during disasters and especially near the holiday's, their contents dwindle to levels that make it difficult to meet that need.

As an individual, it seems that there is often little we can do other than contribute money but that means someone else does the grunt work. This suggestion is aimed at increasing your sense of Eudaimonia (a deep sense of well-being) by initiating, organizing, and following through with a food drive in support of a local pantry.

After connecting with a charity that will accept the donation, it may be necessary to establish a collaboration with your work, school, or spiritual organizations to get energy, commitment, or permission. Generally, it's as simple as placing collection containers in an obvious place and inviting people in that environment to participate by contributing to the cause. Unexpired canned or boxed food items are always appreciated as are paper products that any family could use. Some drives are specifically aimed at children or infants. What a blessing it would be for a food pantry to be inundated with a supply of diapers it can offer its patrons.

This is a common effort during the holidays so as we enter that season each year, it may be something you want to add to your to-do list. Yet I offer the sentiment, "why wait?". Perhaps now... before we're all inundated with people asking, it would be more effective! It doesn't have to be complicated or fancy... a phone call to a pantry or charity to get needs and details... an email or flyer distributed to your cohorts... the actual collection... and then delivery. It could be one box or ten.

It's bound to boost your gratitude level, your sense of belonging, and your overall well-being and that's just the benefit to you! Your energy will most definitely help others and make life easier for someone who needs a boost. I hope you'll consider...

Organizing a food drive.

#200 Get a massage

One of the most wonderful self-care practices you can participate in is the treat of a massage. There are few treats better than settling into a state of complete relaxation while someone gently moves their hands across your muscles in a way that continues to promote a deeper sense of comfort and calm. All this in a quiet room with soothing music and low light. If it's a gentle massage, you're likely to fall asleep.

There are different types of massage and it's important to ask for the one you want with clarity. If you're expecting a gentle rub down but end up with deep tissue kneading - you're likely to be disappointed. A Swedish massage is where many people start - it's wonderful for people sensitive to touch, desiring something relaxing, and soothing. The sensation of long strokes along the lines of your muscles is quite relaxing. It's wonderful for working out small knots in the shoulders, neck, or back and can last as long as 90 minutes on average. A masseuse can use heated stones in place of their hands to ease muscle tension, relieve pain, and improve the flow of blood toward the heart.

In addition to hot stones, your massage may include Aromatherapy which adds a healing boost to your experience. Depending on the type of 'aroma', you may enjoy a mood boost, reduction of stress or anxiety, and/or pain relief just from the aroma in the room while enjoying your massage. Some essential oils may also be used on your skin - increasing the overall health benefit.

A deep tissue massage may be a better option if you have chronic muscle problems, pain, or anxiety. There is a stronger pressure with each stroke and with finger movements during a deep tissue massage. While it shouldn't 'hurt' or leave you feeling sore - it's not the kind of massage you want if you are specifically seeking relaxation and maybe a little nap.

There are several other options available for massage treatments so it's important to have a good conversation with your therapist to decide which is better for you. Massage can be helpful with circulation, sore muscles, lymph drainage, and overall stress management. Do yourself a favor and ...

Get a massage.

#201 Try a facial

If you're headed to the spa for the massage that I've recommended, why not treat yourself to a facial while you're there. A facial cleanses, exfoliates, and nourishes the skin on your face and neck, keeping it healthy, potentially firmer, and younger looking!

There are different types of facials which is why your best bet is to use the services of an esthetician. They are trained to identify any problems your skin may have such as blackheads, level of hydration, and issues with acne. As with other professionals, they are trained to identify a problem and then educate as to the best way to treat or serve that particular issue.

If you experience any acne, excess oil, large pores, dark circles, puffiness, sagging, pigment difference or have fine lines and/or wrinkles - you can benefit from a facial. Different facials offer different benefits. There are facials to firm and lift the skin, calm visible redness, depigment dark spots, detox skin, hydrate skin and other conditions. Considerations about which type of facial is best for you include diet, allergies, lifestyle, medications, activity, stress, and your home skin care routine. Based on all that information, your esthetician will know how to best meet your needs.

Most facials include some element of facial massage, a fantastic benefit as your face muscles get a workout with each sentence you utter not to mention your day-to-day facial expressions. There is typically a deep steaming to cleanse the skin in preparation for exfoliation - removing all the dead skin cells that accumulate. It's often a very soothing and relaxing experience. Next is generally some kind of mask... an effort to pull toxins out of your skin so that is fresh and clean. Lastly, your face will be massaged with a moisturizer designed for your skin type, leaving your face feeling healthy.

If you can make an appointment for a professional facial, don't fret as there are some good alternatives that will accomplish the basic elements important for a facial. Harper's Bazaar recently posted the best 14 Face Masks of All Time - giving us a nice list of alternatives to a salon experience. It may be a great activity for a girlfriend sleepover, a bridal party activity, or a quiet sole evening. Frankly though, for a few more dollars - someone else can do the work!!

If you want to have a do-it-yourself facial evening without all the costs and perhaps from a more organic standpoint, it may be as easy as heading to your kitchen. Homemade recipes for face masks that will detoxify your skin, hydrate, and cleanse with common food items like bananas, honey, oatmeal and milk are readily available online.

Aside from looking better, the time you take to either get a professional facial or a DIY one will be 'me time' - self-care at its best. You'll experience a sense of relaxation, calm, and potentially time away from the daily stressors of your life. According to dermatology experts, facials are the best way to rejuvenate our skin and can prevent premature aging. It's another item to add to your 'wish list' - you know, the one you are making so that when someone ask what you want for your birthday or the holiday's you can tell them you want to...

Try a Facial.

#202 Clean your lampshades

While this may seem like an odd suggestion in terms of creating a 'happier, healthier, and more productive life" ... it does fit into the 'healthier' category. Lampshades are a significant culprit for holding dust. Have you looked at yours lately?

Accumulated dust can be problematic for a lot of us, in particular, those who suffer from asthma. Think of how much dust is wiped away with a weekly furniture dusting. If you don't dust your lampshades equally, the layers build and contribute to pollutants in the air of your home. For the purpose of this article, a lampshade can reference any light cover, so it includes the 'globes' that adorn many hanging light fixtures. They are all rather invisible as we routinely move a dust rag through the house.

I prefer to vacuum mine... when I get the gadgets out to do baseboards, I'm usually in the frame of mind to get the dust creatures lurking in random spaces so the lampshades (who are major culprits of hiding those buggers) - get a good vacuuming also. A microfiber towel lightly sprayed with dust spray or slightly damp will also work as does a good, old-fashioned sticky lint roller. Organization and cleaning experts suggest filling the tub and washing anything that can tolerate water. (A tub is large and can easily accommodate larger shades.)

Dust particles exist everywhere in our environment and while there are some ways that we can reduce their presence, they'll never completely disappear simply because living things release their dead cells constantly. Clean air filters on your HVAC system will help, air purifiers trap more, and frequent vacuuming and dusting support the efforts.

Allowing too much dust to accumulate invites the critter 'dust mite' into your life. Many people are very allergic to mites and experience consistent sinus and respiratory issues. Reducing dust in often 'invisible' areas - such as lampshades - reduces the potential nesting areas for mites; creating a better breathing environment all around.

Would your shades pass the white glove test? You may want to grab the gadget of your choice and do your lungs the favor of ...

Cleaning your lampshades.

#203 Ask friends and family for feedback

One of the most basic tenets of self-awareness is to understand how you are perceived by those in your environment. There's no better way to get honest feedback than to ask people who know you best.

Being open to the constructive criticism people share is a necessity. Your ability to hear their perspectives without feeling attacked or 'bad' can help you understand how you are perceived by others. Try to remember that people who love you offer a view that is shared from a place of acceptance; they love you - anyway! It's always interesting to see things about yourself that can't be seen from the inside out.

Not everything that is observed needs to be changed. You are who you are! If an observation suggests offensive behavior, of course you'll want to consider how it is impacting someone you love and ask yourself if that's what your goal is... It may be just something you want to stay aware of so that you can mitigate its negative impact - where applicable.

Sometimes, we look at something so long that we stop seeing it - having become so accustomed to its presence. The feedback we receive is important for a complete picture. If you're concerned that the response may be too critical - qualify your request by asking this:

"Please offer gentle and constructive critique about my behavior/actions and how they impact our relationship: a mix of positive and negative observations would be appreciated."

The biggest pushback that I typically see to this suggestion is the fear we experience when we think that our faults are going to be highlighted. We have a deep seeded belief that if we bring attention to them, somehow people will think less of us. Interestingly enough - those traits are always exposed... just because we don't acknowledge them, doesn't mean they don't show through. It's always better to brave the exposure. Nothing changes if it stays packed away... even if no change is desired, keeping it out in front ensures that it stays healthy. So, give yourself an opportunity to grow and ...

Ask friends and family for feedback.

#204 Make bread from scratch

Is there anything better than the smell of fresh baking bread? One of my favorite childhood memories is coming home from school and entering a house filled with the aroma of bread in the oven. This is considered an "odor-cued memory" - a smell that, in an instant, propels us back to a fond childhood memory.

For this reason - although not the only reason - the suggestion to make bread from scratch and fill your home with the aroma is meant to create those same pleasant memories for your family. It's a two-fer... you're bound to recall wonderful memories AND eat some hot, fresh bread.

Bread doesn't have to be complicated. The invention of the bread machine simplified the process and eliminated the need to knead, rise, knead, rise... it's automatically achieved inside the machine. No machine? No worries... there are great breads that don't need all that attention. Indeed, some of the no-knead recipes resemble more organic and unprocessed (basically, because they are...) loaves that are more popular and tasty these days.

Of course, with a hot loaf of crusty bread to look forward to, there begs a question as to what you'll serve with it; a hot bowl of homemade soup? A big bowl of chili? A large pot of marinara covered pasta? Regardless of the choice, you'll need a stick of 'real' butter (preferably salted - because everything is a little better with a tad of salt), and potentially some jam or honey for the desert portion of the meal. Freshly baked bed with a little dollop of sweet makes a great follow up if you have any belly space left!

Google *40 Insanely Delicious Yeast Bread recipes* and choose the one that makes your mouth water. Gather the ingredients and treat yourself to the pleasure of ...

Making bread from scratch.

#205 Practice mindful compassion

One of the 'new' buzzwords in psychotherapy is 'mindful compassion'. It's not new really… Buddhists have been practicing mindful compassion for thousands of years and one might even argue that most prayer regiments are akin to this practice. Mindful compassion is the specific expression of empathy, goodwill, and compassion towards oneself and/or others. It's learning how to extend a deep level of compassion, without judgment, to oneself or to others.

Think for a moment of how you would comfort a child who has just lost his mother. Imagine that child sitting on your lap in a deep state of sadness and you are helpless to 'fix' the problem. Your only comfort can be a deep level of empathy and compassion for the pain that this child feels. Now, imagine that you can generate this same level of compassion for yourself each time you experience emotional discomfort or send that compassionate energy - via thought waves - to another human who may be suffering.

This level of comforting - this extension of deep compassion - can be very healing. Cultivating an ability to self-soothe is the focus of new treatments for anxiety and depression. It is also a wonderful way to begin each day - extending compassionate 'vibes' to people in your life who may benefit from a little extra love.

Doing so is quite easy if you sit quietly and imagine yourself in a state of deep compassion; going to your core. Next, create an image of the person you want to send energy to… and offer these words:

"May you be well; May you be happy; May you be free from suffering"

Spend 5 minutes in that space, sending love and energy to one or more people - or even yourself. Practicing this on a daily basis will not only increase your personal depth of compassion, it will calm you, build inner peace, and increase the endorphins that are associated with acts of benevolence.

This suggestion is a mere blip of an introduction to mindful compassion and I encourage you to investigate further. Furthermore, it's free! So, sit quietly for a few minutes and let the sunshine on your face as you close your eyes and …

Practice mindful compassion.

#206 Have your palm read

Palmistry has been practiced for thousands of years and some individuals are very talented in their ability to describe the characteristics about your life and personality based on the composition of your hand. First, they look that the fingers and there are assumptions made depending on a variety of hand features.

Additionally, the lines in your palm represent a variety of areas; marriage, head, heart, fate, sun, children, money, and health. More information is contributed based on moles, the way lines cross, and shapes that they make. Even the size of your hand matters. The left hand speaks your potential, the right hand about what you've done with that potential.

Supposedly, this ancient method of predicting has some merit. Recent science has correlated greater athletic talent in men whose ring finger is longer than his index finger. (I'm so curious to know how many of you just looked at your fingers!). Those men are more apt to be well-endowed and have more children. Those with longer index fingers are more prone to heart disease. Scientists think these elements have something to do with the prenatal testosterone exposure. Go figure!

These 'palm readers' are versed in the thousands of years of similarities and perhaps even the results of modern research, so they notice and comment on those things that are common across individuals with similar characteristics. They may tell you something that you don't know... not that it is 'carved in stone' but that you may be more prone to something that is indicated across the population with similar individuals.

Having your palm read is just a fun... not too serious activity that you can do with friends, sisters, bridesmaids, a partner, or colleagues. It's harmless unless you make more of it than is intended. Take it with a grain of salt... kind of like... Blondes have more fun. For some it's true - for others, not so much. The next time you want something fun and crazy to do, consider...

Having your palm read.

#207 Try a new hair color

One of the easiest ways to 'shake things up' from a personal look perspective is to color your hair. There are a wide variety of options, it's as temporary as you want them to be, and the opportunity to go bold is inherent. Your colorist's ability to create a natural blonde look or a full rainbow is only limited by your desire. Do you have a wish to see what it's like to be a redhead or a beach blonde?

For those of us who use hair color for reasons other than covering gray, it seems that we are demonstrating very specific personality characteristics; using color to make a silent statement.

Making the Brunette choice indicates stability and responsibility. It suggests a mature perspective with an emphasis on hard work and success.

Making the decision to dye your ends with a bright color indicates that you like to 'switch things up'. It implies that you prefer compromise and like to find a 'happy medium'. You're more likely to settle into the 'middle ground'.

Choosing a natural blonde look will highlight the fun side of your personality. The 'blondes have more fun' mantra speaks to your bold side. It tells the world that you're willing to be the life of the party and you're up for a night out or a chill PJ party as long as it's with friends.

Going red is always just 'sassy'. You take charge and make things happen while cultivating the hearts of those who take the time to know you; others step back. Your energy keeps life interesting.

Making the move to do dark and deep boldly tells the world you'll welcome it in but you're not going to chase it down. You wear your heart quietly on your sleeve and home is where you want to be.

There are a lot of great variations to these descriptions that will add a 'side note' whether it's a Balayage, foil highlights, a colored streak, or an Ombre. These playful options are fun and shift the color without a massive change.

If you're needing a little pick-me-up, this may be just the option for you. Consider your personality, talk to your stylist, and ...

Try a new hair color.

#208 Wear a blindfold

Ok... don't get too excited just yet. This suggestion is geared toward highlighting all senses when sight is not available and not just during sex. If you have a 'sleep mask' - go ahead a grab it, otherwise, close your eyes and follow the honor system. Take a few minutes each day this week to experience the conditions outlined below - without sight - to notice elements of everyday life that you've never experienced before.

Stand in the kitchen when someone is cooking - notice how you smell more or differently when you can't see what is cooking.

Sit outside on your deck or porch - notice the sounds that you may not have heard before. What birds are singing? Do you hear traffic? Or people? What do you smell?

Try eating without sight. Do you notice a difference in how quickly you devour your food? Are you more in tune with the smell or texture?

Make love while wearing a blindfold. Do you notice a difference in the level of pleasure that you experience?

Eliminating your ability to see, heightens your other senses. Your brain automatically redirects its reliance to sound, smell, and touch in order to identify the experience. This is one of the reasons using a blindfold during sex intensifies the experience for women. Men, who are more dependent on sight for stimulation, may not enjoy the same benefit.

Wearing a blindfold for a prolonged period can induce hallucinations. Research is discovering that when a sighted person is denied the ability to see - the brain will create visions. We seem to develop an ability to 'see' through our 'third' eye. Indeed, there is a retreat that promotes this process for those who want to 'destress' by using blindfolds to open a path to your subconscious. I would encourage anyone moving in this direction to move with caution and with someone psychologically trained. Going that deep - if there are old wounds - can be more harmful than helpful.

In any event - for a short duration - you can intensify your other senses and develop a stronger sense of being present by taking a few minutes each day to....

Wear a blindfold.

#209 Donate your books

Do you have shelves of books that you've read? Or of 'how-to manuals' that are contain information easier to find on the internet now? Or old textbooks that may even be obsolete at this point? Will you be re-reading any of them? If not... perhaps it's time to clean off your shelves.

There are a lot of places that you donate those books so that they don't end up in a landfill - a thought that seems completely sacrilegious. Here's a few ideas:

Donate them to the Salvation Army. There's been a lot of publicity about the various donation organizations. This one takes the lead in terms of amount of donations that actually fund its programs. Your 'trash' will be someone else's treasure.

Local libraries. Your local library may be interested in your cast offs but check with them first. Some are inundated and stop taking certain genres.

Hospitals & nursing homes. These institutions often have small lending libraries for patients and residents. Even older books may be appropriate for nursing homes as their residents often prefer to read popular fiction from their era.

Underfunded schools. If you're close to a region that struggles to meet the needs of its population - in particular, students - they may be very interested in books that can be used for educational purposes. The Reader to Reader program will take your books from local donation points and distribute them where they are needed.

Book Art. You could try your hand at Book Art... a growing genre of artistic expression that is accomplished by folding the pages of a book in a certain way. You can make anywhere from $30 to $75 per creation by selling them on Etsy. Maybe a great way to pull in some spending money.

Your dusting efforts become more efficient when your bookshelves are decluttered. You'll feel better knowing that those volumes are engaged with more purpose; potentially helping someone or providing relaxation and/or entertainment for another individual or child.

Grab a box and pull out those paperbacks that you finished reading years ago and ...Donate your books.

#210 Do a good deed

Are you a natural do-gooder? Are you the first to stop and lend a hand to someone in need? Do you run late or miss appointments because you donated that time to someone or something else?

Doing good deeds is good for our spirit. They can be cumbersome, quick, free, or pricey. They can impact one or many. It may be worthy to compare the differences between a volunteer activity, a random act of kindness, and a good deed... all of which may cross define. When I think of a 'good deed' it distinguishes itself from a RAK because I may not want to do it, but it's the right thing to do. Same for a volunteer activity, which may certainly be a good deed but it's more of a 'one-time occurrence' than a volunteer activity may be. So, using this criterion - a good deed is an isolated incident of doing the 'good' thing.

Perhaps a good deed is donating a dollar to the guy with a cardboard sign at the intersection or handing him a fresh apple.

It may be taking a random grocery cart back into the store when you see it out in the corner of the parking lot.

Perhaps it is dropping something off to someone on your way to work even if it's an extra five miles out of your way.

Yes, these are kindnesses, but based on the definition above, they are definitely good deeds.

Our daily life offers plenty of opportunities to do a 'good deed' even if it is picking up a piece of trash and moving it to a can when the person in front of you failed to discard it properly. We are more apt to notice the potential deeds when we are paying attention - being present - in our lives. Sadly, this is happening less and less as our faces are turned toward our smart phone more often than not.

Make an effort to be more aware of your surroundings and I'm sure you'll find more possibilities than you'll have the energy to follow through with. As you make time, notice how you feel... making sure to set appropriate boundaries when applicable. Overall, you're sure to notice that you just feel better about life each time you recognize yourself...

Doing a good deed.

#211 Follow the 5-minute rule

Years ago, I was introduced to Mel Robbins and her explanation of the 5 second rule.... A commitment to start those things you've been putting off by counting down 5-4-3-2-1 - and GO. She does a much better job of discussing this and extolling its benefits - it's worthy of attention if you procrastinate. Interestingly enough, as I was explaining it months later - I confused the concept by describing that we can do anything for 5 minutes so go ahead and ... just do it. It's different than Mel's strategy but helpful, nonetheless.

There are tons of things in our life - on our to-do lists - that we simply don't want to do... we may dread it or be annoyed by our need to accomplish it. Perhaps it just feels overwhelming. The idea behind the '5-minute rule' is that if you spend just five minutes on that item you are avoiding and still don't find the wherewithal to keep going - then, stop; redirect and know that you tried.

What tends to happen here is that once we begin to attack something - the enormity of it goes away. We often finish before the five minutes is up, having manifested the 'thing' to be much bigger - more challenging - than it actually was. Additionally, after giving something five minutes of our time and attention, we frequently discover that we can keep going; that it isn't that bad after all or that we're halfway there.

As you go throughout your day and face something that feels overwhelming or too cumbersome to attack - consider using this 5-minute rule and step into it with a timer set. Let me know what the result is! I love to hear the successes or challenges when people make an attempt to ...

Follow the five-minute rule.

#212 Decorate for the Season / Holiday

This suggestion is inspired by all of you who do this year after year because I believe it's something that those of us who don't... may benefit from. Just walking into any big box store confirms that the seasonal decoration business is booming. No matter the season, Fall, Winter, Spring, or Summer - there are distinct elements and/or holidays that prompt us to embellish our homes with seasonal decor.

In the Fall, we are presented with beautiful foliage informed items that bring much of the outside color - in. Without changing the color of our walls or the art we hang there, Autumn color adorns table decorations, window clings, candles and their containers, and porch ornaments as we embellish our mantles, tables, porches, and flowerbeds.

In addition, Halloween decorating has become extremely popular. It is emphasized by the plethora of 'scary' items intended to bring the 'haunted' element to neighborhood homes. It heightens the entertainment value to end-of-month trick or treaters. Almost immediately, we move into the season of 'Giving Thanks' and very quickly, to Winter.

Without almost any time passing, we move from Fall to Christmas - a holiday that brings out the decorations in a way no other time does. From our front lawns and rooftops to the family room and bath - decorating for Christmas is common across the board. I won't spend much time in this area of the discussion as most of us don't need additional encouragement.

After Christmas, Valentine's Day gives us a wintery reason to brighten up a dull and sometimes white, landscape, inside & out. This can be a fun and cheerful way to lighten the mood when the winter 'blues' have taken over.

Who isn't ready for beauty and fun by the time Spring arrives? Generally, Easter gives us a reason to get our creative spirit moving in the decorating department. Here again, marketing gurus have enticed us with a growing body of outdoor options, including giant blow up bunnies that wave to passersby.

If it isn't eggs and rabbits, it can be tulips, daffodils, and hyacinths or religious artifacts celebrating Christian beliefs.

228

And then there is summer, highlighted with patriotic holidays that entice the red, white, and blue color schemes. This is the time of year that truly encourages outdoor decor as that is where we spend our time. From banners across our decks, decorative pillows/cushions on the patio chairs, or string lights that help to create a festive vibe... summer is the perfect time to bring our decorating energy into whatever outdoor space we inhabit.

No matter the season or budget, a little construction paper or fine arts can bring color and fun into your environment, helping to lift your spirit and entice a celebratory energy each time you walk into your home. Whether you live alone or in a house full of peeps, revitalize the heart by...

Decorating for the season.

#213 Make a family yearbook

Scrapbooking has been a popular pastime and in actuality, big business but there's a new kid in town. It's called a Memory Book. The rising popularity of the digital age has given space to an average person's ability to create hard bound books from the collections of digital photographs that are now stored on our smartphones, tablets, and laptop computers. My suggestion here is to begin the tradition of creating a family Yearbook - just like the one from high school but ... about your family instead.

While not as personal or time consuming as the traditional method of noting memories, the Family Yearbook is made in the style of a Memory Book; similar to a scrapbook but digital. It can be as creative as you have the desire, time, and talent to make it so and without a trip to the craft store or hundreds (or thousands) of dollars of machines and materials. There are apps and programs that will allow you to do all of the creating and then there are apps and programs that will grab data from your social media accounts and create basic prototypes that you may edit.

Shutterfly, MixBook, and Snapfish are the big players here. In all three cases, you upload the photos you want to use, pick a layout, and create. They are relatively user friendly and offer competitive pricing but MixBook took top honors in a recent review of similar players.

Of course, there are local options too... in the review above, Walgreens & Walmart made the list. Here, you take a flash drive or photo card to the physical location and use a kiosk to make your book. The creativity may be less personalized plus you are limited by their stock selections.

Certainly, another option is to hire a digital designer to make you a book. I think this is a great option for something like a 50th Wedding Anniversary, or a life celebration where you are collecting stories as well as a long history of photos. If it's something that would be considered an 'heirloom' item - go ahead and spring for the big buck version if you can... you may be more satisfied with a more professional flair.

Why a memory book? They provide the lure, the joy, and the interest of photo albums and scrapbooks with the durability of an encyclopedia volume. The memories may be captured in similar contexts, but the variability, the time constraint, and the robustness of a Memory Book seem to offer a longer lasting solution. It becomes a living journal, a historical record, and a family treasure.

The holidays are fast approaching and so it's a great time to think about all those experiences you had, the photos you took, and laughter you shared this year and how it would all be recorded as you...

Make a Family Yearbook

"Happiness is not easy to find. It's very difficult to find it in yourself — and impossible to find anywhere else."

— Nicolas Chamfort

#214 Send postcards

Remember when people would go on vacation and send us a postcard with the sentiment "wish you were here?" You'd get a little envious or jealous or just happy that someone you care about was in a place that looked amazing.

Today, with social media, the need for postcards is practically obsolete. Yet, they still adorn racks near the cashier of retail establishments in those places that are considered tourist attractions.

I've written about sending snail mail before and the cheer that it brings when we actually receive something significant in the mailbox. A postcard from a place you've been, a place that is meaningful to you, or a place that you may want to share with someone would be a great treat as well.

Postcards can be used as 'thinking of you cards', 'get well cards', or even to send birthday wishes. In this age of image bombardment - the picture focus of Instagram, Snapchat, and Pinterest, the photo element of a postcard seems apropos.

No matter where you are, there's likely to be a place that offers at least a small collection of postcards to choose from. Even non-descript places off a major interstate may offer a few depicting the best features of the state you're travelling through.

You can save a little money too! Sending a postcard only costs $.35 today compared the $.50 of a regular stamped card/envelope. The savings of $.15 adds up over time and those little cost savings is how the rich get richer!

The next time you're at the shore, the lake, in the mountains, or on vacation... maybe even the next time you stop in a Cracker Barrel restaurant... pick up a few postcards and surprise your friends and family with a little mailbox treat! I've written extensively in this series about the benefits of doing nice things, surprising someone, and the effect of receiving good will. In each case, there is a shot of dopamine for both you and the receiver... increasing your happiness level just a tad with the quick and easy effort of...

Sending a postcard.

#215 Fast for a day

Fasting has been a tradition, a happenstance of the environment, a spiritual practice, and a medicinal effort for perhaps as long as man has been walking the earth. At the very least, our bodies are designed to fast overnight as we sleep, and they know what to do when they are deprived. In fact, many illnesses were called "Kings disease" because it was only those who were well fed that came down with particular ailments - attributed to gluttonous living.

While there are significant debates amongst medical professionals about the types of illness that benefit from fasting, one tenet is common; fasting offers the body an opportunity to 'reset' (akin to 'wiping the hard drive'). This may be especially helpful when beginning a healthier eating phase or starting a weight loss program - a kind of 'jump start' for your body by cleansing the system of accumulated toxins.

Fasting (consuming clear fluids only) for a day allows the body an opportunity to enter 'autophagy', a stage meaning the body naturally works to repair damage that it has accumulated. The postulation is that without food to digest, the body organically spends its energy cleaning house. Intermittent fasting (one day a week, for example) has been demonstrated to be very helpful for some medical conditions.

Some people fast for longer durations. Intense fasting sessions should be done under medical supervision. The experience is very similar to detoxing from hard core drugs according to people who have suddenly eliminated sugars and refined carbs from their diets. When the body is denied these 'drugs' and the reserves it has to use run dry - there is a withdrawal experience.

Before you grab the bull by the horn and dive into a fasting experience, pick a day when you will be distracted by things or people you love (to detract your attention away from hunger), do a trial run by...

Fasting for a day.

#216 Try a cleanse

A cleanse is designed to rid your body of the chemicals and bacteria that should not be there and/or is hazardous to your overall lifespan. There are a number of foods that purport to detoxify the body. The concept is to flush the piping system just like good home maintenance.

Ideally, a cleanse is designed to encourage your liver, kidneys, and colon to do their job. *They* are the organs in our bodies that are perfectly designed to naturally keep the good things in and the bad things out. Eating foods that help them process more effectively and work better is the key here.

Your liver filters toxins from your blood at the rate of 1.4 liters per minute. It breaks down alcohol, drugs, and chemicals we ingest. Dark berries and hot peppers (Caspian) will help it work more effectively. The best advice however is to eat cleanly and avoid alcohol of any kind for the best liver function. The liver is divinely designed to heal itself naturally and will do so if there aren't any deterrents

The colon accumulates waste and prepares it for elimination. In order to do so, material needs to move freely and so hydration and fiber are critical components. Dr. Oz says whole grains and fermented food are key elements in this process.

The kidneys filter toxins from the blood as well and are responsible in maintaining electrolyte balance and blood pressure. Hydration is a primary consideration here - a state that most human bodies today fail to balance. When properly hydrated, kidneys don't need to be cleansed. Cauliflower, broccoli, and Soy products will support kidney function naturally.

While there are a ton of products on the market that claim to 'cleanse', there are dangers to riding your body of too many of the nutrients that aid in the proper digestion of good things we eat. Dr. Oz recommends doing it naturally by eating organically available foods over a 48-hour period to assist the natural efforts of your body. A list of his recommendations can be found online.

When your body works the way it was designed, your energy level, your mood, and your spirit are likely to be organically balanced. If you don't want to fast, you can ...Try a cleanse.

#217 Plan a surprise for someone you love

This suggestion will elevate happiness for both you and someone special in your life. Surprising someone is always fun but planning a little (or big) surprise for someone you love is the best! For this particular post, the intent is to up your game romantically.

A lot of us made this part of our early romantic life. We commonly offer the unexpected as a way of initiating romance. We love the dopamine rush when we pull off a surprise and many of us enjoy the experience of receiving these kinds of gestures. Coming home to an impromptu candlelight dinner... a hot drawn bubble bath with spa music... being whisked away for a steamy night in a local hotel room... These kinds of surprises turn up the 'you're special to me' meter in any relationship and they are generally low cost; low effort.

Keeping this type of energy alive in a relationship demands awareness and intent. An awareness of time and activity with the intent to keep our romantic partners needs and interest in the forefront of our mind regardless of the years that have passed.

Perhaps the surprise is being picked up from work and escorted to a coveted sporting event or a favorite restaurant. Perhaps it's bringing in a cleaning team or scheduling a babysitter for a couple's night out. It could be as simple as declaring it "Jane/John Appreciation Day" - and treating that person as if you would on a birthday or Mother's/Father's Day - but for no special reason other than they are 'appreciated'. Everyone receives an endorphin rush by being appreciated.

It's important to specifically consider the individual you are wanting to surprise. The surprise needs to be something THEY would enjoy. Some people don't like 'surprises' so the gesture needs to be softer and maybe less spontaneous. It may be important to have a random and casual conversation with your romantic partner to find out what kind of surprises they would enjoy and then write them down or commit them to memory.

Spice up your life, invest in your relationship, and elevate your mood by...

Planning a surprise for someone you love

#218 Read a book about history

Was History a class that you zoned out on in High School or College? Did you resist listening to the story about Christopher Columbus or Napoleon for the umpteenth time after a while? Have you ever found yourself wishing you knew more about certain time periods now that you are an adult and perhaps more travelled?

Learning about history can be accomplished in a variety of ways but reading a book that is either biographical in nature, a factual presentation of historical data, or a historical novel can offer a great perspective and tons of information you never knew you'd actually find interesting.

Outside of reading about Mary Todd Lincoln and fantasizing about being able to wear hoop skirts, my interest in historical information was minimal until I became an adult. Interestingly, it was my love of historical fiction and generational novels that enticed a wider interest in other time periods. I'm not sure I gave it much significance until Downton Abby rekindled my interest in the fashions of the late 1800's - shortly after hoops were removed from the skirts of ladies dresses.

Since then, and perhaps in tandem with a couple of visits to Europe in recent years, my interest in history has blossomed. I've enjoyed the fiction of Ken Follett and Edward Rutherford - both authors who create magical fictional characters against the backdrop of actual events. I am able to imagine the depth and breadth of historical moments when I am emotionally invested in the characters who are being invaded by the Nords, grieving a war loss, or losing their fortune in a market crash.

Biographies are another way to establish an emotional connection to a character; one who is historical in their own right. These books are stories as well as factual accounts (in most cases) that are shared in the context of the person's life. The need for environmental context is usually present and so we are introduced to this person in relation to their historical surroundings. Thus, we are given a front seat view of an event we may have read about in a newspaper or a textbook at some point.

More recently, I am intrigued by political history and as they say, "history repeats itself". I've searched archived accounts of leaders who demonstrated attributes similar to President Trump. I think I am looking for hope.

History gives us perspective. The older we become, the more we realize that humans don't change dramatically over time. Behavior and intention are those things that make us human. We may do different things, but our motivation is often similar. Noticing this, allows us to experience compassion and empathy when we look backwards. It can also promote deep gratitude for the people who came before us; their struggle, efforts, and intent.

We can always learn and grow. One of the ways to do that is to...

Read a book about history.

#219 Talk with an older person

For the sake of this post, we'll say that 'old' is 80+. So many of the conversations I have with individuals in this age bracket end up at some point with an expression that they feel invisible to society-at-large. Seemingly, our culture doesn't openly value the old-old. If you happen to live in a community where there is a significant retirement population, you may have noticed that there are a lot of active, contributing older people these days.

I have had several clients through the years that are older than 80… people who drive, live independently, and feel the pain of being dismissed by their family and community. And yet, they are generally people with a lifetime of amazing experience, accumulated knowledge, and sound perspective. There must be something that you are curious about - even if it's how they made the transition from big band music to rock & roll - or did they?

If your grandparents are still living, when was the last time you just sat down and asked them questions about their own life? Research tells us that recounting memories in our late life increases overall life satisfaction. It turns out that a 'life review' can be very helpful in allowing us to see that there were meaningful and contributory moments.

If your grandparents are not living, consider adopting an elderly person - at least for an hour or two. The conversation you have may be the highlight of that individual's life. As a volunteer in a nursing home, with Hospice, or in the hospital, you'll have an opportunity to talk with as many elderly people as you have the breath for. If volunteering isn't your thing or if you are cramped for time, just make the time to engage with an old person the next time you see them in a line, at a restaurant, or shopping for groceries. Find a way to acknowledge their presence and listen carefully for a reason to validate their existence.

Doing this one little thing will enrich your life more than you can imagine. There is great joy in watching someone's face light from the understanding that you 'saw' them. There is great learning to be done when you take time to listen to accumulated wisdom. And, there is great joy in giving of yourself in the most unassuming moments. All this because you tried to …Talk to an older person.

#220 Hide a love note

This suggestion is almost always found in lists of 'things to do' in order to perk up your relationship or build trust and intimacy between you and a partner. It's another one of those things we are apt to do in the early stages of romance before our attention and energy get pulled into the day-to-day distractions of real life. Yet, it's another - rather easy - free effort that reaps big payoffs in the long run.

This can be a one liner; a lengthy tribute; or anything in between. It is specifically directed to someone you love and the note points to those emotions; includes any 'loving' relationship. Or, it can be a thinking of you note: Generally, a one liner but may include a romantic suggestion or a good will wish. And don't forget the appreciation note: A note specifically pointing out the attributes of the individual that you especially appreciate; more meaningful if you speak to 'who' the person is versus 'what' the person does.

The notes can be from a sticky pad, beautiful stationery, printer paper, or the back of an old envelope. It doesn't matter what the note is written on - what matters is the time and sentiment that it takes to write and then 'hide' the message. Likewise, your penmanship, spelling, 'writing ability', and writing instrument makes no difference. The sentence: "I luv u with my hole hart" scribbled in crayon is just as sentimental as one that is typed on parchment paper and spelled correctly.

Hiding them is perhaps, the trickiest part. It's nice when they aren't blatantly obvious although if you're only option is to lay it on the kitchen table before you leave for work - it's better than not doing it. The little surprises of finding a note hidden in a towel as you grab your shower, or inside a shoe you only wear on weekends, or at the bottom of a cereal box... those are the moments when you least expect to be presented with something significant or sweet. The goal here is for the note to be discovered in an unexpected way.

Think about the person you are writing to... where would they least expect to find a note of love, appreciation, or a kind thought? Grab something quick, while you're thinking about it, jot something down and then...

Hide a love note.

#221 Give up your favorite beverage for a day.

If you happen to be reading this just as you move your favorite coffee cup up toward your nose, simultaneously enjoying the aroma and the bold flavor of liquid caffeine... I apologize. Yet - any negative reaction to the suggestion is further evidence that it may be just what you need.

We tend to get sewn into our habits and that morning cup of coffee, tea, lemon water, the evening frosty mug of beer, or the stemless glass of wine are easy habits to do without much thought or consideration; and that's the danger. Some habits aren't necessarily good for us. Indeed, it has been postulated that any habit at all is rather detrimental if we have little awareness of it.

Perhaps the best part of deciding to give up your favorite beverage for a day is the subliminal (or direct) understanding that *you* are in control of your being. It's a reminder to your psyche that *you* have authority over your actions. Far too often I hear people say... "I couldn't help it" or "I don't even realize I am doing it" when it comes to habits. Paying attention to something as automatic as pouring a cup of coffee or a glass of wine helps you to raise awareness overall.

It's a simple suggestion and a simple effort that helps you stay focused on the little things. Plan to...

Give up your favorite beverage for a day.

#222 Plant your mother's favorite flower

I cannot see a yellow rose without thinking of my mother - it was her favorite flower. I would buy her a birthday card, months in advance if I saw one with a yellow rose. There is a yellow rose bush planted in her memory in the corner of my flower garden. Each time a bud pops up, I am reminded of the comfort she provided in my life It's nice to glance out my window and capture a quick glance at those roses. In that split second my mind automatically moves to thoughts of my mom, even if for a nano-second.

If your mom isn't available to ask about her favorite flower, think of one that reminds you of her. Fall is a good time to plant bulbs so that they will bloom next year. Certainly, you can plant something and start it indoors, transferring it outside when the weather is warmer. If you don't necessarily want to be thinking of your mother on a regular basis (acknowledging that some people have distant or no relationships there), think of someone who inspires you or reminds you of love (grandma, a friend's mother, an aunt, or mentor).

Flowers are generally beautiful. As such, they ignite endorphins in our brain that connect to happiness and overall feelings of good. They do this even if we have allergies as long as we're admiring them at a distance. When we couple those good feelings with thoughts of someone that reminds us of love - it's a double happy.

Today is a good day to do something that has the potential to bring a smile to your face. Why not...

Plant your mother's favorite flower.

#223 Make that appointment you've been putting off

Almost everyone I talk to speaks to the fact that our lives are over scheduled these days. It's become worse over the last several decades as we have to work longer and harder to meet our obligations or catch the American Dream. Consequently, those necessary appointments - the ones that hold our reality together - are often sliding to the bottom of our priority list.

Do you need to go to the DMV? Have you had your annual physical? Your 6-month dental cleaning? Have you procrastinated on your mammogram or colonoscopy? What about your fireplace or carpet cleaning? Sadly, most of us have to take a full day off - some of us, without pay - in order to accomplish these tasks.

My recommendation is to make a list of all those 'appointments' that need scheduling and make as many of them in one day as possible. It's a practical time management solution to take a day off and get it all done.

Procrastination occurs for other reasons too... particularly with medical appointments. Sometimes it's because we don't want to fast or to clean out our system. We're fearful of what the test may find, or we anticipate bad news or judgment from the doctor. Occasionally people will tell me they don't want to change parts of their lives - knowing that a doctor will make that suggestion (i.e., weight, smoking, drinking, etc.)

Sometimes we don't make an appointment because the things we need to do leading up to them feels cumbersome and/or overwhelming. Something as little as getting a money order for an application can stifle the completion of that task. If you don't need an 'appointment' for the pre-task, get that completed either before or after work.

Getting those things completed that you have been putting off... especially when they are medical related may in fact, save your life. There's always a sense of accomplishment when we get things done that we've been putting off. The appointments you keep for home repair and maintenance are for your welfare and safety. Don't waste another minute... make that list and then...

Make that appointment you've been putting off.

#224 Drop in on a friend for coffee or dessert.

My mother used to say that if you were coming to see her home you needed to call first but if you were coming to see her... you could come at any time. She had an open-door policy and as such - she was loved dearly by all of the people who knew that the coffee was hot in her pot all day long.

These days, we monitor our doorbells from our cell phones and 'dropping in' has become somewhat socially awkward; a lost tradition it seems. Yet, the surprise that someone takes time to stop by and check on us - to lean on us - to engage, is timeless. It's an endorphin shot if we can step back from the idea that our house isn't clean, our bed isn't made, and our mascara is from yesterday.

If you're worried that you may not be received well by just 'stopping in' then I suggest you check with your friends to see if they're game; kind of 'advanced permission' to stop by unannounced. With that consideration, you'll have no excuses.

Another suggestion is to take them coffee or dessert. While this isn't necessary of course, it's a great gesture. These days it can be as simple as a drive through Dunkin on your way or showing up with a pint of Ben & Jerry's Cherry Garcia! In both cases, your thoughtfulness will likely be appreciated in case your friend just drank that last cup of coffee or didn't serve dessert that night.

In the days of social media and instant connection, I think these little traditions could use a comeback... Ask for permission if necessary or just go ahead and ...

Drop in on a friend for coffee or dessert.

#225 Create a list of home maintenance responsibilities

Being a homeowner can be overwhelming when life is pulling us in a gazillion directions. Even if you don't own your home, there are basic maintenance items that make living in a home more efficient and healthy - leading to a higher quality of life and a sustainability of your home's value.

If you don't want to reinvent the wheel, just search Google for a list of House Maintenance Items - there is no shortage of links to investigate but there are a couple of categories you must be sure to include:

Monthly items:

The things you need to do each month such as changing your air filter, are designed to keep abreast of potentially bigger problems. One list suggested moving from sink to sink with a hair drain clog remover ... a proactive stance to remove buildup. Anyone with girls living in the house needs one of those do-dads. It's completely gross but oh-so-worth-it!

Quarterly items:

On a less regular basis it's good to inspect under sinks and around toilets for water leakage. Additionally, someone suggested inspecting extension cords and surge protectors - something that I personally, take for granted. I imagine the one behind the couch hasn't seen daylight in more than a year which, means it's nested in a full out hollow of dust bunnies. When those babies collect extensively, they create hard core matter that can catch fire from a spark. Yup... got to check them.

Bi-Annually:

Get the vacuum out and suck up the dust on your refrigerator coils. You'll have to pull it out to do this, but it will save a ton of money on power efficiency and it will take all of 10 minutes or less. Of course, you'll want to scrub up the spilled milk that's been baking there for months along with spider poop and the dead flies.

Annually:

Inside, you'll want to prioritize vent cleaning (including the dryer vent!). The air you breathe will be so much cleaner if it's not blowing back the dust that has settled in your vents throughout the year.

And… that dryer vent accumulation that you never see and therefore never think about - it's responsible for thousands of house fires around the world each year.

Outside, you'll want to make sure that shrubs and trees aren't up against the house too close. It's especially important to get those climbing vines off the house. The little feeder roots it uses to hold itself to your masonry will break apart the concrete, stucco, and brick over time. It can also make its way into your siding and create havoc as water and ice will have a path to parts of your home where they are most destructive.

Of course, the whole idea of a list is to get organized with these tasks and make sure that they are accomplished. While you're thinking about it - go ahead and …

Make a list of home maintenance responsibilities.

#226 Use white vinegar

There are a handful of antidotes that have survived the ages - white vinegar is one of them. It is derived by fermenting grain alcohol today but it used to be the product of fermented beets, potatoes, and milk. From gardening, cleaning, and cooking, it is used in a variety of ways with success for a number of maladies. Medicinally, it has been a staple of the 'medicine man' for thousands of years. The element of acetic acid found in most vinegars is known to control blood sugar, reduce cholesterol and act as an antimicrobial.

I've always kept a gallon of white vinegar in my pantry and when I am faced with a tough cleaning problem, it's one of the first things that I reach for. Vinegar and baking soda combined are powerful cleaning agents; toilets, silver, and windows shine brighter with vinegar cleaning solutions. It may be one of the best agents for breaking down mineral build-ups occurring in irons and showerheads.

Vinegar is an organic product capable of killing weeds and controlling pests. Poured directly on a weed - it will die. Diluted slightly, it will deter ants from the area. Vinegar dissolves rust and calcium, making it a great cleaner for outdoor fixtures.

In everyday cooking, pickling is accomplished with just a little vinegar and spice. It's the acidic element giving marinades and BBQ sauces that flavor zing. If you want your cake to be cakier or your bread to be airier - add a teaspoon of vinegar to the mixture. Finally, if you need buttermilk for pancakes really quick - add some white vinegar to your milk… the acid causes the milk proteins to separate and 'sour'.

Vinegar is cheap and perhaps more efficient than other products so grab a gallon the next time you're at the store and start…

Using white vinegar.

#227 Clean out your pantry

You may or may not have an official 'pantry', yet it is likely that you have a cupboard in your kitchen that is a 'catch all' - a place to stash those arbitrary ingredients that you rarely use. When was the last time you dug through there and got rid of the old stuff? I'm occasionally embarrassed by how long I've kept a can of water chestnuts or a packet of gravy mix that I picked up for a recipe or overbought.

It's a good idea to pull everything out to clearly see what's what. Experts suggest we attempt this task at least once a year. It makes sense to do it before the holidays when we are apt to buy more groceries and may need the extra room.

Take stock in the items you have that may be on the verge of expiring. Expiration dates on food are conservative as required by the FDA. My family is hard evidence for the fact that people can eat food after its expiration date and live to tell about it (some foods are a hard "no" to this). Anything with a close expiration date can be incorporated into your meal planning over the next couple of weeks. Pasta stays good for a couple of years when it's stored in a cool dry space, for example.

Before you return things, make sure to wipe down the shelves and vacuum up crumbs and dust. Some people tout the use of shelf liner, making clean up really easy from year to year.

As you return food back to the pantry, be sure to check that is securely packaged. You don't want an open bag of rice to suddenly spill and spoil your efforts. For those items that are better in airtight containers, consider Ziplock bags or containers that lock in freshness.

There are thousands of ideas on Pinterest for pantry storage. Many of the suggestions use free or low-cost items to keep things neat and tidy. It's easy to get inspired.

This is one of those tasks that often sounds more time consuming than it really is and your feelings of satisfaction will flood your senses each time you open the pantry door once you make the time to...

Clean out your pantry.

#228 Visit a cemetery

Walking through a cemetery has a strange way of connecting us to our past. The fact is that each of those graves represents a person with a history; someone's child. Maybe they had siblings, fell in love, and worked hard - or not. Whatever they did, they had a story. Even if we are not connected to any of those particular stories, standing in the middle of a cemetery can remind us of several things that are important life lessons to keep in the forefront of our mind.

Maybe it's morbid, but it's also a fact and one that when considered... literally helps us to be present more often. When we realize that our days are numbered somewhere between 0 and 36,000 - generally speaking - we tend to pay more attention.

When we consider that there are perhaps, only 8 or 9 thousand more days to share, people who are important to us somehow take on a new urgency. We tend to sweat the little things a lot less when we think of life as limited initiative.

Walking through a cemetery allows us to see our own lives differently. It's representative of the circle of life and can initiate thoughts of our own mortality. We realize just how dispensable we are and while that may be a little discerning to our ego... it can be soothing to realize that the world keeps turning, even in our absence.

Cemeteries can be cultural learning tools full of traditions which, can be fun to notice and experience. There are religious, ethnic, generational, and socioeconomic differences visibly obvious from the headstones and ornaments that are displayed throughout. All of these variations tend to change across time, making it an interesting archeological study as well.

Architecture may not be the most precise term here yet there can be tremendous examples of architectural intrigue and ornamentation in some of the more elaborate structures. A stroll through the grounds may be visually stimulating - raising an itch in your artistic energy.

Whether it is a famous cemetery or the one in your hometown - there's something for you there so go ahead and make a date to ...

Visit a cemetery.

#229 Eat dessert first

This suggestion is the reason that my mother's mother was by far - the best grandparent in the universe. Most of the days that I was there for dinner - days that were not family events - I was encouraged to have dessert before dinner was placed on the table. She used to preface it that we had to eat what we could before 'Grandad' got ahold of any available sweets. It was also her strategy to defy my parents in a small way - maybe giving them a taste of their own adolescent medicine.

Occasional treats are necessary for our sense of well-being - to prevent a sense of deprivation. If dessert fits that bill - why not? There's a sense of defiance associated with the idea of reversing the order of what is considered the norm. If this is the depth of one's rebellion, it's more than manageable. It's also just downright fun. It's a harmless deviation from typically acceptable behavior and yet it is completely innocent. It's a great treat for kids especially.

It's a simple thought but stimulating, nonetheless. Go ahead and treat yourself tonight...

Eat dessert first.

#230 Create some doodle art

Who hasn't doodled? For some of us, it's a passing time activity that barely has any conscious value. Yet, psychologists say that what we doodle actually says something about us. It's akin to daydreaming in symbols and sometimes it can be downright artistic. Interestingly, doodling can stimulate your brain just enough that it actually pays attention to what's happening environmentally instead of going rogue and into hyperspace.

What do you draw when you doodle? Do you draw faces? If you draw an attractive face it symbolizes that you are in a positive state of mind. Ugly faces mean the opposite or perhaps that you may be feeling distrusting of something. People who draw profiles are more apt to be introverted and those who draw wide circular faces tend to be innocent and needy.

Flowers are the most popular doodle and imply a gentle or even passive frame of mind. Flowers made of circles and soft lines signify a happy doodler. If there are thorns or sharp petals surrounding a round center, there is a possibility that the doodler is feeling defensive. Stairs and ladders suggest that your inner self is focused on a goal. Psychologists infer that the style of this doodle indicates the level of significance or struggle you are experiencing in reference to this goal. Your doodles describe your inner most thoughts, fears, and considerations. They suggest how organized or disorganized you are; how motivated or uninspired you may be; whether or not you take a passive or aggressive stance; if you are generally selfish or benevolent; whether you feel trapped and isolated or free and loved.

Very similar to dreams, this is not an exact science and the goal isn't to be self-conscious while you're drawing... just let your mind do the work. Keep a pad of drawing paper near your work desk and allow yourself to doodle at random times without too much forethought. Once the paper is full, consider adding some color.

As you're doodling, consider using different color pens or pencils for the color element. Maybe the easiest doodle style art is simply a random long squiggly line that intersects repeatedly and then colored in a stained-glass fashion. Need a break? A way to mentally vent? An inside view to your deeper psyche?

Create some doodle art.

#231 Believe in yourself

As a therapist, I see lots of people who are challenged with this ability. When our self-esteem is damaged or underdeveloped, it can be quite difficult to have faith in your ability to achieve success. I'd like to suggest that success is relative and that the only person whose opinion matters - is yours!

Our self-doubt is often a seed that was planted in childhood either by parents, peers, or society. I've heard children make the comment "I'm trying" and an adult in the vicinity says "no you're not" or "not hard enough" which, is hard to reconcile if you feel as if you've given it all you know to give. Unfortunately, these patterns often continue into adulthood and become hard held beliefs that are challenging to reframe.

We, as individuals, intrinsically know if we have given it our all or not. We *know*, regardless of what others comment - even as children, we know. What we have to do is believe that if we think we've given it everything there is to give - it was *enough*, regardless of whether or not it met an outside standard. If we gave it our all... there wasn't any more to give and we need to learn to simply believe that as a fact.

When we don't have an established belief in our ability to succeed, we become afraid of trying because our culture promotes a fear of failure. One thing is for sure - if you don't try - you will not succeed so the first rule is to TRY. The second rule of thumb is to assess your willingness to work for the success you want. When we say "I can't" - most of the time we are saying that we don't want to do the work required in order to become successful.

Almost anyone with dexterity can learn to play the piano - this fact is illustrated by all of the young people who perform at recitals all over the world. It's only those who diligently work at their craft that become proficient, however. Somewhere along the line, those people believed in themselves.

It's the 'Little Engine That Could' mantra... "I think I can, I think I can..." that makes the difference and becomes an overall mental health - healthy perspective. If you don't already, try to grow your esteem and learn to ...

Believe in yourself.

#232 Practice loving kindness

The practice of loving kindness stems from the Buddhist practice of the Metta prayer. It's a specific method of meditating that promotes compassion for others and for the self. It's easy, and it makes a difference.

The essence of a loving kindness meditation is to conjure up a sensation of deep love, of significant loving energy and then metaphorically - send that love out into the universe toward humanity as a whole or to specific people. There are a number of amazing websites and YouTube videos that can walk you through in a guided meditation as you get started.

As in many other mental health wellness practices, loving kindness utilizes imagery. It is suggested that as you begin your meditation, you imagine people who love you, surrounding you and sending vibrational hugs toward you until you can essentially feel the loving energy coming from them. You may imagine the swell of love that you felt as you held each of your children or married your spouse. Each of the meditations begins from this place - deep in the experience of sensing love.

Each phrase found in most scripts begins with "may you.../may I". The concept is that while in an envelope of loving energy, you send some of it out or reflect it back to yourself in phrases that represent wishes.

"May you feel loved, may you be happy, may you be healthy'

"May you find acceptance, may you feel joy, may you live with ease". In each phrase, the "you" can be replaced with "I" for the experience of self-compassion. The objective is to build upon the empathy and compassion that is an innate element of your spirit. The more you practice, the more it grows.

Those who cultivate a practice of loving kindness speak about the sense of inner peace that develops over time. It is attributed to a deeper sense of happiness. It works to evaporate anger, resentment, and past pains. It becomes a coping mechanism for those times when our humanity loses perspective and emotions become overwhelming.

There is much benefit for you personally, for those people you love, and for the collective consciousness that comprises our universe when you commit to the... Practice of loving kindness.

#233 Make something for someone

There are few things better than being the recipient of a gift made with you in mind. The holidays are fast approaching and this suggestion is designed to encourage you to consider one or a few homemade gifts this year.

Personally inspired, homemade gifts have always been big in one branch of my family. The time, consideration, and attention to a gift that was created from a loving perspective has always been highly appreciated.

Of course, many of these items are derived from crafty hands but they don't have to be. A homemade gift can be cookies, or a soup mix. It can be bath salts, vinegar, or infused oils - none of which take much talent outside of a Google search and assembling a few ingredients. Indeed - those particular suggestions are quite simple.

Make Your Own Vinegar
Infused Oils
Dry Soup Mixes

It can be more involved though, depending on your talents. Do you draw? Paint? Crochet? Sew? Build? Of course, artwork is always nice for young people just setting up house. A commissioned drawing or painting is great if there is a beloved pet, home, or photo that is meaningful to someone. Everyone needs an afghan for the couch or a cuddle blanket. It only takes a bit of time and talent to build a blanket ladder, a gift that most of us would love.

If your talent is more service oriented, then make an I.O.U. Create a card, a certificate, or a coupon that offers your time to someone. The gift of babysitting, cleaning, yard work, cooking, home decorating, etc.... the list is endless. Anywhere that an extra pair of hands is needed would be a welcome 'gift' to most all of us.

The holidays don't have to be stressful on the budget - not to mention, birthdays or other special occasions when we can...

Make something for someone.

#234 Embrace aging

On a rather gloomy day in my late twenties - maybe after I noticed a significant patch of grey settling in - I spent an entire weekend pampering myself, my skin, and my eyes. I exfoliated, scrubbed, hydrated, and massaged every part of my body that showed any signs of aging. The next day, I stopped for a bottle of wine on the way home from work and got carded... I was elated - beyond - that my efforts at disguising my advancing age (!) had worked!

Our culture values youth so much that we tend to fixate on staying young, for women at least and more than one client, friend, and relative has lamented on the aging process weekly for as long as I can remember. Even though we see more and more examples of middle aged and older individuals in the media, there is an acute undercurrent of anti-aging in our current culture. Everywhere we look, we are exposed to ideas of how to 'stay younger, longer'.

In practice, I think the most troublesome part of aging is that it is out of our control - this seems to be the component that most people have difficulty with. Even if they attempt to control their health - people are acutely aware that there is an absence of control over the years - time - slipping by. My suggestion for all those things that we can't control: Embrace or let go!

Perhaps to some, these are one in the same. Embracing, for the purpose of this suggestion is to see aging as an honor; a testament to strength and perseverance. It means accepting that our bodies change as the years pass. It means to stop fighting the organic process and to stop wishing for a fountain of youth. It may also mean that we stop spending money on wrinkle removal but see them as honor lines; earned through the years as we loved, laughed, and lived.

It doesn't mean to give up on self-care; to let our bodies atrophy. It doesn't mean that we give up the goal of making each day count or the joy of learning something new with each week that passes. It doesn't mean that we surrender to the term "I'm too old".

Letting go doesn't mean that you should necessarily 'go gray' - although that may be a stunning option - or to give up on your physical health. It does mean acceptance and letting go of critical thoughts about your appearance as it relates to age. It means to silence any disparaging comments about getting older. It may require conscious effort to be present and find joy in the present rather than lamenting over the past. Letting go requires you to stop comparing your current self to your younger self with disdain or regret.

With every day that passes, wisdom grows. Each day is an opportunity to learn and to love - both allowing us to embrace life more completely. In our older years we are the Autumn of life - where we burst into full color, demonstrating maturity and seasoned perspective. Hold onto this ideology and make the effort to...

Embrace aging.

#235 Sleep on the other side of the bed

I will occasionally recommend this suggestion to clients who have difficulty sleeping and/or couples who are attempting to inject new energy into their relationship. It is sometimes met with resistance and declarations that they won't be able to sleep yet, when they report back in, I often hear how making that shift was a new and interesting experience.

We are creatures of habit and without realizing it, we tend to slip into comfortable routines that create the potential for chunks of monotony to set in. The side of the bed we choose is one of those 'chunks'. It's necessary to notice comfortable, unconscious patterns and challenge them from time to time; to force a 'shift'; to shake things up! In doing so, we are organically more present; more conscious of our being; and more aware of our power.

In 2015, a survey concluded that people would rather give up the TV remote than to change the side of the bed they sleep on. If you share the bed with someone, this suggestion will need to be a team effort. Consider sharing this post with your partner and make the suggestion. It doesn't have to be a permanent change, or even a long term one. It can be for a night, a weekend, or however much time you may need to experience an awareness of the difference.

Changing bed sides may be good for your mattress assuming that different body sizes and shapes are on the new side - mattresses tend to conform to our bodies over time and changing it up will work to smooth out the ingrained shape. You may also find that sleeping is easier on one side versus the other. Perhaps you will change the side you sleep on - shifting the pressure points to which your body is exposed. You may find more romance by shifting sides... it could feel like you're in bed with a different partner - playing into fantasy or simply refreshing a staleness in your relationship. You may snore less, be warmer, cooler, or be on the side with less light.

At the very least, you'll be challenging your brain and the way it remembers - an activity that is all over healthy for your memory and it reminds your psyche who is running the show! Maybe start on a Friday night so that you'll have the weekend if it totally ruins your sleep pattern. Generally, people consider it an interesting experiment when they... Sleep on the other side of the bed.

#236 Stargaze

There is a lot to see in the evening sky. The bulk of us attempt this with the naked eye during summer evenings when we can comfortably lie outside and gaze above. In the fall, the brightest star is Fomelhaut, the overall 18th brightest star in the sky. It's sometimes called the lone Autumn star as it seems to be all alone. As Fall transitions into winter, the Milky Way gives way to the constellation of Orion and all of its neighboring stars. And if you've never taken the time to notice, the winter sky looks very different from the summer one.

Knowing what you are looking at is easy these days with a smartphone. iPhone users can literally just point their phones at the sky using the SkyView app and identify precisely what is there. The apps NightSky and StarChart are also good options if you want to know more detail about the space beyond.

Another way to participate in stargazing year-round is to view the sky through a telescope. Depending on your interest level, you can spend anywhere from $50 to several thousand in order to get a better view. A telescope magnifies and clarifies your view, allowing you to see much more than you might with the naked eye.

Stargazing is a fantastic family activity that allows for fun and learning simultaneously. There's always something to glean about the stars and planets we can see because our view changes as the earth turns. It's constantly changing month after month. Break into sections and deeply explore one quadrant at a time.

The next time you are outdoors in the evening, take a few moments and do a little…

Stargazing.

#237 Be vulnerable

As a mental health counselor, I spend a significant amount of time encouraging people to 'be vulnerable'. By definition, being vulnerable means that you "expose yourself to the possibility of being attacked or harmed, either physically or emotionally." It means that we must be willing to lose love, admiration, safety, respect, attention, etc.... It is not possible to love without vulnerability.

Dr. Brené Brown has spent much of her career researching and talking about being vulnerable. In fact, it is at the core of her famous TED Talk. She has several books documenting her stance on how life is best lived through the state of vulnerability. Indeed - one of the most popular quotes is "vulnerability is the core, the heart, the center of meaningful human experience."

While it can be scary and uncomfortable, the experience of being vulnerable is healthy for us in many ways. We are our most authentic selves when we are vulnerable. In that state of mind, we are able to experience intimacy in our relationships more fully. Our sense of self-worth increases, and we become more accountable for our actions. We are apt to experience more compassion, be more motivated, and share our ideas more freely. Maybe most importantly, when we accept the feeling of vulnerability, we tend to let go of our need to be in control... opening doors in most areas of our life.

For most of us, the key to vulnerability is in learning to let go. Letting go means that we have to trust in the process most of the time, trust in the people we've surrounded ourselves with, and trust in our own abilities to manage life and relationships. We have to be willing to be a little afraid and accept a bit of discomfort as life unfolds in unknowing ways.

In general, life is better all the way around when we allow ourselves to ...

Be vulnerable.

#238 Identify your triggers

An emotional trigger is something that provokes you. It may be a person, an opinion, a situation, or an environmental condition. When we are 'triggered', we generally *re*-act emotionally - often with a defensive behavior. We experience a swell of emotion and it may or may not be specifically connected to the experience at hand.

In order to properly manage your emotions, it's imperative that you know what your triggers are. Ninety-nine percent of the time, our triggers are based in fear. Fear of losing something, having less of something, or never having something - that 'something' being anything really... trust, respect, time, money, love, etc... When we understand 'why' we are reacting - managing our reactions is much - much easier.

Once we know 'why' we get triggered we can learn how to communicate and manage our reactions. Often, it's about learning how to be present - not allowing our histories to overrun the present moment. It's about communicating our truest emotion - that thing we fear (i.e., not being loved, having enough time, etc....) By being aware of our immediate thought, engaging our breath, and making an intentional choice in our response, we can stand down those automatic responses that tend to stand at attention when we are triggered.

In order to change anything - we need to be aware and know what needs to be changed and so, to improve our reactions, it is imperative that we make an effort to ....

Identify our triggers.

#239 Eat healthier

This sounds like a New Year's resolution at first glance and yet it may be the cornerstone to living a happier, healthier, and more productive life. The concept is only new to you if you've been living in a cave for the last couple of decades. Indeed, over that time, the Surgeon General and most of our health care practitioners, have touted the benefits of making healthier food choices while the average size of children and adults continues to escalate.

In our fast paced, modern world - the most basic element of survival has become more and more difficult to monitor. We are inundated with food choices almost everywhere we go. Even at my children's orthodontist office - right next to the coffee pot (a valued added service) there are cookies, cake, or doughnuts ready to be gobbled up by waiting parents, siblings, and hungry kids ready for their after-school snack.

Instead of picking an apple off the tree on a walk home from school, our children ride the bus around a corner and into a subdivision. They get dropped off at the driveway, grab a processed rice Krispy treat or a bag of Doritos, and plop on the sofa to play video games. Sadly, that morphs into a quick dinner with a 'hurry up and eat' before someone has to be somewhere more evenings a week than not. It's the 'way of the world' these days and we are all guilty at some point of wanting and making meals to be quick and easy regardless of how healthy they are.

It is beginning to change with healthier options on menus everywhere, yet our size continues to grow. Even though we have healthy options, we don't choose them enough of the time for it to make an impact. Consequently, grocery stores still sell the processed stuff; restaurants still offer the 2000 calorie burger & fries, and deep-fried Snicker bars are sold by the thousands at every fair/carnival around the country. All because we keep buying them!!

In the interest of honesty, I must disclose that I too, cave to the pressure - the smells - and the flavors that tempt and tease me. I can definitely commit to making more consistent healthier choices. In talking with clients who are challenged here as well, the common similarity is that we lack will power. It's challenging to walk into a mall where Cinnabon has just finished baking a tray of toaster sized rolls. The air is fragrant with the smell of cinnamon and yeast. A glance in that direction identifies the source. One can hardly ignore that they are frosted with a decadent amount of cream cheese sugary goodness. So much so, that if you've ever tasted it - and loved it - your mouth instantly begins craving another fix. Just one classic bun touts 880 calories and the equivalent of 15 spoonsful of sugar. Would you sit down and shovel 15 teaspoons of sugar into your mouth on purpose??

Instead of succumbing to the temptation of my olfactory inclinations, I make an effort to command control and convince myself that carrot sticks are sweet too. I then seek an eating establishment that offers 'fresh' non-processed options and each time I sit down to eat or stroll through the grocery store I make another concerted effort to...

Eat healthier.

#240 Realign your priorities

Why do you do what you do? What are your priorities? Do your actions - your behaviors - demonstrate your priorities? Are you engaged in the activity that you say is the most important thing?

When asked this question, people often respond family, friends, home, work, etc.… and often in that order. (Many people put God ahead of them all). Yet, as I ask a client to describe their day to day lifestyle, there is often a discrepancy between what I heard described and the values they shared to begin with. If someone tells me that their family is the most important thing on Earth but then works sixty hours a week, they are demonstrating that it's not 'time' with family but 'providing for' family is the priority. This is a great example of what one person says and what the other 'hears'. Jack and Jill both 'say' that family is their number one priority, but their actions/behaviors delineated that further by drilling down to 'time with family' and 'providing for family'. Often - those specific values work in contradiction to one another.

We could drill down even further to examine the nuances of each by describing 'time' more specifically. Is it family weekends and soccer games? Or is it story time and date nights too? Does 'providing for' mean any old roof over our heads or does it mean 3000 square feet and quartz countertops? Does it mean private school and full college tuition or public schools and grant money?

The fact is, our priorities develop and morph over time. If we are good communicators who are present and who spend time 'going deep' with our partners, they stay in alignment both with our actions/behaviors, and in tandem with our partner. I find that this is rarely the case - at least with couples who seek therapy.

Many of us fail to remember to check in with ourselves from time to time - let alone with sour partners. In our crazy busy world where we are constantly seeking more, we get stuck on auto-pilot - somehow thinking that because we got on 'this' road, it will take us where we want to go without more direction checking on our part. We set course based on the information we have garnered - at - that - time. Along the way, there are distractions, chaos, change, temptations, etc.… And we often lose sight of the original objective or we adjust course and forget to share that information.

262

Getting realigned takes little more than some self-assessment, a discussion, and honesty. It means revisiting your values and priorities to be sure they are still valid and then assess our actions/behaviors to evaluate their efficiency toward manifesting the priority. If '(quantity) time' with family is above all else, working 60-hour weeks isn't the route to that goal. It will require an honest conversation to realign the priority or to realign the action/behavior so that they work in tandem with one another.

We see our doctor for an annual physical. We get systematic reviews of our professional performance. Our corporations are assessed for proficiency and profitability on a regular basis. As an individual who is ultimately responsible for backing up our words with action - it's imperative that we do the same. Make it at least an annual habit to take a step back and …

Realign your priorities.

"If you are depressed you are living in the past. If you are anxious you are living in the future. If you are at peace you are living in the present" — Lao Tzu

#241 Make a new friend

Life is just better when we are sharing ourselves with other people who are like-minded. Some of us who are more introverted may hesitate to reach out in ways that allow us to make new friendships. Others are challenged to keep up with the friendships that already exist. And for some of us, the friendships we have may no longer be meeting our changing personalities or needs.

Friendships are built upon like-mindedness; shared interests, values, and inspirations. When our daily activities or the things we value change, so may our friendships. It might be that as we grow into a new interest, we discover surrounding ourselves with people who also like those things inspire us to go further than we thought we could.

Sometimes we realize we need to make new friends, yet our opportunities to meet new people appear limited. This is when we need to break barriers of comfort and habit. It becomes necessary to branch out and create opportunities to get introduced to people like us via clubs, groups, volunteering, etc.

If you know that new friendships will enrich your life, be brave enough to make the first move... ask someone to lunch with you or suggest a get together. Initiate conversation or invite them over for an evening that encompasses that 'thing' you share. Take the initiative in opening up - be vulnerable!

It's not possible to have 'too many' friends - people that really matter to you and that share common ideologies. If you've noticed a void in your connections to people, perhaps it's time to ...

Make a new friend.

#242 Adopt a new coping skill

Coping skill - those things that help us deal with the crap that life throws our way. They happen sometimes without much awareness and at others, with great intention. Some are healthy - others ... not so much. Self-awareness of the coping skills we use to deal with things are super important. It's necessary for us to distinguish between those things that work for us and those that don't.

There are several great ways to work through stress, problems, and life challenges that are immensely effective and have overall positive effects. Exercise, Me Time, and Self Care are at the top of the list. They are some of the things that create balance in life.

These strategies are perhaps the most efficient and effective when it comes to an overall sense of feeling better. Research about mindfulness and its helpful effect on health, emotions, stress, and pain is overwhelming but it takes practice and perseverance to be truly beneficial.

Learning to laugh, to find humor in the mundane, and to appreciate silly is also a great coping strategy. When we become so stressed that our tempers flare, humor can generally take the edge of negative feelings if not neutralize them all together.

Just when we may feel like we would be better off in our sour mood alone, or when we don't want to trouble anyone with our 'issues', that is the precise time to lean on our social support system. The friends and family members that love us, that know us at our core... those are the people who can stand behind us when times are tough. When we need to ask for help... they are the ones we ask. And yes... learning to *ask* is a functioning coping mechanism.

Assess your current repertoire of positive coping skills and research one that you've yet to develop. Practice, practice, and practice in the pursuit of

Developing a new coping skill.

#243 Go to a high school play

I was a 'drama geek' in high school as were several of my children and what I know for sure is that everyone involved in these productions - no matter how elaborate it may or may not be - works their fanny off and gives great heart to the project.

The community support of these endeavors is paramount to the performers on stage and the hardworking teams that keep them there. This is where young stars are born, and others confirm their lack of passion for the commitment necessary to build careers. It's where self-esteem is cemented, and friendships are fostered. It's where confidence is built and where for a few minutes, getting lost in fantasy is healthy.

These high school kids may not be seasoned actors, they may not have acutely tuned voices, or the best comedic timing but they have heart. Their courage, spunk, and energy are generally undeniable.

Making the effort to fill the auditorium of these local high school productions makes the statement that not only are 'they' important, but that support of the Arts is a priority. We're telling our local school boards and elected officials that being a well-rounded student is more than grades and sports. We are both proactive and passively encouraging.

If you don't have a high school student, gathering information about the productions in your community is only a phone call or a web visit away. Take some time to find out what productions are scheduled this year and put it on your calendar. It makes a great night out and it's usually very affordable. Do yourself - and your community - a favor and...

Go to a High School Play

#244 Make a list of positive affirmations

The idea that positive thinking is at the core of positive developments and manifestations is now more than one hundred years old. It is thought to have been born out of Wallace Wattles's 1910 book, The Science of Getting Rich. One of the primary tenets of the ideology is the value of affirmation.

By definition, an affirmation is "the action or process of affirming something" as well as "emotional support or encouragement". In the New Thought movement, an affirmation is defined as "a carefully formatted statement that should be repeated to one's self and written down frequently". As they are formulated, attention is directed so that they are "present tense, positive, personal, and specific". It needs to be: Personal, Positive, Specific and Present. *Example: I am (Personal) always (positive) extending compassion (the 'thing') as I breathe (present moment).* It doesn't have to be in that exact order or using only those words of course. The internet has a gazillion examples if you need help choosing the ones that are meaningful to you.

For many of us, the use of affirmations is a way of teaching ourselves a new language. It's a way to overturn critical and negative self-talk with something encouraging and healthy. Instead of a personal beratement of "I never do anything right" - the affirmation of "I am always learning from mistakes I have made".

I recommend making a set of flashcards - just like you would if you were learning a new language vocabulary and practice them on a regular basis. I've had clients who kept them in their car, their purse, on their nightstand, etc. and reviewed them several times a day. Eventually, they become memorized and etched in our mindsets just like the vocabulary we learned as students.

Consider for a few minutes, those positive elements that you want to become more pronounced in your day-to-day life and …Create a list of positive affirmations.

#245 Use imagery

The goal behind imagery is to use your brain's ability to imagine in order to foster thoughts and feelings more conducive to your goal. For example, if you are feeling overwhelmed and stressed, it is helpful to imagine yourself sitting on a beach watching the waves roll in or by a waterfall, listening to the sound of the water hitting the rocks below.

If you've read The Secret or if you are a follower of the Law of Attraction, then you know that both promote the use of imagery by using vision boards or manifestation meditation in the pursuit of future objectives. The concept is "if you can 'see' it, then you can believe it - and ultimately manifest it as reality.

When getting started, guided imagery is often the best way to go. Three are thousands of guided imagery videos on YouTube and thousands of other scripts available online that you can record and listen to yourself. If you are challenged to create a descriptive monologue that depicts exactly what you are hoping to achieve, then something recorded may be the best option to start with.

Imagery is used in the treatment of anxiety, stress, and high blood pressure. It's been shown to reduce blood loss and pain after surgery. It's used with athletes to improve coordination, develop skill, and increase confidence. It can benefit self-esteem, deepen intuition, and bolster creativity. And, those are just the areas with empirical research substantiating the benefits.

There are some people who have claimed to 'cure' their cancer via visualization and The Simonton Process is now used in a number of hospitals across the country in cancer care. It's a consistent practice of imagining cancer cells evaporating, getting swept away, or being attacked and destroyed by other means. Many of the patients who saw improvements - and an increase in immune function - were those who committed to the practice.

Think of a change you'd like to see in your life and search YouTube or find a practitioner to help you get started. There's a lot to gain when you learn how to...

Use imagery.

#246 Get hypnotized

While 'under hypnosis', the hypnotized individual is in a heightened state of awareness, temporarily rendering the person fully susceptible to suggestion [but only to the extent that the individual is willing]. It is during this state that the individual is able to zero into the subconscious, mostly due to the absence of environmental chatter - eliminated by suggestion. Some people call this state a 'trance' and is easily recognized by the state we all commonly experience when we arrive at a destination but have no memory of actually taking the route there.

Sometimes, there is so much internal or environmental 'chatter' that it is extremely difficult to get to the data stored in our brain. Hypnosis helps us dive through the noise. At other times, we are so consciously resistant to going 'there' that hypnosis allows us to bypass the auto-diverters that our psyche has created; allowing us to get 'there' [a memory or a feeling]. In other cases, hypnosis allows us to get underneath the ego or established defenses and to the place where we are vulnerable and receptive to new ways of thinking.

When we can reach the deepest part of our psyche, we are able to touch the truest power of our brain. There, we can divert pain, established beliefs, and dysfunctional thinking. Hypnosis can attack phobias (irrational beliefs), sleep, depression, stress, and other mental health struggles. It can help us visualize, remember, and concentrate.

Some people question the validity of the 'memories' that are reportedly recalled while in a trance. Since these memories are often unable to be substantiated, it is helpful to consider the 'point' of the memory, what is the 'meaning' that may be attributed to what the brain has created, regardless of the truth or fiction. I find that under some circumstances, a fictional 'memory' may be just as valid a message as a literal recollection - like a dream.

If you are challenged with an addiction, an unidentified nagging feeling, or a curiosity about childhood - consider finding a therapist qualified to practice hypnosis and take the step to…

Get Hypnotized.

#247 Lower your expectations

It has been said that the single quickest way to obtain a sense of happiness is to lower your expectations - allowing most of the disappointment you feel to disappear. You see, when we experience disappointment, it's due almost exclusively to an expectation that wasn't met.

Here are a few areas where high expectations can make life more difficult:

Expectations for perfection.

Expectations for people to think like 'me'.

A belief that there's only one way - the right way - and an expectation for people to adopt that belief.

An expectation for people to 'do what I do'.

We are raised with expectations. We are required to meet expectations at our place of employment and are constantly exposed to social expectations. The challenge of determining which ones are appropriate to meet and which ones we can dismiss can be overwhelming. Some of us - in light of this - try to meet them all... often with disastrous consequences to our mental health.

Consider the ones that do *not* fall into any of the above categories. Then, look at which of the remaining ones are a priority to *you*. Meeting those expectations at work may be necessary if you want to generate an income that sustains your lifestyle yet making your bed every morning may be a leftover from mom.

Meeting expectations feels good but failing to hit the mark generally, does not. If you are going to establish expectations, make sure they are reachable for the people to whom they apply. It may be too big of a goal for your C student to get straight A's next semester. Expectations need to be clear and verbalized when they exist and for that to happen, they need to be in our awareness. Many of us have subconscious expectations that are represented by ideas of 'should'.

Discover your subconscious expectations easily by recording those things that are 'should's' in your life... you'll be amazed. Only then can you know when to ...

Lower your expectations.

#248 Practice appreciation

Early in relationships, whether they are employment, romantic, or just personal - we tend to be observant of the 'niceties' that are exchanged and comment on them in appreciative ways. In many cases, that energy quickly wanes.

In the age of the Gratitude movement, it is apparent that people are using the term gratitude when they mean appreciation. We believe because we appreciate something, we are automatically grateful for it, but it is different. They are not one-in-the-same.

The Oxford English Dictionary explains that Gratitude is the "readiness to show appreciation" and then goes on to define appreciation as "the recognition and enjoyment of the good qualities of someone or something". Key into the phrase 'recognition of the good qualities of someone' - seeing the good - as that is commonly the area to dissolve first.

I love the way Esther Hicks explains appreciation - "seeing something through the eyes of the source (creator)". It is to 'notice' and once we do... we can be - and often are - thankful for what we are appreciating (gratitude).

In order to practice appreciation, we must direct our attention away from ourselves and engage in the present moment. As you recognize the good - comment on it.

"I appreciate that you got up with me this morning."

"I appreciate that there is always cream in the fridge."

"Thanks for being willing to work every day. We appreciate the way you care for us."

And the list is endless. Hearing appreciation for our 'being' and for what we do, helps us to feel recognized, loved, and valued.

The next time you feel salty with your partner or they are being cranky with you - stop and assess three things that you appreciate about them and share. Even in that no-so-perfect moment, you can find something to appreciate and expressing it will pump some loving energy into the negative space between you.

It is always helpful and potentially relationship saving when you...

Practice appreciation.

#249 Give someone a backrub

Remember that saying "it's better to give than to receive"? While most people I know enjoy receiving a backrub, it's also quite nice to earnestly give one.

Back in the day - before 'hookups' were a truly a casual thing, this is the 'intimate gesture' that often served as a 'hint' that more touching might be welcomed. At least that was my experience. However, initiating sex is *not* what this suggestion is really about.

When we gently and slowly massage the bare skin of another human that we feel connected to, it can be a very intimate experience. This exercise is encouraged as a way to build physical intimacy with someone without the expectation or culmination of sexual activity (although if you are moved... by all means).

When I make this suggestion in couples' therapy, I will sometimes hear resistance by an individual's declaration that they have weak hands and I send them directly to the internet to learn how to give a back rub. It turns out that strong hands are not a requirement for a relaxing, stress reducing, or even a seductive backrub. They may be if you are seeking sore muscle treatment in which case, see a trained massage therapist. Indeed, a good back rub is more about the caress of the skin, slight pressure moving in a particular direction, and the intention of the touch. Most anyone can give a good backrub with a bit of practice.

At first glance, one might think that the receiver is the only one who tends to benefit from a backrub but for the giver - there's opportunity as well. Making a connection with someone you care about may be the most obvious. Making the time for your friend or partner lets them know you put them first from time to time and that gesture reinforces the relationship you are also a part of. Initiating a selfless gesture of providing pleasure to someone you care for keeps you grounded and focused beyond only your needs, encouraging a eudemonic sense of well-being. The act of physically touching another person with compassion and gentleness can be physically (not sexual) pleasurable for you as well. Indeed, there's hardly a downside when you make the effort to ...

Give someone a back rub.

#250 Make wine

Since the beginning of the current millennium, the number of American wineries has more than quadrupled and wine of some variety is now grown in all 50 states. With this type of availability, one might ask why bother to make your own and yet there are a number of us with devout curiosity about our ability to make a great glass of vino.

Making your own wine doesn't actually require a massive number of grapes. It can be made from grape concentrate and it's completely possible to purchase concentrate from almost any grape producing part of the world. Certainly, you can do the research, buy the grapes or concentrate, add the proper ingredients and chemicals, ferment the juice, and then bottle the result.

You could take on the entire process yourself or... you could find something like The Wine Room in Cherry Hill, New Jersey where wine experts - having all of the ingredients and equipment available - are able to help you make a wine consistent with your tastes; you do the composing - they activate the process.

This is one of those things that offers the opportunity for people to come together in their shared interests. It's like a book club but winemaking instead. It is the kind of thing that can motivate conversation, pique curiosity, and encourage cooperation all at once. It is a great activity for couples who share a liking for wine. It's a great family project or special occasion effort (The Wine Room).

There is a lot to learn and an entire industry to explore if you become curious about winemaking. There are annual amateur competitions to be entered, tastings to win, and grants to be granted. It could become a passion you never knew you wanted to pursue and overall a grand adventure! If you have an interest in wine, you may consider making the effort to ...

Make wine.

#251 Paint the woodwork

As I look around my home, my first thought is that I must add this suggestion to my to-do list *asap*. How does the woodwork in a typical home get so beat up? You'd think a herd of antelope have charged through the doorways and against the chair rail in almost every room.

Some people don't like painted woodwork and have gone to great lengths to adorn their home with cherry or walnut stained woodwork throughout the house. Others have cursed those oil-based stains as they attempted to paint over them years later with washable latex. Stained trim is beautiful, especially in older homes where the quality of wood used was high end. It can be both dark and comfortable as well as dark and dreary. If dark and comfortable is the feel you want and have... read no further. If it's dark and drab or if your woodwork is already painted - read on.

In Colonial style homes, the tradition of painting trim a darker color than the walls is still practiced. The contrast of dark colored trim against a light wall can create an artistic feel. Painting detail trim (dental molding, etc.) a darker color draws attention to that architectural feature.

In many of the modern homes where trim was mass produced, it's rather nondescript and acts more as a simple frame for a door or window. It is commonly white. Although, white may not be white - or so says Better Homes and Garden Magazine. In an online article, they remind us that 'white' comes in a variety of tones. They vary across a spectrum of cool to warm; each one complimenting the primary wall color differently. They recommend taking a paint chip of the wall color to the paint store to see which 'white' works the best and then make it consistent throughout the room. Personally, I prefer cool white throughout the whole house. It seems chaotic to choose a different white color for each room.

Perhaps the most important part of choosing a paint for trim is in knowing to get a hardy, washable paint. This is where quality matters. Bob Villa, one of televisions most beloved home improvement specialists, suggests an alkyd-oil based paint in either semi or high gloss for most traditional household trim work. It is by far, the most durable and the most washable - tolerant of harsh cleaners.

Personally, cleaning up with oil-based paints is cumbersome and it doesn't come off easily after drying on areas it wasn't supposed to be in the first place (my hands, the floor, the doorknobs, etc.) so I use water based paints in semi-gloss but go for high quality and high durability. Behr paints have been rated highly by consumer reports over the years and have been satisfactory in my personal experience. It goes on well and blends well if all I am doing is random touch ups.

Take a walk through your house and glance around at the trim in each room and then grab a paint brush and a fresh can of paint and...

Paint the woodwork.

#252 Binge watch a show

'Binging' is not often attributed to a suggestion that might increase happiness and yet there are times when too much of a good thing ends up being even a better thing. Sometimes, taking a 'down' day offers our body, mind, and soul a much-needed vacation from daily life and its stressors. One of the ways to escape is to binge watch television.

"Binge watching" is a relatively new term and yet it's akin to the concept of 'marathon'. Seemingly, one has a derogatory connotation while the other was much of a contest of sorts. When 'reruns' came into being, there would be weekend 'marathons' of Star Trek that captured the full attention of Trekkies all over the world. When the AMC channel was introduced and ran one Hallmark movie after another all day and night long, we'd hear about someone watching a 'marathon' of Robert Redford movies. Year ago, movie theaters would offer marathons of Spencer Tracy movies or newsreels. With one you could sit as long as you wanted and leave when you were finished enjoying the experience. Today, we do it without commercials on channels like Netflix and Hulu, but we call it 'binging'.

Binge watching is a great way to destress and regroup. Pick an old favorite, a classic you never saw, or a series that you've had a hard time following (sometimes it is easier to follow if you don't have to wait a week to reconnect to the storyline). For some, there's barely a difference between digressing into the dramatic world of television or devouring three Nora Roberts novelettes in a weekend.

When making the decision to 'binge'... allow yourself an honest evaluation of the motivation. If as described in the paragraph above - give yourself permission to unplug and recharge. If, on the other hand, it is to *avoid* something... you may want to reconsider using the binge suggestion as a reward for meeting the responsibilities at hand first. Avoidance rarely offers constructive consequences. Indeed, it is at the core of much dysfunction and the accessibility of binge watching on countless devices makes it an easy out when we are looking for excuses.

It may be appropriate to set limits for yourself as you enter a binge-watching session. Personally, hanging out on a winter afternoon in front of the fireplace in my jammies and curled up in a blanket on my sofa watching reruns of Fixer Upper is one of the most relaxing things I can think of to do. If I were to do it every weekend, many of the things that are important to me would never get accomplished so it's key to set a limit. I generally have an hour limit... once it was the entire day - 12 hours of a docu-series that I got hooked on right away. Most times it's capped at 4 or 5 hours and I might do that a couple of times a year. I might have felt guilty that first time because there was a long list of 'should' playing in my mind, but I've learned to silence them and use this suggestion as a form of 'self-care'.

Try it! You may find that it is fun to ...

Binge watch a show.

#253 Run or walk a 5K

No matter the season, you can generally find an organization that will be hosting a 5 K. Why not make the effort to participate?

To put this into perspective - most walkers will complete a 5K in about 45 minutes. It's only about 6000 steps for the average stride (a piece of cake - or pie - for all of you who seek that 10K step goal) and you'll burn 300 calories. Running of course, will be faster and burn more calories.

While walking a 5K once and only once will feel like an accomplishment to those who participate, making it a regular practice has tons of benefits for your body and mind.

Walking improves your mood.

Walking improves your body strength.

Walking improves your cardiovascular strength.

Walking improves your balance and coordination.

Motivation

Maybe the best thing about these 'organized' walk/runs like a 5K is that they motivate us to do it with others - to be 'a part' of something. We tend to do these kinds of things more frequently if we have moral support in the form of crowds. It's easier to participate with someone than if we have to make the decision to get up and out all on our own.

So, gather some friends and jumpstart your holidays with something that is good for you...

Run or walk a 5K.

#254 Learn origami

When was the last time you even had a thought about folding big paper into little paper? For many, it was the last 'cootie catcher' you made in middle school or the last paper 'football' you made for the high school lunch table. Some of you may have folded paper in more appealing shapes in girl scouts or a crafting class, perhaps as part of a scrapbooking project. Origami though, takes folding paper to a whole new level.

Origami is a true form of art. It's attributed to the Chinese dating back to the 1600's but there is reference to the process in different forms as far back as 1000 A.D. in a couple of cultures. Today, there are a number of world-renowned artists whose only medium is paper and whose primary method is to fold.

Paper folding is a favorite de-stressing activity for a lot of hobbyists. It's recommended as a 'tool-box' item for anxiety and depression. It's attributed to lowering blood pressure, increasing attention capacity, and improves dexterity in people who've had injury to their hands. Some therapists recommend Origami for ADHD, Addictions, and raising self-esteem. It fosters creativity.

Origami can be instrumental in the development of mindfulness as it brings your attention directly to the present moment and it can be done anywhere, anytime, and by anybody who has a piece of paper. It can help us let go of our need to be perfect and may foster a form of meditation as the skills develop and focused attention is deepened.

Some of the basic Origami folds can be accomplished by children as young as four years old. It's a great activity that can bring the entire family to the table with very little - if any - expense. It has the potential to become a family hobby - or one that is shared in an adult relationship - fostering time away from electronics and societal noise.

Origami as an art, a hobby, and a therapeutic tool is a real thing. There's a National association, several annual conventions, and Meetup groups that allow lovers of paper folding to connect and share. So, if you saw the title of today's suggestion and raised your eyebrow, I suggest you find a piece of paper and find out what all the fuss is by getting started on a basic fold as you watch the a YouTube video and...

Learn Origami

#255 Try a new perfume or aftershave

Have you been a creature of olfactory habit? Have you 'smelled' the same year after year because you're fearful of finding another scent that works? Many of us have fond memories that relate to scents. I can't smell Old Spice without thinking of my father and my mother, Estee Lauder. They wore those scents so long that they were synonymous with their roles.

It's interesting to note that over time, our bodies chemical composition can change just enough so that the way it interacts with the chemicals in the cologne, it may smell different on us. Likewise, manufactures can tweak even one element of the scent structure and it interacts with us differently - changing the way it smells. It's always good to have a fall back or another 'go to' scent.

While there are those that will never change - it's not necessarily true that one scent fits all occasions. A light fruity scent may not be the most appropriate one for a winter holiday party. Likewise, a sexy soft scent probably isn't a great choice for an important board meeting. Men also need to consider how strong their aftershave or deodorant is as compared to their environment. And ladies - when you spray, try to remember a little on the wrist goes a long way.

This suggestion is for those of you who know how to take a risk, who want to try something different, and who aren't afraid of change. Of course, starting with samples is probably the best approach until you find something you enjoy. There's no reason to accumulate a dozen bottles of scent that you won't be wearing.

The next time you walk through the cosmetics department or find a magazine filled with samples - grab them so that you are ready to ...

Try a new perfume or aftershave.

#256 Ask for a hug

Connection is one of the most fundamental needs that a human being requires for survival. In fact, researchers in Chicago have postulated that not feeling connected to a 'tribe' may be more devastating to our life expectancy than smoking or obesity. There may be no better way to signify a connection than by hugging.

Often these days, we are racing around attempting to complete our own agenda and don't take the time to stop and consider those around us. Consequently, we may fail to notice that people in our circle - our tribe - our family, are feeling disconnected from us. We may not feel comfortable speaking out when we are the ones feeling on the outskirts. And so, it goes... we brush past one another, maybe with a smile but disengaged from a sense of belonging.

It is during those times that it becomes imperative to 'ask for a hug'. Whether you're the one feeling disconnected or you are noticing that someone appears to be detached or unplugged from the group/family. Either we notice that we are in need or there is someone in our tribe that can tell we are deficient. Either way, the gesture of a hug will likely break the isolation and pull us into at least a temporary circle of comfort.

Because a hug can generate that sense of belonging and compassion, it fosters calm. It allows us to feel protected - if even for that moment. Consequently, our immune system may function better, our fear is reduced, and we feel happier. More hugging may help with heart health, depression, anxiety, and overall life satisfaction.

That's a lot of benefit so go ahead and take the time to think about your needs and ...

Ask for a hug.

#257 Have a girl's/guy's weekend

This suggestion is another that will help foster the sensation of 'belonging' by bringing together those people that constitute our tribe.

Our need for friendship and belonging doesn't change as we mature. It does however, become more difficult to get those needs met as we marry, have children, full-time jobs and the daily responsibilities of home life. Our giggling late-night conversations with our best friends are few and far between. Those nights that metaphorically 'fill our gas tank' are rare unless we make them happen. Hence, the need to have a girl's or guy's weekend.

While it's great to get out and 'do' things while you're with friends, some of the best parts of a friend weekend is to keep it simple. Life is busy enough as it is so a getaway weekend may best be served by taking it easy next to a beach, swimming pool, or fireplace with a bottle of wine or a bowl of popcorn. If there is too much planned activity, there may not be room for the conversations and connection for which the weekend was designed.

Likewise, the goal is friendship and bond strengthening so it can be short and inexpensive - one night at a campground; or longer and deluxe - a long weekend in Cabo. It can be just one friend or a dozen as long as drama, personality differences, and complaints stay home.

Generally, men like to 'do' things and can find comradery in building a barn, hunting, skiing or gaming. Indeed - plenty of gents' splurge on annual outings for many of those reasons and for some, it's the only real 'friend' time they get during the year as family responsibilities prevail. Women seem to be better at planning short and sweet visits together more often, saving the long and expensive trips to enjoy with their significant others.

No matter the style, budget, or program - fostering, building, and strengthening a sense of belonging is the ultimate goal when you make plans to ...

Have a Girl's/Guy's Weekend

#258 Check your posture

Posture affects our balance. Balance affects walking, going up and down the stairs, getting up and down from chairs, getting in and out of the car, carrying things, and even turning our head. Hence, good posture is vital to many of the things we organically do throughout our day.

Good posture plays an important role in our mood and also in the interpretation of our mood. It reduces neck and back pain and helps us look slimmer. Additionally, it helps us breathe easier by allowing our lungs sufficient expansion room. When we are well oxygenated, we may learn and retain information longer (improved memory).

What signifies good posture? Your chin will be parallel to the floor and your shoulders, even. Your arms will be down and your elbows, straight. Your weight will be distributed evenly across both feet on even hips. It will feel good unless your muscles have already begun to adjust to an abnormal configuration.

Certainly, you can resort to the traditional 'book on your head' method of practicing posture. The goal is to find the position that puts the least strain on your joints and muscles. Or, you can imagine a straight line running through your body and it's connected to the ceiling. Without standing on your toes, make yourself as tall as possible. You can strengthen the ligaments in your back by doing a 'shoulder blade squeeze'... move your shoulder blades as close together as possible and hold them there for 5 seconds. Repeat ten times.

There's also the Upright posture training device (this is not a commercial for the product - just passing along info). It's a wearable device that vibrates slightly when your posture is out of alignment. It's part of the 'wearable' technology that monitors our body for optimal health and is a great way to retrain yourself to stay aware of good posture if you've gotten a little lazy about it.

The goal is awareness and good health. A simple piece of that is to be diligent and...

Check Your Posture

#259 Stop complaining

I read somewhere that complaining was like emotional farting - a description that resonated with me. It turns out that when we complain, it's as if we are in a closed elevator - essentially impacting everyone in our vicinity with the negativity of our comments. Yes, complaining is contagious. When you complain, a black cloud of dust settles in, over, and around everything within earshot.

The adage at play is "what we focus on ... grows". Science has demonstrated that as electrical charges are sent through the brain, the speed with which the charge travels gets faster and faster. This makes it easier for the brain to think the way it is thinking. In this example, "grows" refers to the ease with which thoughts are triggered. When we complain a lot, complaining becomes second nature.

Based on this logic, the reverse would also be true. If we compliment - or notice the positive - over and over, they are the elements that become a natural part of our thought process.

Negativity begets stress... stress is hazardous to your overall health. When we are surrounded by complaining, stress levels increase. When we are complaining, stress is elevated. In both cases, the overarching effect on our system is negative which, in many cases - become another focus of our complaint.

Complaining is easy. We are hardwired to look for what's wrong in life. It's a mechanism that supports our survival and some complaining - is healthy. The truth is that some aspects of life feel negative and expressing frustration effectively is a necessity for good mental health. Expressing the emotions we feel constructively is more difficult than it appears.

The antidote to complaints is to recognize the good in each experience. Expressing gratitude for even the most difficult of scenarios is at the heart of healthy functioning. It is akin to finding the silver lining in every storm cloud and describing it - instead of the horror of the storm. Noticing the good and allowing it to take center stage instead of complaining about the element that wasn't perfect... can be where the focus goes. And as it goes... "what we focus on... grows" so...

Stop Complaining.

#260 Ditch gossip

If you're human, you've probably - at least once in your lifetime - participated in a round of gossip. By definition, gossip is the "idle talk or rumor, especially about the personal or private affairs of others". It is differentiated from asking a friend if they've 'run into' another... or asking about the welfare of a joint acquaintance. It's speaking about someone's life without explicit permission to do so.

By speaking about things that are considered private or deeply personal, we are likely to insult or hurt the targeted individual even if that wasn't the intent. It may promote shame for that person and ignite feelings that lead to depression, helplessness, and sadly... even suicide. Gossip can injure esteem and confidence. It can lead to feelings of loneliness and cause people to isolate further. It often leads to embarrassment when someone's private business becomes the focus of outsiders. The anxiety that results can paralyze.

When we gossip for the sake of having something to say, we breach the trust that others have in us for keeping their secrets. How many times have you questioned whether someone is talking about you by the way they are talking about another? If they are willing to betray the interest of John Doe, what keeps them from doing the same to you? Without trust and respect, it's difficult to sustain a relationship.

Do you want your personal and private affairs to be the center of discussion between people not involved? If you think that may be bothersome, make the effort to change your energy into something more productive and compassionate. Make a conscious decision to ...

Ditch Gossip.

#261 Learn to trust

Our ability to trust others may be one of the most primary elements that makes life good. Counting on people, trusting them to be where they say, do what they say, and get things done when they say… that is a component of a good life. It feels reliable, consistent, and dependable. It speaks to our need for some level of security.

And then we find out that not everyone is 'trustworthy'. It's disappointing for sure, and we become skeptical of trusting again. Sadly, for some, trust isn't easy to rekindle. It may depend on the situation or circumstances to some degree but even for simple or superficial infractions - trust can be difficult to reestablish.

I've found that most healthy people are indeed - trustworthy. Notice, I said healthy. People who betray us, people who lie, people who steal, people who trick and coerce us -generally, they are unhealthy. Healthy people - most people - don't do those things. And so, if you've crossed paths with an unhealthy person who has proved to be untrustworthy… put it into context and realize that they are not like 'most people'.

There are plenty of emotional benefits when we allow ourselves to trust. Perhaps first and most importantly, we are able to have more meaningful relationships. When we trust people and they demonstrate trustworthiness - our confidence increases. Our stress level is lower when we know that someone has our back. It offers us peace of mind.

This suggestion is "learn to trust" because it's a necessary component regardless of how many times people in our environment have been untrustworthy. It's about allowing each person that you cross paths with to establish trustworthiness on their own - not based on someone else. Regardless what has happened in the past…

Learn to trust.

#262 Create a personal space

I grew up knowing that the back room in my Grandparents house was "Granddaddy's Room". It was the part of the house where he could sit on the couch in dirty farm clothes, leave his boots where he took them off, and keep the newspaper open - if he chose. My Grandmother even had a room dedicated as an 'office' way before it was chic, even though she didn't work from home. Today, the terms 'Man Cave' and 'She Shed' are common. They are used as enticements for buyers desiring dedicated personal space.

Our ability to establish personal spaces like the ones described above means we have a place to 'regroup' when necessary. It is a place for us to collect our thoughts, calm down, and gain perspective.

Dedicated space can be a 'pit stop' for us... a refueling space where we go for quiet time, reflection, meditation, prayer, or exercise. It's a way for us to temporarily shut out the outside world.

Creative expression is an important element in many of our lives and it can get loud, messy, or downright dirty! Having a dedicated space to participate in a beloved activity not only 'refuels' us but also saves the sanity of other family members by not exposing them to the mess or noise. It can act as an adult 'play space'.

A home is often an integration of what she likes and what he prefers. She may not paint the bedroom walls pink out of consideration of the fact that he sleeps there too. Likewise, his vast collection of baseball paraphernalia may not be a mutually desirable choice for family room decor. A personal space offers people the opportunity to have a dedicated area that is completely representative of their own personality.

When we have personal space in which to regroup, refuel, express our creativity and express specific parts of our personality, we are likely to feel happier in general. When we are happier, our relationships benefit, our health benefits, and our productivity increases. Indeed, the list of advantages is long.

If you haven't done so already, take a look around your living quarters and think of how you might...

Create some personal space.

#263 Get inspired

Understanding that inspiration is an internal energy that drives action is an important concept. Dr. Wayne Dyer described it like this... *"Inspiration is when an idea gets hold of you and carries you where you are intended to go."*

Because inspiration comes from the inside, it is an authentic energy; one that we need to find and listen to. How do you find inspiration as you move from day to day? Are you in the habit of noticing when you are inspired?

There are people in your life that encourage you to 'act'. Inspiration often comes when a suggestion resonates deep within. For example, when someone encourages you to do something and you experience an inner drive to go 'do' it... that's inspiration. "She inspired me to run a 5K."

Nature is full of inspirational energy because it is living and moving. We can be inspired by what we see, hear, feel, and smell as we move through nature. I remember standing at the edge of the Grand Canyon and feeling quite insignificant against the backdrop of one of nature's most compelling creations. That feeling tugged at my core in a way that inspired me to find a way to be more significant in the world... to give back.

Dance, music, sculpture, paint, theater... all the arts are filled with opportunities to discover inspiration. It may be color or form... posture or voice that moves you from the inside out. Even if the arts don't inspire you to create art - they may tug at your heart in a way that moves you to support the arts or participate locally in a way that benefits others.

Literature, poetry, and lyrics offer, perhaps the most common, form of inspiration. Quotes from these bodies of work are daily inspirations for thousands of people around the world today and there is no shortage of places to find them.

No matter the source, make it a habit to listen to your 'heart'. Those internal vibrations are signals that your most authentic self has recognized something on which to focus your attention. It is the voice that allows you to...

Get Inspired.

288

#264 Quit a bad habit

Bad habits are those things that we do that we know aren't helping us; the things that nag us more than our moms. These malicious behaviors are quite obvious and include doing anything in excess: drinking, eating, spending, smoking, nail biting, and snacking. They are the things we 'know' we need to stop doing for our health and overall welfare. These habits can literally put our lives in danger. They impede our self-image, our confidence, and esteem.

Some habits have developed underneath our awareness. Some of us twirl our hair incessantly or click a pen to the extent that our co-worker wants to jump across their desk and snatch it away. Or how about that foot that shakes or the leg wiggle that indicates nervousness? Constantly smacking gum, or slurping coffee are common habits that go unnoticed by the habitour but are obnoxious irritations for those in the vicinity.

Some of our bad habits are verbal... Saying the word "like..." far too often and contextually inappropriately; speaking too loudly for the environment; and using the sound "um..." in more than just an occasional sentence. While not directly verbal - many of us don't make eye contact while speaking - a habit that is considered downright rude in many cultures.

As with anything, in order for it to be changed, you must be aware. Ask friends and family members for their observations to catch the things you aren't aware of. Make a list of the items that you may want to work on and consider which ones are priorities - don't try to make too many changes at once.

In order to break a bad habit - replace it with a good one. If you are trying to stop smoking - chew gum instead. If you're trying to break the habit of nail biting - find a way to keep your hands busy; crochet, knit, play with a fidget spinner or stress ball. If you can eliminate your bad habit for at least 66 days, the odds of beating it is greatly improved.

Don't wait for the New Year and a resolution that will likely be broken quickly. Make the effort today so that you will go into the next year without that annoying behavior. Take a minute to pick one and then make a decision to...

Quit a bad habit.

#265 Step back from negativity

Are there any 'Debbie Downers' in your life? Any Eeyore types? People who find the dark clouds in life and describe them in detail without ever looking at the liner? Have you ever noticed how you feel when you spend time in the company of these people?

People often report feeling 'drained' after spending time with negative people. It's not surprising. When we are exposed to negativity for any length of time, it can feel like an attack against our system. Our instinct is to defend against the negativity and so we spend subconscious energy blocking it. The longer we have to keep our shield up, the more exhausting it can become.

Of course, negative things happen and occasionally they are significant, rendering it almost impossible to distract our focus. It's important to be realistic and see things for what they are. Yet, the negativity being called out for the purpose of this post is actively finding and commenting on what's wrong. It's expecting the worse. It's assumptive failure no matter the condition. It's expecting the worse.

Constant exposure to negativity is downright unhealthy. Negativity produces stress. Stress produces Cortisol. Elevated levels of Cortisol interfere with our immune function. Compromised immune systems are susceptible to disease, bacteria, and viruses. Negativity stunts creativity. Negativity exposure has also been demonstrated to decrease the power / effectiveness of the Hippocampus - the brain area responsible for reasoning and memory. It keeps us from taking risks necessary to invent, discover, and explore. It stifles our self-confidence, our self-esteem, and our perseverance. It is destructive to relationships. It destroys hope and encouragement. When covered in a shroud of negativity, it's almost impossible to feel happiness.

If you find yourself exposed to negativity that feels / seems unbalanced or overwhelming, set boundaries. Engage the tenets of self-care and create an exit strategy that allows you to ...

Step back from negativity.

#266 Read the Bible

If you are a Christian, you've probably already done this. If not, scholars around the globe have spoken about the rich value of the bible as literature and it may be a book you want to read. It is rich in history and parables. It is full of life advice and insight about the human condition.

Perhaps for no other reason, the objective of reading the bible is to understand the call and drive of the Christian community; a significant percentage of the world. Additionally, because of its contribution to the culture at large, it helps us to comprehend embedded nuances. The bible is filled with lots of practicality about life. For example:

In the New Testament, James writes... "my dear brothers and sisters, take note of this: Everyone should be quick to listen, slow to speak and slow to become angry.

At the end of the day, that's just good advice - believer or not.

The bible is the world's most recognized sacred text. It's a historical document. If you remove any emotion one may feel about its 'religious' attachment - there is great value in seeing it as a great antique; responsible for much of the governing history across time. It may help in understanding the development of other cultures. It is the foundation of Western Art.

Of course, if you are a Christian - then you may see the bible as a literal interpretation of the Word of God and for that reason, the bible is a textbook for living life as a Christian. Years ago, someone recommended that we may find value in reading the bible ourselves - from cover to cover and then... attend a bible study group to dive more deeply into various chapters and stories.

If you are seeking a new book - a historical account that covers thousands of years and proves to be a sociological overview of cultural development and ideocracies, then there is only one option...

Read the Bible.

#267 Disengage a toxic relationship

Toxic refers to any behavior that results in harm - either physical or emotional. We may think it goes without saying that physically abusive behavior is toxic and cannot be tolerated yet there are thousands of people in relationships that are physically abusive. If your relationship is - *in any way physically abusive* - disengage, get out, leave... *now*. Your very life may be in jeopardy.

Perhaps worse, because there are no apparent bruises, is emotional abuse. Emotional abuse also comes in a variety of forms and *must not* be tolerated. No one deserves to be the target of emotional abuse. Any form of communication (speech, text messages, email, letters) that is controlling, punishing, manipulative, degrading, or derogatory - is abuse. When people use the silent treatment to coerce, withhold love and support for specific outcomes, and use money to bribe or entice - that is abuse.

Other people use less apparent tactics to 'abuse'. Gaslighting is one of the most common - providing false information so frequently and with so much conviction that you begin to doubt the truth; to distrust your own knowledge or instincts. Isolating and ignoring someone can also be considered abusive - especially if it is a parent/child relationship. It doesn't 'look' inappropriate yet when someone is dependent on our attention and care - to withhold it intentionally is an abuse of power.

Relationships are toxic when we no longer can trust, feel safe with, or feel appreciative of - the person with whom we are relating. It can be a romantic relationship, a friendship, a sibling or other family member, a parent... When we continually feel powerless, humiliated, defensive, criticized, belittled, unloved, unappreciated, etc., and our efforts at communicating and resolving those feelings go cold - it is time to *get out*.

Healthy relationships are reciprocal. They are not self-focused. They employ communication - even imperfect - to resolve differences. They are light and easy although, every relationship has some level of challenge. They are supportive and compassionate. There is a mutual respect and encouragement.

Disengaging means creating distance. The amount of distance may be determined by circumstances and/or the relationship. At the very least - learning how to set boundaries and demonstrate self-respect is imperative.

No one - absolutely no one - deserves or causes abusive behavior. Abusers are responsible for their behavior. If they fail to make a healthy choice when they relate to you - make sure you demonstrate self-respect and make the healthy choice to...

Disengage from a toxic relationship.

People are just as happy as they make up their minds to be.

Abraham Lincoln

#268 Mentor someone

What do you do with all your accumulated knowledge, experience, and wisdom? Is it just there? Untapped except for your own judgment? Why not make the effort to share it by mentoring someone?

A mentor is defined as someone who establishes a trusting relationship with a younger, less experienced individual and provides guidance, support, and encouragement.

It doesn't matter how old you are, there is at least some accumulation of information that can be helpful to those younger or less experienced than yourself. Children in a homeless shelter, teens attending an after school support program, college students looking to enter the workforce, Twenty-somethings just starting out, new mothers, new fathers, first time home buyers, startup entrepreneurs, and the list goes on… can all benefit from the insight generated by someone who's 'been there… done that'.

Children, in particular, benefit from mentoring. A child who's been mentored is 53% more likely to go to college and 130% more likely to hold a leadership role of some kind. They are 81% more likely to engage in extracurricular activities such as sports and 46% less likely to use illegal drugs. A primary advantage of being mentored is the emotional support and approval received. It's a significant contribution towards an increase in self-esteem.

Graduate students who have defined mentor relationships as strong and successful demonstrate more satisfaction with their graduate programs and postgraduate well-being. Research indicates that the stronger the reported mentoring relationship - the more professional success attained by the mentee. Adults entering the corporate marketplace also report higher job satisfaction when mentored by seasoned workers.

Often, the things we teach are things that we need to remind ourselves to do. It's similar to picking through an old file and discovering something there you'd forgotten or are just happy to be reminded of. This is true for both industry knowledge and life skills in general.

Additionally, mentoring offers you the opportunity to gain perspective. It is a blatant reminder that the world goes around, and around again. As we gain experience, we understand more intently, how to prioritize. We learn to trust our intuition and decisions. Working with mentees can demonstrate how far we've come in our own journey, thus increasing our confidence.

This is a suggestion that is a win-win for all parties involved so look at your schedule and research some of the opportunities where you live where you can...

Mentor someone.

#269 Stop comparing

One of the potentially troublesome elements of our humanness is the tendency for us to compare ourselves. Comparing what we look like, our incomes, our homes, our jobs, our families, or the like often allow for feelings of unworthiness, envy, and jealousy - none of which are healthy contributors to our emotional frame.

When we compare, frequently we are measuring ourselves against observations that are unfair. We equate the worst of our person (or situation) to our assumption about the other - generally a perspective that is seldom accurate. We may think that our friend's marriage is perfect because when in public - the couple appears laughing and engaged yet they may simply be hiding great pain and shame of a poor relationship under that laughter. Others may have a large home, go on lavish vacations, and drive fancy cars - allowing for assumptions about their large incomes but in truth - are deeply in debt.

The reality is that we are each unique and perfectly imperfect people who have a personal story unlike another's. No matter how similar one may be to another, the likelihood that we can be the same or would really want to be the same... is farfetched. What would the world be if we were simply duplicates of one another?

People's lives are often like icebergs... only the tip is exposed to the world and we don't know what is happening below the surface. Measuring ourselves against only part of the whole, sets us up for false perceptions.

When you find yourself comparing - the quickest antidote to any negative feelings that may occur is to express gratitude. When we take the time to be grateful for what we *do* have - for who we *are* - and for what is *real*... we stop getting caught up in other people's lives because we notice the blessings in ours.

While the temptation to compare may not entirely evaporate from your life, remembering that you see only what people what you to see and not what is real may help. Add that to an expression of gratitude for everything that works in your world and you'll quickly learn to ...

Stop comparing.

#270 Celebrate a friend

Friendship is a gift. In the longest longitudinal study of human development ever conducted, it was ascertained that friendship is critical to our mental health and directly impacts our physical health.

A good friend wears many hats by helping us make critical decisions, cope with stress, and rebound from illness. A good friend may literally make the difference between life and death. Whether it is holding our hand during an emotionally weak moment or donating a kidney, bone marrow, or genetic material so that we can start a family, a good friend deserves to be celebrated.

When was the last time you demonstrated solid appreciation for the friends in your life? If you've been remiss, now is a great time to reconcile your gratitude. Consider hosting a "[Barbara] Appreciation Day". It may look very simple - a handwritten card with expressions of acknowledgement. It could be a PB&J picnic or treating him/her to a nice lunch at their favorite restaurant. It could be a full-on surprise party or a celebration for the sole reason that they've been instrumental in your life. The point is to acknowledge their contribution to your overall wellbeing as you...

Celebrate a friend

#271 Be a cheerleader

I've written about mentoring, appreciation, and friendship and in each case, there is potential for this suggestion - to be a cheerleader. Of course, I don't mean the high school sports variety. By cheerleader, I mean someone whose focus is championing for another, directly encouraging and supporting.

We all need someone in our corner cheering for us - egging us on for a win - for success. Cheerleaders don't criticize or correct, they inspire, urge, celebrate and rejoice in each little maneuver that delivers someone closer to the goal.

For some people this comes really easy - we all know one ... that person (often a Grandmother) who encourages you no matter what - even if it's not all that great of an idea or goal. And then there's the rest of us (often parents) who say, "that's good, but...". A true cheerleader eliminates the "but". A cheerleader leaves their personal opinion out of the equation. Unless someone is headed in a direction of self-harm or violence - they are pure support.

While there has been a lot of controversy in recent years about building people up - sometimes without merit, it's an important element of developing and sustaining self-esteem. It feels good to know that someone is 'on our side' and that there is a person who 'has our back' no matter what. Trust is established in this manner as well as confidence. Yes, it's true that blowing smoke at people isn't helpful because the real world doesn't always 'cheerlead' for us. It's all in the delivery!

It's possible to be a cheerleader without going overboard and unrealistically puffing someone up. Instead of saying "you were great!" (if they really weren't) ... say "Your effort was amazing!" or "You'll get it next time." Instead of claiming that a negative isn't present at all... focus on the positives. Instead of buying into the disappointment that a 'big' thing that didn't happen - celebrate all the small victories.

I'm sure there is someone in your life that can benefit from your decision to...

Be a cheerleader.

#272 Plan a surprise getaway

I've written about Surprising someone, but this suggestion is just a bit more specific and tends to crank up the appreciation scale significantly.

Your partner may be the most obvious choice for this suggestion as they are the often the most deserving of your unannounced benevolence. It's a great way to spice things up; to let them know how important they are; how much you appreciate their contribution to your life together, etc.... It doesn't matter if it's only an overnight at a local Holiday Inn or a week away in Sedona - the fact that you thought of and planned for his or her absence (leaving no detail unchecked) will garner points for months - if not years - to come.

Next to your spouse, for many of you it's your parents that have devoted themselves to your success. If you're going to plan a surprise getaway for someone, why not a spa weekend for mom or a golf outing for dad? Maybe they'd enjoy a weekend at the beach or a chalet overlooking a ski slope. It could even be a camping cabin with a fire ring all set to light. Surprises don't have to be fancy to be meaningful. If money is tight - try an Airbnb or call in a favor from a friend who has a place that mom and/or dad may like.

One of the best gifts I ever received from a friend was when she surprised me by taking my kids for a weekend. She brought a big pot of soup, took my kids, and left me in my own home - alone - for the whole weekend. It was a great reprieve at a difficult time in my life to have a 'staycation' without any responsibility. It was - in its own right - a surprise getaway even though I only 'got away' from responsibility. I've never forgotten how good that felt.

The key element here is that a big part of the surprise is not having to plan - a thing! I've heard some stories about guys who even packed a suitcase and had it in the trunk of the car - almost like a love kidnapping. The babysitter was arranged, the meals were planned, responsibilities covered, etc..... It's a true escape for the recipient.

If you can't think of anything to get your loved one this year for the holidays - consider a way you might...

Plan a surprise getaway.

#273 Have your palm read

Even if you don't believe in someone's ability to 'see' into your hand find a palm reader with good reviews and take the plunge - it's fun! Palmistry has been practiced for thousands of years and some individuals are very talented in their ability to describe the characteristics about your life and personality based on the composition of your hand. First, they look that the fingers make assumptions based on:

The length of your various fingers and the space between them
The thinness of your fingers
The shape and state of your fingernail

Additionally, the lines in your palm represent a variety of areas; marriage, head, heart, fate, sun, children, money, and health. More information is contributed based on moles, the way lines cross, and shapes that they make. Even the size of your hand matters. The left hand speaks your potential, the right hand about what you've done with that potential.

Supposedly, this ancient method of predicting has some merit. Recent science has correlated greater athletic talent in men whose ring finger is longer than his index finger. (I'm so curious to know how many of you just looked at your fingers!). Those men are more apt to be well-endowed and have more children. Those with longer index fingers are more prone to heart disease. Scientists think these elements have something to do with the prenatal testosterone exposure. Go figure!

Palm readers are well versed in old antidotal and more modern research. That information as well as commonalities across individuals with similar characteristics are used to predict. They may tell you something that you don't know... not that it is 'carved in stone' but that you may be more prone to something indicated across the population with similar individuals.

Having your palm read is just a fun... not too serious activity that you can do with friends, sisters, bridesmaids, a partner, or colleagues. It's harmless unless you make more of it than is intended. Take it with a grain of salt.

The next time you want something fun and crazy to do, consider... Having your palm read.

300

#274 Host a game night

Do you or your friends get together for Poker, Bunko, Caton, or D&D? Have you spent any time at a board game cafe? Are you a Monopoly fanatic? Board games are making a comeback and Game Night is a 'thing' in many twenty-something circles. What is your favorite game?

Gathering the family for a night of gaming is a great break from electronics and television. New York Magazine has published several lists of popular board games - among them, many of my family's favorites; Codenames, Sequence, Ticket to Ride, and Telestrations. Telestrations in particular, is great for a crowd and we are always left belly laughing the night away. When my kids are gathered (adults now), they love Ticket to Ride and lovingly call it the 'train game'.

Game nights can be several people playing the same game at different tables competing for a final spot (Bunko) or just a couple of people vying to be the champ (Monopoly). It can be serious and committed or rowdy, fun, and lighthearted.

By planning and arranging a game night, you'll be connecting with like-minded people. You'll be creating opportunities for belonging and laughter, and you'll be making memories. All of these things lead to feelings of happiness and well-being.

If you don't have a favorite game, experiment a bit or visit a local game store to get recommendations, or ask friends for their suggestions. Get your family together and involved with one another more often by ...

Hosting a game night.

#275 Attend a concert

I'm sure many of you have - at least once in your lifetime - been to a concert of some type. There's a wonderful element about music that helps us feel better, no matter the genre. And there are so, so many options regardless of your preference: Country, Rock, Opera, Acapella, Easy Listening or Jazz. Additionally, there may be almost as many different types of venues where you can enjoy the music.

My personal favorite is attending a concert outdoors, preferably at the beach where I can combine the sensations of both the sun, sand, and music all at once. Smaller outdoor venues can be a lot of fun as well and it's there that we often find new bands just getting started on the circuit. Often, outdoor concerts won't have a seating capacity - especially at locations like the beach but you are always vulnerable to the weather.

Indoor venues vary from small and intimate to covered Superdomes. There are venues with front stages, stage-in-the-round, and others with no stage at all. Indoor venues generally do have limited seating and there's a special energy to a 'packed house', especially because special effects generally have more of an impact inside. Of course, weather isn't an issue indoors, but crowds can be.

I'm always a bit surprised when I see bands that I loved as a young adult still pull in packed houses entertaining an entirely new generation of music lovers. Some newer musicians are drawing great audiences also and we're never too old to enjoy good music.

Perhaps you've discovered a new genre that you'd like to see in concert. Don't forget colleges, casinos, and State Fairs when considering concerts - they often book new artists that are gaining momentum.

Look at TicketMaster, VividSeats, or StubHub (rated #1) and see who's going to be in your area - or consider traveling to see a much-loved band and make a weekend of it. A great gift may be tickets that allow you to ...

Attend a concert.

#276 Stop worrying

A few years back, a famous survey illustrated that 40% of the things we worry about never happen! Thirty percent of the things we worry about are from the past and can't be changed; 12% relate to other people and are therefore - none of our business; 10% relate to illness which, may or may not be real. And only the remaining 8%. of the things we worry about are worth the energy spent. ***eight percent***

Worry has been vital to the survival of the human species. It is part of our flight or fight response and for that 8% of the time it acts like a warning system for our physical or emotional safety. For this reason, we can't ignore worry altogether.

One of the first questions I ask a client when we talk about what their worries is "what are the actual 'odds' of it happening?". We discuss the possibility versus the probability. If it's not actually probable... then strive to redirect or let it go. Anything is possible but many times, the things we worry about are literally, not probable.

Based on the survey, 12% of the things we worry about are things that we have absolutely no control over because they are in the hands of another person such as a family member getting home safely. Therefore, it is often necessary to ask ourselves who controls the outcome of the thing we're worried about. If the answer is anyone but us... turn around and walk away from the worry. The key here is to trust that the people in control of the situation, have it in hand (like the pilot of an airplane).

For those things that are within our realm of our control, our worry is often mitigated with a plan. *If* the thing we are worried about happens, it's good to know how we'll handle it. Generally, I recommend a plan B as well... planning for contingencies is a good practice.

Worry is most often about the future and so learning how to stay deeply in the present moment will also mitigate much of the agony we experience when we feel concern. Mindfulness brings our attention to the 'here and now' - breaking the cycle of considering things too far from this point in time.

In the best interest of your own physical and emotional health, take some of these suggestions and learn to...Stop worrying.

#277 Investigate new restaurants

For years, my partner and I had a habit of dining in the same favorite restaurant every week. It got mundane and stale after a while and we knew something had to change so I turned to friends and family to find out what their favorite eatery was and why. I started a list. It's always nice to have a personal recommendation when visiting someplace - especially by someone who knows you and is considerate of your time and budget. Most people are candid if they believe you won't enjoy a certain experience.

Another option is Yelp. It is a great 'recommendation' app for smartphones. Generally, you can access menus and see photographs that have been taken by people who've eaten there. Additionally, you can read 'reviews' and determine if it's a place you want to try. I've found that its necessary to read through a number of reviews in order to get a balanced perspective. Sometimes, people are having a bad day and will leave a solid derogatory review for even a small infraction.

OpenTable is another smartphone app used mostly for reservations; you won't find every restaurant here but those who are will typically leave a table or two specifically for people who request tables through the app. Case in point: on a beautiful spring day in Baltimore, we strolled along the waterfront and decided to have lunch. When we approached the maître d' of the one we were interested in, he told us it would be a 90-minute wait. We knew we didn't want to wait that long, so we found a bench and I checked Open Table to see what was available in our location. That very restaurant had a table for 4 available in 15 minutes. We thoroughly enjoyed our lunch overlooking the Baltimore harbor that day and I spent a few minutes being just a little smug about the work-around.

If you really need inspiration, start a dinner club with a couple of friends or family members. Plan to meet once a month at a different restaurant each time. There's a certain sense of adventure that you'll experience in doing so and even if there's a less-than-great meal now and then - you'll at least have had fun with people you care about.

Be brave, trash the routine, and give your taste buds an adventure by...

Investigating new restaurants.

#278 Go solo

In a world where we talk so much about belonging, I am going to recommend that - at least for some time - you 'go solo'.

Depending on who you're talking to, the term 'go solo' may refer to several things. Some people immediately take it to the far side and assume you're spending some 'intimate' time with yourself. Others wonder if you are going to 'go out on your own' professionally. Still others conjure visions of sitting in a movie theater or a restaurant by yourself. A few may even imagine travel.

No matter the definition, in fact, any of the above can apply... the goal is to find a comfort level with spending time with yourself - and only yourself. It may be uncomfortable for some of you to think of this from the perspective of sexual pleasure. Yet I'd be remiss to omit this suggestion. Indeed, personal pleasure time is very important to a healthy perspective about sex and a satisfactory sex life. If you don't understand how your body experiences pleasure, how are you ever going to introduce another person to it? The key is to explore and experiment in the privacy and safety of your own company so that you can engage more fully when you are with a partner.

In almost every memory I have of attending the movies, I recall seeing at least one person there solo and I've always admired their courage to sit there by themselves. My mother preferred going to the movies by herself because (she said) no one would interrupt her experience by asking questions or talking in the middle of the feature. Another friend prefers to eat lunch alone every day and seeks restaurants that are quiet and less crowded. She asks for a booth where she can 'hide' from the world for that hour and she considers it a reprieve from her stressful job.

If your career is in the trades or professional services and you've considered or made the decision to 'go solo' - bravo to you for taking the initiative of entrepreneurship. It takes considerable courage and commitment to step outside the safety of a group or organization and accept the risk of not knowing where or when your next client will surface. Not everyone can or will be open to existing in that arena but for those that do... the reward is often worth the risk.

I've read blogs and talked to people who have experienced solo travel as "one of the highlights of their lives" and indeed, some prefer it. I stepped out on my first solo travel trip with much trepidation. While I can admit that there were fun moments, for me... the jury is still out. I love adventure and hesitate to submerge myself in unfamiliar situations without a safe harbor close by. It's part of my current development plan and a 'work in progress'.

Learning to spend quality time with yourself is vital to your overall emotional health. It's too demanding on our social systems to provide 100% of the comfort that we need as individuals. Therefore, it's imperative that we learn how to be still with ourselves. No matter the platform, consider including some 'solo time' into your self-care plan. Eventually, you're sure to establish some comfort in your ability to ...

Go solo.

#279 Go ahead and veg

Do you know how to relax? Do you feel guilty or restless when you spend time doing 'nothing'? It may be time for you to learn to let go and experience the pleasure of occasionally 'veg'ing'.

According to Urban Dictionary - to "Veg" means to "relax all day", or to "be in a vegetative state". Most people think of this in terms of 'doing nothing' or 'not accomplishing anything' and I can't help but wonder why most of us are so compelled to constantly 'be accomplishing' something.

The concept is easily considered if we imagine spending a day on the beach with our feet in the sand, a good book in our hand, and our mind fully content listening to the surf and seagulls. For some reason, we give ourselves permission to spend the day on the beach 'vegging' but deny ourselves that relaxation when we are at home.

Some might argue that in contemporary societies, we simply do not rest enough. Many studies have pointed out the perils of sleep deprivation with attention to the fact that it is at epidemic levels in the American society. Sleep then, would be the most beneficial way to obtain rest but so too... is fostering one's ability to 'veg'. This is a time when we are not focused on things linking daily stressor items such as work, money, family, etc. It may be reading a nonsense fiction book, or sitting on the deck birdwatching, or channel surfing - any activity at produces a resting heart rate and allows your mind, body, and soul to be on auto mode.

Vegging helps you recharge. It settles your body and brain from the demanding performance levels one frequently experiences day-to-day. It is a 'plugging in' of sorts - breaking away from energy draining activities to recharge and regroup. Thinking of vegging in this manner may help you dismiss any derogatory feelings about letting those hours slip by unaccomplished.

This is not to say that constant vegging will be good for anyone. Indeed, vegging should be utilized in those times - other than vacation - when it's obvious that your tank is empty or when you feel the stress level about to overflow. Those are the times when it's imperative that you give yourself permission to let go of the 'to-do' list and ...

Go ahead and 'veg'.

#280 Attend a mystery night out

Are you a mystery lover? Do you like to solve problems? Are you seeking a new idea or an alternative for your next 'date night'? While murder mystery 'game night' boxes have been around for decades, the idea has taken on a very different vibe with museums, galleries, restaurants, and others getting in on the fun.

If you want to invite a few people over for a fun night at home, consider a box game - readily available from a variety of places. You'll get everything you need to invite a few friends over and role play a real-life game of Clue. You don't need the box though - you can download a game and all the necessary information to play.

Not into hosting? Want to be a partygoer? Keep an eye out for a Murder Mystery night in your community. Local theaters, tourist train companies, galleries, libraries, and even small townships have hosted murder mystery nights with themes ranging from Casablanca style nights to Old West Gold Rush motifs.

A simple Google search for "Murder Mystery Night in YourTown" will hopefully return a number of options in your community or nearby. Sites like Eventbrite and Yelp also returned local options and Yelp of course, offered some reviews and comments about the events themselves. A warning for those comments: The fun is often determined by the people involved in the experience and as such - will be different for each group.

It's yet another way for couples to enhance time together in a unique way. It's an opportunity for families to disconnect from electronics and do something fun. It's an entertaining way to spend time getting to know new friends or building comradery with business associates or team members.

Do a quick search for opportunities in your area, gather one or more peeps, and ...

Attend a Mystery Night out.

#281 Create a plan

Any good life coach or business development coach will tell you that the secret to success is a plan. We can easily relate to this concept when we understand that many aspects of our life are akin to building a house. Every house that's ever been built began with a vision and then moved into the planning stage with a blueprint.

The blueprint is the base 'plan'. It's a conceptual illustration of how things 'could' work with all systems in place and in the absence of major changes. It's a starting point and a visual from which to work.

In your plan, this means writing things down... make a list - create a binder - build a vision board, etc.

The next step is to lay the foundation. This may be the most important piece as everything else is supported by this base and many of us have witnessed firsthand what happens to a house when there is a deficiency in the foundation.

In your plan, this means education - training - experience, etc.

Few of us have ever built a house single-handedly. Indeed, most of them are built with the cooperation and coordination of people who are there in support of the entire project and they are aware of the 'plan'.

In your plan, this means family - friends - experts, etc.

Sometimes, as we move about the construction, the plan on paper doesn't work the way we thought it would in real life. When something needs to be changed there's a mini plan developed to accommodate the shift. Most often, it's no big deal. Sometimes, it's a major repositioning and we need the support of everyone involved and potentially a bolster to the foundation. Some houses get built with very little deviation from the primary plan. When I did it, there were 22 work order changes; the irony of it is not lost on me.

In your plan, these modifications may be health - relationships - money, etc.

When the foundation is in great shape, the alterations are handled efficiently. When it isn't, you may need to go back to square one and adjust the original plan in detail.

It's really very simple. Life is just one big, personal house that we begin designing in adolescence with a vision of who we are and what we want for ourselves. The biggest mistake that we make is going into adulthood without a blueprint for how it will unfold. Maybe you did but there've been so many 'renovations' along the way that you now need to go through each room to make sure that they meet the conditions set forth with the current revision. It's a process many of us can benefit from every couple of years.

If you never did implement a formal design... it's never too late. Take the time to consider your future and ...

Create a plan.

#282 Stop overthinking

Do you think a thought and then 'run with it'? Do your thoughts ever take on a life of their own? Do you find yourself getting anxious or worried? Do you have a hard time focusing or sleeping? Do thoughts get stuck in your mind and go around and round? These are all symptoms of overthinking.

Overthinking is generally not good for your health. It can cause anxiety, depression, and persistent worry. It promotes obsessive and/or compulsive behaviors. It can strain relationships, work performance, and self-worth. To cope, people try to escape by abusing food, alcohol, or drugs.

The first step in stopping the pattern of overthinking is to notice when you do it. Take another look at the list in the first paragraph and honestly assess your own processes. When does it happen? About what topic(s)? What is your response? How do you (if you do) get them under control? How do they prevent you from living your best life?

Are your thoughts based on facts? Or Fears? Are they happening now? Or at some point in the future? Stay focused on the facts that exist in the here and now. When you are facing facts, it's easier to problem solve. There aren't any solutions to imagined or fantastical problems.

Get busy! There's only so much space in your brain for active thinking. When your thoughts go into busy mode, overrule them with direct action on something else; pulling energy away from the overrunning thoughts. The more involved you are in the distraction, the better.

When we are overthinking, it's not really the thoughts that are problematic, but our feelings and associations we have with them. If we can learn to become observers of the thoughts, their impact is reduced. Meditation is one of the best ways to achieve this. It allows you to detach from the thoughts so that they become nothing more than something moving through your brain.

We all do it from time to time but if your life is negatively impacted by too many thoughts too much of the time, follow these steps to … Stop overthinking.

#283 Take the long road

While this advice may not always be in your best interest, sometimes taking the long road offers a range of opportunities.

Taking the long road home allows you to gather your thoughts and partition work related stressors away from the energy you want to greet your family with.

Taking the long road on vacation allows you to experience the culture and ambiance of the location you are visiting in a vastly different way than a freeway or interstate does.

Taking the [figurative] long road in responding to a hurtful remark will allow you to make sure that your return comments aren't ugly and spiteful.

Taking the [figurative] long road to consider ethical challenges will most often allow you to feel confident that your considerations were well thought out.

Taking the long road may help you bypass the frustration of traffic congestion.

Taking the long road may allow you to explore a conversation that might otherwise get interrupted. Some of the best conversations happen in a car when parties are somewhat captive.

Taking the long road may allow you to contemplate a problem or run through solutions because driving and heading home are such rote activities

Of course, taking the long road may also use more gas, put more miles on your automobile (except when using the figurative sense) and ultimately cost more money. Yet, there are times when it's a clear advantage to...

Take the long road.

#284 Go to the library

In this digital age of Kindle, e-readers and Amazon's ability to deliver hard copy books to us in 48 hours or less, jaunts to the library are far and few between for most of us. Sadly, I must admit that it's my loss - not taking the time to enjoy browsing the rows of hard bound books - running my fingers along the spines and choosing carefully, a new book to read.

There's something whole-hearted about being in a library. The smell, the aroma of paper and glue, of dust and ink. If it was a glass of wine, it may have hints of acidity and grass or vanilla and smoke. The old ones are my favorite as that aged scent is inviting and seems to permeate the walls.

Many libraries have nooks and crannies that allow you to hide or escape with a book. It's one of my favorite places to go if I need to concentrate on a project as I tend to hope that the collective wisdom, represented by the volumes of information there will guide me.

The hushed quiet is reassuring in some way. It's as if we must be still in order to absorb what our eyes are experiencing. The complimentary noises of books opening and closing, of being moved around on the shelves, and of people searching, connects to our brain in a way that may remind it to scour for its own collection of information. It's as if sitting in a library urges us to dig deeper into our own knowledge banks.

There's a bit of history in libraries that has yet to be captured by the world wide web. Certainly, we're not yet at the point where each book has been scanned electronically. There are historical collections of newspapers, magazines, and lessor known copy that exist in libraries - especially the larger ones - offering a historical perspective unavailable in our technology. There's something magical about holding a book published in 1940 and understanding that it's been moved around our culture and literally shared by thousands of people since. Touching it connects you to that history - joining your combined energy and adding your own historical fingerprint.

If we don't make the effort to continue to support these institutions, they will disappear, and the world will lose part of its vitality; an element of its heartbeat. So, the next time you pass by... make the effort and take some time to...Go to the library.

#285 Revisit your childhood home

Many of us go 'home' during the holidays and are reminded of childhood memories and the places they represent. Often, just driving past a movie theater or a diner will elicit fond memories of times past; those places where we giggled over infatuations and had our first dates. The place we caught our first fish and the location of our first kiss; all the 'firsts' of childhood are there to induce one memory after another.

A trip down the memory lane of childhood can be beneficial on many fronts. It reminds us of where we came from. Sometimes, a little humility feels good. It can refresh our memory of a simpler time; allowing us to reflect without all of the complications that have settled upon us since. When we are reminded where we came from, we can make the effort to reconnect to that younger self; to remember our purest beginning.

Sharing the place, it all started is fun. Children are humored by the stories we tell about a time they can only imagine. They enjoy getting to know the person behind mom, dad, aunt, or uncle. Our significant other can garner a better understanding of us if we are open to giving them a tour of our early selves. Moving through our childhood habitat allows them to gain insight about how we came to be who we are.

Knocking on the door of the home you grew up in will introduce you to others who are sharing many of the same kind of memories. People have been known to offer tours of the house in its current state and are frequently quite curious about the history of those who came before them!

Some people don't have great memories of home and may avoid going there. The benefit of closure is considerable if you can visit without reliving the pain or discomfort that may have been a part of your childhood. In these cases, I recommend clients prepare to watch the memories as if they were a movie with an arbitrary actor instead of personalizing the memory. This technique can be very healing, especially if you are with someone safe and supportive as you move through the recollections.

When you go 'home', consider taking a significant other or a dear friend and ... Revisit your childhood home.

314

#286 Switch hands

Want to give your brain a quick boost? Spend a day primarily using your non-dominant hand. Try using it to zip, button, and snap. Soap your body, brush your teeth, and comb your hair with your 'other' hand. Keep going. Try buttering toast and reaching into the fridge opposite from how you usually do it.

This activity is considered exercise for your brain. Scientists tell us that if we are using one side of our body more often than not, we are using only one side of our brain more often than not. Something as simple as using a different hand will help you develop the other side.

In the same way we strive for better physical health, it is imperative that we are attentive to keeping our brain healthy. If we change those little things that we do automatically, it forces us to use brain power. It's literally exercise as the brain attempts to think about how to do something that's not automatic.

If you're right-handed, your right bicep is probably stronger. You are likely right footed as well with more developed right leg muscles. Shifting things into your left hand will activate the left side and balance the muscle development in your body.

Researchers have suggested that we tend to 'lead' based on our dominant hand; meaning that we will lead to the right when we are moving through a store, an amusement park, or generally anywhere we go. Watch what direction people tend to move as they exit an escalator or at the entrance to a concert hall. One of the most helpful tips I read when going to Disney World the first time was to go left as soon as we entered the park because most of us will automatically go right. [More than 70% of the world's population is right-handed.] And, by the way, it worked.

You may be surprised to discover the benefits of exercising your brain by making a commitment to simply...

Switch hands.

#287 Keep a stress diary

I've spoken several times about the deleterious effects of stress and offered numerous tools for its management. However, I've yet to comment about recognizing stress and tracking it as a coping mechanism. A stress diary is the perfect way to do this.

Essentially, it is a record of when you feel stress, what was the triggering event, the intensity of the stress response, and how it manifested. Lastly, identify how you attempted to manage it and whether it helped. By tracking each of these elements, you may discover a pattern that enables you to shift or make a change that eliminates the stress.

When - Is there a time of day, or a week of the month, or a time of year that stress is magnified?

What - What triggered your stress? Was it a person? A task? A thought? A sound? Go deep here… what about that person? What about that task? Exactly what was the thought? Etc.

Intensity - Rate your stress response on a scale between 1 & 10 - 10 being pure panic. Here again, we're seeking to identify those stressors that are manageable and those that need attention or adaptation.

Where - Where does stress appear in your body? Do you perspire? Rapid heart rate? Shallow breathing? Back or shoulder pain? Headache? Do you have a nervous twitch? Do you cry, yell, shut down?

Management - What did you do? Here, we're trying to notice what helps and what doesn't. Often, when we're stressed, we're not paying attention to how we worked it out and yet this is truly helpful information that we can use over. Keep track of the techniques that you used. Did you take a walk? Meditate? Breathe? Journal?

A stress diary can be formal or not so much. It can be a simple notebook, a bullet journal, or an excel spreadsheet depicting the key elements discussed here.

Keep the diary for 30 days during a typical period of your life and then analyze it for patterns. You'll be amazed by what you discover when you…

Keep a stress diary.

#288 Check for vitamin deficiencies

When was the last time you had a physical? And in particular, did it include a full vitamin panel to check for deficiencies? Our bodies have a method for letting us know when we're running low but when we don't know the signs, we aren't able to 'hear' what our body is saying. Some vitamin deficiencies can lead to extreme health problems - others can create chronic difficulties.

Here are the things to pay attention to:

Omega 3's

Fatty acids are essential for our skin. They act as lubricants for our body and when we are low, we are likely to see flaky skin, especially on the scalp. Cracked and peeling skin on the hands and feet are also a fair sign that your body may be low in Omega 3's.

Fixing this problem is primarily accomplished by eating foods containing the vitamins; fish, nuts, and oils up to just over a gram a day for most adults. An average piece of salmon will contain almost a week's worth; throw in a few nuts and a little oil and you'll be all set.

B Vitamins

We need several of the B vitamins; B1 (Thiamine), B6, and B12. Beginning with Thiamine, a deficiency is rare in the United States but people who drink alcohol excessively are susceptible to Wernicke-Korsakoff syndrome and may experience tingling and numbness in their extremities, weight loss, confusion, and weakness to name a few symptoms.

Eating meats, whole grains, and beans as part of a normal diet will generally offer enough of this vitamin

B6.

People with kidney dysfunction, autoimmune disorders, and alcoholics have difficulty absorbing enough Vitamin B6 from their diet. Poultry, fish, and non-citrus fruits will help but so will adding a supplement (do so only with a doctor's recommendation).

B12

As many as 15% of Americans don't absorb enough vitamin B12 - they may consume it, but lots of factors may prevent the absorption. Symptoms include fatigue, weakness, loss of appetite and weight loss, numbness, tingling, depression, poor memory and a few others.

Most multivitamins contain B12 and a doctor can prescribe an additional injection if a deficiency is found.

D

The human body needs more vitamin D as it ages and the food we eat doesn't naturally contain a sufficient supply. As you probably know, the sun is actually the source for most of our vitamin D supply and yet depending on where you live or how much exposure you have to daylight, you may not be getting enough.

Deficiencies in vitamin D causes brittle bones and leaves people susceptible to breaks and fractures. It can, in extreme cases, cause Ricketts.

It is easily remedied with supplements, but you can also get too much so it's imperative to have your levels checked before adding supplements.

These are the major vitamins that affect your mind and body but certainly not the only ones. A blood test will give you more information so the next time you see your physician, be sure to…

Check for vitamin deficiencies.

#289 Find a therapist

I don't mean this suggestion to be self-serving in any manner. I have always touted the benefit of having a confidant; professional or otherwise. The difference between a psychotherapist and a best friend is that the latter most often cannot be as objective.

Objectivity is important because someone needs to call us out on our shit. Not that assertively of course but hold us accountable when we lie to ourselves. They are the ones that have no emotional connection to the outcome of your decisions and therefore, can give you an honest perspective.

Therapists offer insight - a chance to see the forest *and* the trees - so to speak. Sometimes, we are so caught up in our own scenario that we cannot get a full view of the situation at hand. Other times, everything gets tangled and a therapist can help us pull pieces apart so that they can be seen clearly.

One of the benefits of therapy is to discover that you are not alone. Not that the therapist tells you specifics about other people in similar circumstances, but they are often able to share general information they have collected over time. Knowing someone can relate to our struggles has great benefit, especially when they can share how others may have handled a similar situation.

One of the challenges about therapy is finding a therapist who is a good fit for your personality and issues. In many ways, a therapist becomes a kind of friend. Not the kind you have dinner with or invite over for birthdays but the kind that knows you and your vulnerabilities but continues to support and offer advice without judgment. The therapeutic relationship enhances healing opportunities immensely

When I think of the price of therapy, I think about the roof on my house. If it leaked, I wouldn't spare any available expense to fix it lest the problem gets worse and ruins the entire home. I've heard people excited that they bought the newest flat screen television, iPad, or cell phone; booked a cruise, a weekend in New York City, or Disney yet they deny their ability to cover the cost of a few counseling sessions. These choices speak only to the order of priority of mental health and well-being. Many challenges are addressed in a matter of those same costs even if insurance is unavailable.

A lot of clients stay connected with their therapist over long periods of time. Not to say that they are actively working on something all the time, but just like they take a car in for an oil change – they sit down with a therapist once in a while for a 'tune up'.

Nothing is more important than your emotional and physical health - without it, your best life is just out of reach so, just like you make the effort to find a good dentist, a good attorney, and a good accountant, spend some energy and...

Find a therapist.

#290 Hire a physical trainer

Are you a faithful gym goer? Are you completely sure your workout is the one that best fits your body and goals? For a trainer to work with you and establish a set of exercises that will help you reach your goals and efficiently develop your muscles, you will spend anywhere between $40 and $90 an hour. Considering that a trip to the emergency room can run in the thousands, a trainer makes more sense.

Perhaps one of the most beneficial elements of paying for a personal trainer is that he or she holds us accountable for reaching the goals we establish. On those sets where we can't seem to bring ourselves to finish - the trainer is there to encourage us and help see us to the finish line.

When we get used to a routine, it's good for a while but then it can become boring and when something is boring - we're less likely to pursue it. Additionally, a trainer is versed in several different workouts that aim at the same goal and can help us change things up so that our goals are achieved without the workout becoming mundane.

Trainers are experts in knowing how to get those spots on our body that remain resistant to self-motivated reduction. Whether it's belly fat, arms, or the small back rolls that pop up with a few extra pounds - a trainer may have a trick or two that can address those problem areas.

Hiring a trainer is an ultimate form of self-care. Its demonstrating that you are important enough to invest in yourself. It's not only the professional advice, but the dedication to pursue a workout that helps you to reach your physical health goals.

No matter your age, indeed - at every age - an expert directing your workout can provide benefit beyond what has been mentioned. Give yourself a boost and commit to ...

Hiring a personal trainer.

#291 Learn to label emotions

We are born knowing how to emote. We laugh, cry, squirm, babble, etc., in perfect expression of our feelings from the moment we enter the world. At some point, an adult in our life tells us to sit down, shut up, suck it up, pull yourself together, etc.... and we are told not to do that thing which, comes so naturally. Consequently, we learn *not* to express ourselves effectively.

Making it more difficult is the way we learn to string words together to describe things. We may say "I feel like a maid" but 'a maid' isn't a feeling so we really are not expressing feelings with this statement. We may say "I feel like you don't care" and similarly, 'like you don't care' isn't a feeling.

Instead, we can learn to use emotion words and the sentences become clearer ... "I'm really frustrated that I need to pick up after everyone" or "I'm not feeling very loved today". In these examples, what we say is more easily digested by the listener because we are using literal language to express our feelings.

There's more to life than happy, sad, and mad. There's disappointment, frustration, defensive, betrayed, anxious, excited, nervous, and dozens of others. How would your communication change if you were able to say "I'm feeling pretty defensive right now" instead of attacking with defensive and projecting language?

Feelings are neither right nor wrong, they just are. Having said that, they don't necessarily represent the truth. Someone can 'feel' stupid but that doesn't make it true. We can get caught up in the feeling without validating if it is a fact or not. When we feel something that isn't based on facts, it's a clue for what we must work on. The less time we spend there, the better. Life is better when we concentrate on what is real.

When learning to express feelings more effectively, I recommend that you keep a list of emotions (there are thousands to choose from online) handy and begin by describing your day with as many of those as possible. Think about your feelings before you express them to make sure the words you are using describe the sensation. Break the habit of happy, sad, mad and...

Learn to label emotions.

322

#292 Do it again ~ don't give up

Remember the proverb "If at first you don't succeed, try, and try again"? [attributed to William Hickson but thought to originate from Thomas Palmer]

Many of the most successful people in the world attribute their success to perseverance. Indeed, it is simply required to succeed on most levels. Time and again we hear stories of people who applied numerous times, who auditioned over and over, or who replicated experiments nonstop until success was achieved. While we certainly must have limits and set boundaries for our emotional and physical health, as long as there is something to gain - having the grit to continue is typically a good idea.

Is there a time to give up? Most experts agree that it is a healthy decision to redirect when we no longer have advantage in the endeavor. Obviously, if continuing would generate harm from either a physical or an emotional perspective - it's O.K. to refocus in a different direction. That's the whole point behind a 'pivot'.

How important is this thing that you are trying to accomplish? Are you working to discover the next cancer treatment? Are you attempting to learn a new language? Getting into physical shape? Or learn a new crochet stitch? These are examples of things that may certainly be within your reach if you keep trying. Spend your perseverance energy on those things that serve your interests. Sometimes, the cost of continuing far exceeds the potential benefit. Focus on the things that you value and let go of those that you do not.

When you get frustrated or tired in your pursuit of a goal it's great to have a motivation kit. It's not as neat and tidy as it sounds because we often need different motivations for different tasks. When you're going to the gym and want to give up - that's when you hire a trainer or get a gym buddy. Create a support system that is also invested in your success - mom, dad, your best friend or your boss. They are the people who will often blindly encourage you in the direction of your dreams. Create a vision board to help keep you steered in the direction you want to go. Always define your priorities and make a list - keep it in front of you.

Whatever it is - go for it and find the strength to …

Do it again ~ don't give up.

#293 Splurge on nice sheets

Considering that we spend somewhere around one-third of our life in bed, it's not presumptuous to think that it needs to be a place of comfort. An element of a great bed is the sheets that we lie between. This is one of those treats we never knew we needed until we've had the experience. Once you have the pleasure of sleeping on nice sheets, it will be a goal.

What determines how nice a sheet is? The experts say that the very first thing to look for is the fiber of the sheet - what is it made of? The higher quality of fiber, the more comfortable the sheet. 100% cotton sheets may wrinkle and be more expensive, but they will absorb moisture better than anything else. If you perspire a lot while you sleep, cotton sheets are a must. They're easier to keep clean as well because polyester blends tend to hold dirt and stain. For the most comfortable feel, choose a long fiber sheet generally labeled 'Pima' or 'Egyptian long staple'.

After the material, you want a high thread count. [note that lower thread count 100% cotton is better than higher thread count poly blend] In my experience, typical sheets are in the 200 range (the number of vertical and horizontal threads per square inch). Thread counts can go as high as 1000 but sheets in the 500 - 800 range are really nice.

The method of weaving those threads is also determines how the sheets feel. The most common is Percale, equally woven between horizontal and vertical threads. Percale sheets are known to be crisp and breathe more easily so they're cooler in summer months. Sateen sheets are woven tighter and are therefore much thicker. They will keep you warmer in the winter months and are generally thought to be softer.

January is known as the month when linens are deeply discounted. If sheets aren't the priority right now, you're likely to find great prices at online retailers like Overstock.com throughout the year. It's been my go-to site for linens for years. Like the strategy many of us use for electronics - buy the most exquisite you can afford. Treat yourself to the thing you never knew you wanted...

Splurge on nice sheets.

#294 Send a card of connection

Several years ago, I befriended - via an interesting set of circumstances - a resident of a nursing home who had no known living relatives. She is a sweet old lady in her nineties with a very simple life who dedicated her career to pediatric nursing. Today, her memory isn't very sharp and she sometimes receives cards from people who have passed through the nursing home; prior roommate family members, employees who came to love her, or strangers who've heard of her story through the Facebook page I made for her years ago. It is the highlight of her day. She calls me with sheer delight to ask me who the person is that sent the card. Even if I don't know, she pins it to her bulletin board and adds the address to her little book so she can send a Christmas card the following year.

This tiny little act of kindness impacts the entire day in the most positive way by connecting her to the outside world.

There are thousands of people, maybe tens of thousands, like my friend who would love to get something in the mail even if they don't know you. Some of our relatives, our neighbors, and our friends may also fall into this category; people who could use a little pick-me-up. Churches and nursing homes know of dozens of people who could benefit from receiving a little sunshine in the form of a card. If you don't want to be identified, it could be an anonymous message: *"Here's hoping your day is filled with light. ~ a caring stranger"*.

This idea isn't so creepy or strange. It is in line with the program that encourages us to send Christmas cards to soldiers or care packages to those serving overseas. This act of kindness sends the message that *"the world hasn't forgotten about you"*, *"someone cares that you're still here'*, and/or *"you still matter"*. Who can't benefit from that kind of reminder?" The effort is small, the cost is minimal, yet the reward is great when you...

Send a card of connection.

#295 Take a cooking class

Are you looking for a last-minute gift for that family gathering or birthday? Are you wondering how to change up your date nights? This suggestion may be just the thing that sparks a new passion or a shared interest.

Cooking classes are for cooks of any ability. They are not to be confused with culinary schools as they typically range from just a couple of hours, a full day, or at most - a week. They are generally designed to introduce you to a new skill, new ingredients, and new methods.

It's likely that there's a local opportunity for you to take a cooking class if you live in or near a major metropolitan area. A quick google search for a location in Baltimore returned several options. The Schola Cooking school offers technique classes ranging from butter making to bread baking and from sushi to fresh pasta. You can take classes that focus on Cuban cuisine or treats from the sea.

If you don't live near a major city and/or you want the options of a specific location, consider a destination getaway with the intent to specifically take a cooking class. What a great thing to do for a girl's weekend, a bachelorette celebration, or a mother/daughter day out. It could be an anniversary event that you do together and carry the skills home as a shared interest.

Do you love Italian or French food and want to learn local favorites or from an infamous internationally acclaimed chef? A trip abroad for the purpose of learning cuisine from that region is a great reason to plan a trip. Like schools in the states, international classes are designed for all levels of knowledge and can accommodate the most uneducated beginners.

Even if all you really want to do is eat well, consider grabbing a friend and ...

Take a cooking class.

#296 Change the pillows on your sofa

One of the quickest and least expensive ways to freshen up the look of a room is to change out the pillows on your sofa. After a few years, they get lumpy or flatten and no longer offer the comfort for which they were intended. Even if the pillows are in good shape, the room may benefit from a change of scenery and pillow covers can easily handle that objective.

A standard couch pillow is 18 inches square and are frequently available as large as 24 inches. The larger and 'comfier' the sofa, the larger the pillow can be and still have style. Go with a variety of sizes for the best look and make sure it's an odd number of pillows overall.

If you want a pillow designed for lounging comfort, a feather pillow will fit the bill best. Other fillers may hold shape better, but they are much stiffer and not necessarily the best choice for a sofa that is used for snuggling and relaxing.

For the ultimate design experience, consider using pillows that offer variety in texture, color, and pattern. Of course, you'll want to use colors that contrast your sofa. If your sofa is a solid color, you can use a combination of complementary patterns and colors. If your sofa has a pattern, choose colors from the pattern for pillows of different shapes. It's a great time to consider texture; chenille's, leather, and fringes offer a variety of textures to add contrast and interest to your design. Make sure that each of the seating options in the room has a complimentary pillow. Chairs are great options for oblong shaped pillows that can act as lumbar support. Adorning chairs with pillows also allows for a more complete and pleasing addition for the entire room.

Pillows are another one of those things that can be purchased during January's white sales and great options can be found at discount retailers such as TJMaxx or Marshalls in addition to online sites such as Overstock.com. A fresh look feels good and may offer a sense of newness or freshness for you. If you can catch a sale, it shouldn't take much more than $100 to ...

Change the pillows on your sofa.

#297 Make a collage

I typically end up with quite the collection of Christmas cards - some of which are quite beautiful. Normally, I cut them up to make gift tags but either I am getting a lot of cards lately or I am giving less gifts because they are starting to pile up.

It makes me think of a craft project that I had my girls do one year. After my grandparents passed away. I gave the girls a pile of condolence cards and asked them each to make a collage. They turned out to be a beautiful collection and ultimately, a bit of a tribute to the pair we had lost.

A collage is cleaner and less complicated than a scrapbook as it is usually just one page or piece - as big or as small as you choose. It can be neatly organized into squares, rectangles, or circles or it can be haphazard and random. It can be a kind of word cloud - cut outs of sentiments or words grouped together in a way that conveys meaning.

A collage can be made from most anything or a combination of several things. I've seen beautiful picture collages that have included brooches and hatpins as well as simpler designs using only white paper with black text in a variety of fonts and sizes. It can be decoupaged, glued, or epoxied. It can be under or on top of glass; in a frame or not.

Along the lines of memory boxes; those deep frames that contain a collection of mementos from a specific year or occasion, a collage makes a wonderful gift. It can be comprised of all the little yellow sticky notes that helped you reach a goal. Or, perhaps it is a collection of the poetry that your father wrote your mother while they were dating - a phenomenal gift for a significant wedding anniversary or commemorating a life well lived.

Yes, a collage with take a little time and perhaps a lot of thought as you move through the memories and decide what goes where... remember there are no rules and creativity is not that important. It's more about composing something meaningful in the way that you give it value. Other opinions are unimportant.

As you move through your year cleaning out drawers, purses, and pockets - consider items that are memorable and put them in a jar for that day when you can finally sit down and... Make a collage.

#298 Digitize your old photos

This item has been on my to-do list forever. Every time I think of doing it, I find something else that has a much higher priority; often watching reruns of Game of Thrones. It seems that anything would be better than attempting the gargantuan job of digitizing my collection of photographs. The fact that I have a huge collection certainly dates me as anyone in their twenties or younger barely remembers the challenge of buying film, taking a photo, and then remembering to drop it off to be developed. For those of you still thinking about the money you spent to print all those film shots, here are the reasons you'll want to engage this tip and ideas of how to go about it.

Keeping all those photographs takes up space and forces you to be protective of them because paper prints are easily damaged. If you eventually get them out of shoe boxes and into albums, the amount of space they require quadruples. In reality, only a fraction of the photos that we have are keepers. Many of them are random scene shots from a location we visited a decade ago and/or of people we barely knew. As you go through them, if you can't remember who is in the photo or where it was, discard it.

The best part of having the photos is the ability to share the memory years later. My children loved sitting down and looking at photos of me growing up and they like to reminisce about their own childhood now. A paper photo is difficult to share however, unless you are sitting side by side. Digitizing them allows you each to have a copy with ease and sharing is accomplished with a couple of digital clicks.

Perhaps this is the very best part about digitizing your photo library, it's available to you at any time and with very little effort. Whether you opt to store them on a flash drive, a hard drive, or the cloud - digital photos are only a swipe or click away. While there are varying opinions about cloud storage, I use Google photos and absolutely love it. I know I can't lose it, it's available on my phone at all times and it does some pretty cool things like grouping similar faces together so that I can access only photos of the person I want to see.

Now here's the hard part. Getting all those paper photos into digital format... There are several options. If you have the time, it's probably better to do it yourself. That way you can 'clean out' the ones you don't want and/or send along paper copies to those who may love them the most. You can do it with a scanner designed exclusively for photos (the easiest way), with a regular scanner [the one incorporated with your printer] or you can use a smartphone app. All of these methods will take some time and dedication.

Or... you can pay someone else to do it. A service like GoPhoto.com or ScanCafe.com will do it for you if you send them your photos/slides/negatives and there are local brick and mortar services in most areas as well. Some allow you to bring whole photo albums in and will do the tedious work for you!

No matter the direction you opt to take, the benefit will be great as you realize the joy of being able to stroke the keyboard a couple of times or swipe a couple directions on your phone and access all of your life memories because you made the effort to ...

Digitize your photos.

#299 Clean out your kitchen cabinets

Have some spare time? Consider taking a good look through your kitchen cabinets for all of those things that you may not have used in the last year. Unlike cleaning the pantry, this entails sorting through your plastic storage containers, matching lids with bowls; cleaning out the junk drawers that have accumulated more than the pens, paper clips, and batteries you want there; and tossing anything at all that has begun to rust.

Whenever I do a lot of cooking or have a big family gathering, my kitchen is a mess. Mostly because there are a number of different helpers putting away dishes. I'm usually lucky if I can find the most basic items. Everyone has a way that they like their kitchen staffed and it feels good to reorganize your cooking tools so that they are in the places that make sense to you. It's also a good time to reassess if things work where they are. Do you need the Vitamix on the counter day after day or do you use your mixer more? Do you like the toaster out or would you like a cleaner line going forward?

Cleaning the cupboards means taking stock of your pots and pans. How worn are your cookie sheets? Do your muffin pans have rust spots? Are your cake pans warped? How scratched is that frying pan that gets used every day? Even if you aren't in a position to replace what's tired, you can make a list so that you're aware the next time you stop in at TJMAXX or you see a great sale (May is a good time to purchase cookware).

Several years ago (ten maybe?) on Black Friday, I purchased two boxes of white dinnerware that was deeply discounted. In all, it was service for 16 - which, I've never needed to use. I put 8 place settings in the cabinet and then each year as I do inventory for chips and cracks, I dip into the box of extras. White was universal and has been a staple in my kitchen, no matter the changing decor. When I clean out the cabinets, I check for cracks and discoloration and then replace damaged or missing items to bring my stocked selection back up to a serving for eight.

The same goes for my silverware. Each year it seems that I still have all the knives and tablespoons but for some reason, the forks and spoons are always down one or two. In my younger days, I had a haphazard collection of whatever patterns my parents were discarding and a few Goodwill additions. When I could, I picked a pattern and waited for it to go on sale - then I bought two. I use the same strategy as I have for my dinnerware.

One look at the cupboard containing glasses and cups demonstrates how eclectic I really am. I've attempted to fix this over the last couple of years, finding mugs that I like and getting several; updating the glassware so that there is more than one of any one kind, and ditching all the kiddie plastic cups that were collected from restaurants.

The wine glass and to-go cupboard are the same... somehow, I adopted all the containers my children made at birthday parties and graduations over the years and there are more than a couple depicting sorority letters. The fact that they are still there indicates my reluctance to purge that cabinet, but time is running short!

It's harder to think about than it is to do, I promise! Find a little time in your schedule and ...

Clean out your kitchen cabinets!

#300 Help a friend

I imagine many of you do this without encouragement and yet in our very busy lives, we either fail to notice when a friend needs help and/or we don't offer for fear of offending their autonomy. For some, a fear of stepping into another's business creates hesitation in offering assistance.

Of course, helping out is common when someone is sick, having a baby, or moving. We extend a helping hand eagerly. This suggesting is designed not for those times, but for the others that are not as obvious.

When you discover someone is spending their weekend painting the living room or weeding their gardens, a dinner would be very helpful. After all, who wants to spend all day working up a sweat outdoors and then go inside to pull together a meal? Childcare or lending a hand may also be welcomed help. Do you have supplies that may make the job easier? An offer to come with the proper tools could prove to be invaluable. One of my dearest friends offers to come by and share my cleaning chores just to be helpful even though I like to think she's just there for the company!

Before deciding what you think your friend may need, make the effort to know what activity would be helpful. Some ideas of 'help' hinder without intent, sometimes, making a task even more difficult. What may seem as if it would make things easier for you, may not seem so by your friend. Perhaps the easiest way to do this is to ask, "How can I help?", "I love to [weed] - can I help?", or "Let me help you".

This kind of help really goes beyond just 'doing a good deed' or a 'random act of kindness' as it is less impulsive and more intentional. It's a way of 'being' with a friend while giving the most important gift. It's never too late or a bad time to make the effort to be more aware of when our friends can use a helping hand and commit a piece of ourselves to…

Help a friend.

#301 Ride a horse

I enjoy watching dramatic television where the only method of transportation is horseback. It reminds me of the couple of times my grandfather pulled me up onto his saddle and pranced me around his farm and also of a single trip down a Caribbean beach later in early adulthood. Both times, I recall feeling the horse beneath me and being amazed at the sense of power there.

Horseback riding is good for you. Sitting on a horse, whether you know 'how' to ride or not, will challenge you physically. First, you'll experience body awareness as you need to sit on the horse in a specific way in order stay balanced. As you do so, it's likely you'll use muscles that aren't used to being used - also, good for you (and those muscles). There's an element of coordination required of riders that is good for your body and posture.

Additionally, the mental aspect of riding is quite beneficial. If you are a recreational rider that only occasionally takes a trail ride - at the very least, you are outdoors. Indeed, you are most likely in a beautiful location where there are endless opportunities for appreciation and gratitude.

If riding is a full-blown hobby for you, the additional benefit is the connection and ultimately the relationship you have with your horse. Very different from that of a house pet, the energy shared with a horse takes trust to a whole new level when you are the rider. Often, that horse is five to ten times your size. Even though you are communicating through body movement and reign management, that horse can still do darn well what it wants. When you work together, the symbiotic energy of the relationship is evident and can be quite lovely.

Obviously, we don't all have the ability to step out and hop on a horse after we finish our morning coffee. However, the next time you are on vacation and have the chance to take an excursion that involves a horseback ride along the beach, through the forest, or around the foothills, I hope you have the courage to...

Ride a Horse

#302 Use your voice

The phrase 'use your voice' is interpreted differently across gender, culture, and age. For the purpose of this writing, it is specifically referring to the effort of speaking the words that run through your mind and heart. You may wonder why this isn't universally automatic. Certainly, some people speak with consideration and yet, so many do not.

As quickly as we learn to speak, we realize that there are things not to be spoken. It's not polite to verbally address someone's size or age; to ask about their income or sexual interests; or to openly condemn or criticize. We've learned how to be politically correct and how to keep the peace. All of this, however, comes at the price of forgetting how to 'use our voice'.

When we discover or realize that by speaking our mind or sharing our heart - we may experience negative consequences, we tend to adopt coping mechanisms to make communication easier. In many cases, it stimulates the reflex of shutting down and silencing those thoughts and feelings that might otherwise be shared. We may have grown up with a parent who wasn't open to other opinions or lived with a spouse who lived within rigid parameters. We might live in a strict culture.

There may also be internal factors that keep us from vocalizing our thoughts; 'will people still love me?', 'will I sound stupid?', 'will anyone pay attention?'. Sometimes, it is the inner voice that controls our courage to vocalize.

The first step in learning to use your voice is listening carefully to your thoughts and deciphering what you want to say. Clear out the clutter and get to the heart of the matter. Once you do that, make sure to deliver the message in a clear and constructive manner so that it can be heard. Learn how to avoid blaming language, use "I" statements, and offer solutions. Learn to have confidence in your thoughts, knowledge, and presence.

Using your voice doesn't mean that you automatically say everything that comes to your mind without thought and intention. Making sure to speak with clear intention is the most important element. When confronting a problem, choosing each word is often the key to a successful outcome. And right behind that is the requirement to speak everything in kindness. Confrontation doesn't have to be ugly to be effective.

If you find this is an area of your life that could use more resolve, consider a resolution to more effectively...

Use your voice.

"There is no path to happiness: happiness is the path" — Gautama Buddha

#303 Keep it simple

I'm sure many of you are familiar with the KISS principle [Keep It Simple, Stupid]. It was first used by the US Navy in 1960 as a slogan for design considerations. Since then, it's been a staple concept in business theory by driving home the point of simplifying. Here, I am recommending that we remember to use this principle at home and in our own lives.

For our purposes, we'll define 'simple' as uncomplicated and easy and since I don't generally use the word 'stupid' - I'll say that this post is really about uncomplicating and simplifying your life.

It's frequently surprising to me that we tend to complicate our communication by 'beating around the bush' and 'hinting'. We use passive aggressive speech and get wrapped up in defensive postures. How amazing would it be if we simply said what we mean (compassionately, of course)?

Here are a couple of examples:

V1: It would be nice if you thought about asking me on a real date some of the time, like taking me to the movies.

V2: I'd like to see a movie on Saturday, would you like to go with me?

Or

V1: Do you think you can put your phone down long enough to pay attention to me?

V2: I feel pretty lonely when the phone gets most of your attention.

In both cases, V2 is a more simple, clear, and distinct than V1 and also less provoking. When we keep things simple, it's often much easier to be understood.

Many of us tend to think that more is better but 'more' only tends to complicate things. I've heard dozens if not hundreds of times *"Life was simpler before we had money"* or *"The only thing that came with this big house is bigger problems"* and *"I have too many responsibilities"*. In each case, having more only served to increase the complexity of a situation. Of course, having [more than enough] money may sound good when your pockets are light - it frequently comes at an emotional cost.

The concept of 'keep it simple' is perhaps best thought of in this arena as we so often tend to reinvent things that don't need reinvented. Here are a couple of examples:

Borrow a tool instead of buying a new one you may only use once

Read the directions before you attempt to assemble something
Ask for direction
Ask for help
Stop trying to please everyone
Eliminate the need to be perfect

These six examples are areas that often get over complicated and I imagine we all have a story that starts with "If only I had.... [asked for directions]". If you can relate at all to this post, it's a sign that you may need to sit back and consider how you might reevaluate life and work to ...

Keep it simple.

#304 Start a collection

This suggestion may seem counterintuitive or even contradictory to the last suggestion 'Keep It Simple'. It appears that having a collection of something promotes happiness for some people and it doesn't seem to matter 'what' kind of items are collected.

From Coca Cola paraphernalia to cars, and beanie babies to rare tins, a collection is generally something that has emotional rather than monetary value to the collector. Perhaps it's representative of a hobby (cars), a fond memory (beanie babies) or time spent with a loved one (Coca Cola). It may also be something that stimulates our winning reflex - the thrill of the hunt (finding rare tins). Still others may be inclined to collect based solely on the social aspect, a shared interest either with a friend or a larger group (Boy Scout or Military items).

A collection can meet many of our psychological needs. It can be comforting and relieve anxiety. It can help us feel a sense of belonging. It can induce fond memories. Moreover, it may function as a hobby which, is important from the perspective of broadening our interests and offering distraction from daily stressors. A collection can be a statement of who we are; introducing us to the world in a non-verbal manner.

Collecting things with intent and purpose is generally a healthy activity. It becomes unhealthy when either of those elements disappears. When we accumulate things out of a fear of letting go or a fear of not having enough, we may be approaching or experiencing unhealthy behavior. Hoarding is a good example of what people may describe as a collection but without intent or purpose. Also, potentially dysfunctional is when we become 'too' attached to the 'things' that we've collected; if/when we identify through the material elements. These are the 'dark side' conditions of collecting but are much more often the exception rather than the norm.

In most cases, having a collection of something meaningful is a rational, healthy, and potentially helpful past time. What would you collect if you were to …

Start a Collection

#305 Build a sandcastle

Building a sandcastle may is an activity that often epitomizes childhood. It uses brain energy and as children, we don't seem to care how many crooks and crevices get filled with sand.

It teaches cooperation. Most of us don't build sandcastles alone. When we enlist the help of others, we are automatically thrown into the task of cooperation. It's a great way for children to learn how to work together and to delegate. It's an opportunity for a group of people to see how individual efforts contribute to a bigger project and outcome.

It may be obvious that building a sandcastle employs a certain level of creativity. Most of us have not studied castle structure or architecture. We are building based on memory from books and television; maybe even solely from our imagination. We can design anything that we fancy and so it's a great outlet for creativity.

It's a time when dimension, volume, and depth become important to the overall task. It forces us incorporate vision and adjust for scale - at least a little. Our brains will naturally attempt to make modifications when an element is too distorted and so it is good practice for spatial awareness.

Working in the sand engages your brain in a couple of other interesting ways. Our senses are often intrigued with the juxtaposition of water and sand and even more so when they are combined to create an entirely different texture. It's a great time to be intentional and savor the experience. Additionally, there's a certain level of motor skill involved; both gross and fine. Shoveling sand to build a mound and then carving the sand for detail uses different muscles as well as different areas of your brain.

I've outlined why building sandcastles is good for your brain and dexterity. It's also a fantastic family experience and it doesn't have to be a summer beach day in order to enjoy it. A sandbox in the backyard or at the park can be accessed at any time. If you can get past the idea of sand covered clothing (it is easier to wash off with a dip in the ocean) ~ it's a wonderful treat for the entire family.

Treat yourself to a free play day by getting outside in the fresh air and ...

Build a sandcastle.

#306 Repot your plants

This is often a spring activity but for houseplants, why wait? Especially if they are dropping leaves, not flowering, or quickly drying out - potential signs of a root bound plant. Some people think that as long as plants get enough water and a little sun - that's all there is to it. Not so!

Over time, sun and water allow the plant to grow, developing a nice root system as it does. Those roots can take over the entire pot as it absorbs nutrients from the soil. You may notice roots poking through the bottom of the pot or starting to lift at be base of the plant. Both are clear indications that the plant is desperate for a bigger home.

It turns out that there is a right and wrong way to re-pot a plant and the internet is full of videos and articles that explain the best method for the type of plant that you are working with. In some cases, you can literally saw the root ball in half and make two out of one.

For others, transitioning the plant into more comfortable digs means that you need to loosen the soil around the roots as it often gets compacted. Think about how good it would feel to stretch out in your bed after being cramped on a long economy flight and you'll be able to empathize. Fresh soil is to a plant what nice clean sheets are to a tired traveler. Once your plants have taken up residence in their new home, they'll need a little extra tender loving care until the root system takes hold in its new environment.

Bound roots aren't the only reason you may need to repot your plants. The leaves tell a story too, about the soil conditions and potential problems that may require a fresh mix. TheSill.com is a great resource for plant lovers and problem solving. It's really a one-stop shop for house plant care.

Live plants add good energy to your living environment and help to keep the air fresh. A little love goes a long way so take care to show them some and ...

Repot your plants.

#307 Birdwatch

Early one summer I found myself sitting on the deck in my backyard enjoying the early morning with a cup of coffee. I noticed something yellow fluttering just outside my direct line of vision and ultimately realized that a pair of yellow finches had taken residence in the rear corner of my yard. It didn't take long before I was mesmerized watching them move through their morning routine.

The contrast of the bright yellow against the summer green foliage was striking and I had to try and capture it. My phone wasn't cutting it, so I grabbed my more elaborate Nikon and added the telephoto lens. It became a sort of binoculars and I found myself zeroing in on those finches - enthralled with their movements.

I was birdwatching.

And I'm not a birdwatcher.

That single experience and the deep pleasure that I felt convinced me that there is joy in birdwatching - something I never thought I'd admit. I understood that morning, what people loved about the sport - or hobby - of watching these creatures move about their environment.

I took to having my coffee on the deck more frequently and noticed a pair of woodpeckers. I had heard them of course but had never bothered to get out there and see for myself - their pecking. I saw bluebirds and robins. My curiosity increased and I found myself on Google to try and identify the female birds too as they aren't as colorful, and I wasn't sure which was which.

I was really birdwatching - and I was loving it.

There was an unexpected pleasure in the activity even though it was so solitary and quiet - perhaps that was it. I was a voyeur into the lives of those creatures, and they didn't care at all. I found myself wondering about their habits even though animal behavior was the least of my interests when I was pursuing my psychology degree. I wondered about the casual and carefree sensation of being able to fly and move to the top of trees. I got it. There's really no way to explain the feelings or the benefits. I accidentally learned why people pull out their binoculars and I highly recommend that you make the time to …

Birdwatch.

#308 Visit a Zoo

I was able to walk through the Central Park Zoo on a warm spring day one year and really loved being there. Prior to that, the last Zoo I had visited was when my kids were young and we had an annual pass to the Philadelphia Zoo which, after falling in love with the San Diego Zoo... was a disappointment. We bought the annual passes because I am a big believer in educating children about animals, especially those that aren't house pets.

Zoos have struggled in recent years. There has been a lot of publicity about the mistreatment of animals, poor conditions, and lack of funding for several zoos across the country. It's thought to be the leading reason that zoo attendance is down overall. Certainly, it's difficult to support an endeavor that wasn't meeting minimum standards. The downside is that we're not there to support the animals nor are we introducing a younger generation to the benefits of saving endangered species.

When a zoo is managed and funded efficiently, it offers a plethora of benefits both to the animals there and to the surrounding society.

Zoos connect animals to people in a way that is no longer viable in most urban cultures. We simply don't get the opportunity to see Buffalo, Elk, or Giraffes running across our sight line. Indeed, we barely see turtles and fox unless you live close to farms and water. Visiting a zoo offers you an opportunity to experience this life form no matter your environment.

Zoos fight against wildlife extinction. They are staffed by professionals committed to the survival and propagation of species. They often collaborate with one another to solve urbanization issues that prevent the animals from organically sustaining their population.

Zoos educate the public and seek to attract benefactors that are committed to helping and sponsoring continued advocacy. They inspire children, teach differences, and motivate respect for animals in general.

Of course, spending time at a zoo is a great family activity. There are usually wonderful programs to take advantage of and it's just nice to stroll through the property to see something new and different than before. Being in a zoo can be a 'getting back to nature' in an odd sort of way. Yet it can challenge your senses as there's always a little dichotomy to this as you walk from one kind of habitat to another.

Going alone may offer a great opportunity for some great 'me time'... away from civilization but inside the energy field of living beings. It can provide a chance to sit back and savor the simplicity of a lions walk across the stone or to observe the complicated maneuvers of barn swallows as they nest in the rafters of an Avian center.

After the horrific zoo experiences identified in the past, I believe we've come to a better place and the zoos of America are a thoughtful, instructional, and compassionate playground for animals that people get to enjoy. If you haven't been in a while, go ahead and treat yourself - if not your entire family and ...

Visit a Zoo

#309 Be introspective

Perhaps the single most important aspect of personal growth and development - the cornerstone of authentic happiness - is the ability to be introspective. The willingness to observe one's own emotional and mental processes demonstrates courage in many cases... sometimes, there's a lot going on in that brain.

When making the effort to look within, it's important to be curious - not judgmental - about the five W's... Who? What? When? Where? And Why? It goes like this:

Who is triggering me?

What was the behavior?

When did it happen?

Where were we?

Why is it a trigger?

Or

Who are the people of my tribe?

What do I like the most about them?

When do I feel the most supported?

Where do I feel it [in my body]?

Why is it important to me?

You may not ask the same questions about each and every situation. Sometimes, you also want to ask How? How much control do I truly have?

Introspection develops self-awareness. It's an attribute necessary for growth and development in both your behavior and your spirit. As we ask questions and seek awareness, it's important to be an observer, not a judge. If you discover something that you don't like, ask more questions about how you might change it and take action.

If you get stuck, ask for professional assistance. Sometimes an objective fresh perspective is all that is standing in the way of discovery.

If you're looking for more joy, for better relationships, and for increased self-awareness, start with the effort to ...

Be introspective.

#310 Host a PJ party

One of the best parts of a girl's weekend getaway is the opportunity to slip into PJ's, grab a glass of wine, and giggle with our besties until we can't keep our eyes open any longer. Well, you don't have to 'getaway' for that to happen! Host a PJ party at home.

I don't know many kids who grow up without the experience of looking forward to the weekends for opportunities to invite friends over for the night. Girls may do this more often than boys, but the allure is always the experience of spending as much time with your friends as you can. We may reach the pinnacle of this in college as couches and floor space are dominated by friends who can't or shouldn't be driving home. Once we step into adulting, our friends' sleepovers give way to sleepovers of a different nature.

One of the most elementary benefits of this kind of comradery is the sense of belonging that it instills. Strong feelings of belonging are helpful to us in many ways. When we feel as though we 'belong' to a group, our self-esteem is higher; our sense of trust is stronger; our immune systems work better; we sleep more effectively; and the benefits continue...

When we spend quality - stress free - time with our friends, it strengthens our bond; our sense of belonging. Overnight visits are a wonderful way to make this happen.

Hosting one, or a group of friends and taking the time to truly interact with them in a carefree manner is a great way to practice self-care. It's gathering your tribe; lifting yourself up; and surrounding yourself in love. It's a wonderful healing exercise, even if you aren't actively thinking about 'healing'.

Friendship is to emotional stress what the ocean is to mosquito bites - an organic healer.

If you need a friendship boost or if you are aware of a friend that does - I highly recommend getting back to basics, employing some self-care and...

Host a PJ party!

#311 Eat dessert first

I think the concept of eating dessert first is centered on knowing how to treat yourself. My grandmother understood the concept of self-care and while I'm not sure everyone in her world saw it as such, she didn't hesitate to meet her own needs. She was a strong woman who understood what was good for her and what wasn't.

For her, eating dessert first wasn't about indulging in sugary treats versus nutrition, or giving in to fanciful whims of confectionary concoction on a regular basis...

It was predominantly a consideration of understanding balance; that sometimes, as a treat, you could set aside the rules and do what you want instead of what you 'should' (with consideration, of course).

I used this strategy occasionally with my children and offered them an "upside down dinner" - starting with dessert, moving to an entree, and then offering a salad to end the meal but of course, no one ever opted in for the salad selection!

Today, as I move through the buffet line at lunch, I am going directly to the dessert section and select the yummiest option as my first course justifying it as the pursuit of self-care! I strongly recommend - for the sake of life balance...

Eat dessert first.

#312 Check your auto pays

For many of us, the days of sitting down and writing out a check for each monthly bill that comes due, are gone. Electronic banking has allowed us to set up scheduled payments for almost everything that needs to be paid. We can 'auto pay' our mortgages, Venmo our rent, and establish an automatic payment plan to pay down the balances of our credit cards. Most of us do a fair job at keeping those things in check.

What I've found harder is to keep track of is those little $4.99 and $9.99 charges that we agreed to when we wanted something but then realized we would never use it. I've heard stories of $10 gym memberships that people paid for years because it was an automatic charge on their credit card, and they didn't pay close enough attention to the debit each month.

Another way we end up with those pesky payments are from all the times we go online and sign up for a 30-day free trial - only to have to agree to subscribe to something in order to get it. Of course, if you cancel your subscription in the first 30 days - the time you used it was free. I think they count on thousands of people forgetting to log back in and cancel something they really only wanted to use for free.

The trick here is to have a discerning eye when it comes to your bank account and credit card statements. I've been lackadaisical too, especially since most of my accounts are now "paperless". I'm less apt to open the account statement and give the activity a good hard look, especially if the email gets opened on my phone first.

If each of us have a deduction of $5 that really isn't getting spent for the use of something... someone, somewhere - is collecting a pretty penny!

Make it a goal as you prepare for your tax return this year to sit down and give your financial statements a once over... looking especially for those things that you're paying for - but not using. I suspect you'll save a few bucks just because you took the time to...

Check Your Auto Pays

#313 Go to open houses

One of the most enticing reasons to attend open houses if you're not house hunting, is to get real time and real people decorating tips. Even when you see a couple of homes in a 'cookie cutter' community where the floorplans are all identical - you are exposed to different configurations and design elements that give entirely different looks to the homes. Model homes are great for professional flavor. In most cases they have had the personal touch of an interior decorator and offer a well thought out idea of what your home could look like.

Going to open houses allows you to see how other people manage storage quandaries. It offers real world visions of a room when three kids and a dog take up space with their belongings. Yes, these days many open houses are staged, and a good real estate agent will have you 'de-personalize' the home a bit but, your experience will most likely be more 'real' than a visit to a model home.

If you are keeping your visits to homes in your general socioeconomic bracket, you may fall in love with a place and find out that it's entirely affordable. I've heard from real estate agents that a fair number of people who visit open houses aren't in the mindset to move but there to satisfy curiosity. Once in a while, that backfires and you discover a home more welcoming than your own.

Potentially helpful is attending open houses in your own neighborhood. It's always advantageous to understand the housing market where you live. Scouting out sales comps and talking with a realtor who is experienced with homes in your community is a way to be informed about the value of your own home. It's doing the preliminary homework for selling your house, someday.

You can attend open houses for sheer curiosity as well. Is there an architectural beauty in your town you've always wanted to tour? Is there a view in a Penthouse that you've often wished to see? Are you simply curious about the outcome of all that construction noise you listened to all summer? Go ahead and walk through the open house. Just be considerate and tell the agent you're "just browsing" so that neither of you waste time or breath.

Looking for something interesting and free to do this weekend? Use a realty app or one of those free "Homes" magazines and …

Go to an open house.

#314 Do a science experiment

When I think of this heading / topic, I immediately think of my refrigerator and all the items that made their way into the far back. Those things that are currently growing various forms of mold and each qualify as hazardous substances. They are unintentional science experiments and not the kind I am recommending you try.

As many people - especially your 7th grade science teacher - will tell you, science is cool. From observing and understanding magnetic properties and chemical reactions, basic scientific principles are interesting to observe and promote our sense of wonder and curiosity. Both are elements that contribute to feelings of happiness.

Some science experiments are magical. There are several YouTube videos that will make you the most amazing aunt, uncle, grandma, pop-pop, or parent in the world if you can pull them off. Most of them use household items and create rather magical effects - even though they are all the result of science happening.

If you don't have a scientific background, I recommend that you stick to those things that you can find in books or online. Attempting to mix chemicals without knowledge of their interaction can be very dangerous. There are frequent news reports of people killing themselves because they lit something or mixed something that shouldn't have been.

Whether you get a book or go online, there are hundreds of experiments that you can conduct to satisfy your curiosity or perform magic at the next family party. All you have to do is gather a few supplies and practice. Grab a friend, a kid, or a neighbor and surprise them as you...

Do a science experiment.

#315 Window shop

This term is probably on the brink of being obsolete as very few of us can identify at all with the notion of walking down a street lined with shops that promote wares in a store front window. It's a stroll that inspired the substance of Christmas lists of yesterday. Today, we 'window shop' by browsing through the ads injected throughout our social media accounts.

Window shopping offers inspiration for several different areas of your life. It can inspire design when you see complementary colors positioned together. It can inspire a haircut you saw on a mannequin or it can prompt you to go home and recreate the skirt it was wearing. Window shopping can inspire you to cook more, read more, or exercise more just by glancing at the 'message' conveyed via the storefront display.

Likewise, it can move beyond inspiration and sincerely motivate action to do any of the above. It can motivate you to clean house, organize, and redecorate. It can motivate you toward a goal after seeing something you would really like to have.

Window shopping can encourage and teach patience. With big ticket items, we may spend time discerning the best time to get the best price. Walking past a display two, three, or four times across a few days, weeks, or months may be just the amount of time we needed to make sure that our purchase wasn't impulsive. A decision made after waiting and thinking is typically a better decision.

Window shopping is one of the ways that we can stay abreast of current trends and styles. Merchandise design is a specialty in and of itself. Consequently, we are often exposed to the newest thing when we walk past a storefront - a cleverly designed space to lure you into the shop where you are welcomed to spend your money.

Since many of us don't have a 'main street' to stroll down, window shopping is taking on a whole new meaning. Certainly, we browse through the mall from time to time - that counts. We can also internet browse by scrolling through Pinterest and the sites of our favorite stores. I will sometimes open those ad emails that get stuffed in my inbox and peruse the sale items… just looking to see if there is something that commands my attention.

Yes, there can be a downside to window shopping… if you have no impulse control - don't do it. If you lean into greediness or jealousy - don't do it. If you are resentful or bitter about your financial situation - don't do it.

That being said, it's a pleasant way to spend a little time now and then. If you're in the market for something, need some inspiration or motivation, or just need to connect with the times, all you must do is…

Window shop.

Happiness is not something ready-made. It comes from your own actions.

Dalai Lama

#316 Monitor your body language

Sometimes, our bodies do the talking for us. Non-verbal communication is one of the ways we create context and emotion in our communicative exchanges. Think about your last conversation. Do you know what you were saying with your body?

Psychologists have studied body language for eons. There are several generalizations about what certain body positions mean. Are you aware for example, that crossing your arms while someone is speaking typically means you are not open to receiving the message? Even if that's not your intent, the person who is speaking may perceive that you are closed off and develop a defensive reaction. When I am conducting couples or family therapy, I often hear comments such as "I can just tell by the way he looks at me" or "when she stands like that, I know what she means".

Most therapists receive specific training on how to posture their body so that clients will feel heard and safe in a session. Essentially, we are taught how to be aware of our body language so that it fosters an inviting atmosphere. This suggestion is designed to help you develop an awareness of your own body language. Do you stand straight - representing confidence? Or do you slump your shoulder and shy away from your environment? Do you sit straight or slouch? Do you maintain eye contact when speaking with someone, or do they dart around and glance away? Do you roll your eyes? How does your face register disapproval?

While counseling a teenage girl and her mother for communication issues, we discovered that mom raised an eyebrow whenever she was interested in a topic her daughter was speaking of. The daughter interpreted that body movement as disapproval and would often shut down the conversation. While generalizations are a place to start - do *not* make assumptions based on them. Check in with the person you are talking to… "are you thinking/feeling [this] way?"

Body gestures have been found to be genetic as well as environmental. We all know the classic… Italians talk with their hands. Twin studies have demonstrated that twins separated at birth will often still demonstrate similar gestures; often with similar meanings.

Obviously, good communication requires that we develop awareness of and take responsibility for the message we intend to send when we speak. Part of that message is delivered with our bodies. Because so much of our body language is innate and/or unconscious, it's important that we give someone we trust permission to highlight or identify those gestures that communicate meaning. For example, how does your spouse interpret a 'sigh'?

As a side note, I would include tone of voice in the body language awareness project... Some people are perceived as yelling when in fact, they are simply expressing their message with passion or enthusiasm. Still others, seem to lack any excitement in their voice at all and are interpreted as to be unmoving, or uncaring. In both cases, an understanding of one's tendency is important so that we are delivering our messages accurately.

Make the effort today to become a better communicator and ...

Monitor your body language.

#317 Ask more open-ended questions

How many times have you asked the question "Did you have a good day?" - receive a "yes" and then felt disappointed because you got a one-word answer? Frankly, you asked a one-word question and set yourself up for the disappointment. Changing the way you ask questions will likely dramatically change the answers and therefore, the information you receive; giving depth to your conversations.

"Tell me about your day, what was good about it?"

"What was the best part of your day?"

"What are you plans tomorrow?"

"Why are you irritated?"

Asking questions that start with who, what, where, when, why, & how are always going to require more than a one-word answer and will generally give you the information you seek. They are conversation questions and when you keep them going, so too... does the conversation.

Open-ended questions require more thought to answer. They generally elicit responses that move beyond the surface, deepening the connection between those who are speaking or at least, providing more detail. They are one of the keys to better communication and feelings of belonging.

I find this helpful when talking with kids - especially teens - who are short on describing activities, thoughts, and feelings; especially with parents. Dinner conversations are much more interesting when we ask, "If you could redo any part of your day - what would it be?" or "What are you looking forward to tomorrow?"

If we don't consciously make this effort, we tend to discover that our conversations aren't fulfilling. A quick and simple attempt to ask for information differently will dynamically change the way you interact; all because you...

Ask more open-ended questions.

#318 Hone your good manners

Good manners are defined as polite or well-bred social behavior. My mother used to call them "social graces" and my grandmother preached "you don't have to have money to have good manners". Simple things such as saying "please" and "thank you", not interrupting people, not demanding attention, asking permission, and knocking before entering are the most basic. They are the proverbial cornerstones of politeness.

Emily Post was the Queen of manners, also known as etiquette. For more than fifty years, she taught the us how to behave within traditional and acceptable social parameters. On her website, it good manners are described "as sensitive awareness of the feelings of others" and I couldn't agree more about this as a guiding principle when it comes to considering how to behave.

I often hear older people speak to the fact that younger generations haven't upheld familiar manner standards. Frequently, they are talking about 'thank you notes' and the absence or neglect of younger people sending them. Everyone wants acknowledgement and appreciation. When we receive a gift and/or a benefit from someone, a thank you is the least of the considerations and "awareness of the feelings of others". Today, it is acceptable to send an email instead of snail mail but your grandmother may prefer something the postal service can deliver.

When culture changes, those things that constitute manners may change as well. Others will remain but with adaptations. It was never courteous to jump up and answer the telephone when it was attached to the wall if you were in the middle of a different conversation. The same courtesy remains even though the phones are no longer attached to the wall. If you are conversing with someone, turning your attention to a cell phone is simply rude.

Good manners used to designate social class, but they certainly don't have to. Behavior is a choice and the classification of manners is available online and in library books, free of charge. There is no excuse, or reason that basic manners can't be observed so take a look and make an honest assessment of your own behavior. If it can use more sensitivity and awareness of the feelings of others it may be time to… Hone your good manners.

#319 Make eye contact

Eye contact during conversations is a type of communication in and of itself. It's a social skill. It's good manners. It's a sign of interest and attention. Indeed, according to the research, people who can make and sustain eye contact are perceived as more dominant, powerful, warm and personable, qualified, trustworthy, honest, confident and emotionally stable. Who wouldn't want to be associated with those characteristics?

People who engage in direct eye contact make more sales, date more frequently, and report more satisfactory interpersonal interactions. Each one of these consequences can improve the quality of our lives. It's postulated that our eyes are have evolved specifically to assist in our ability to communicate. Communication

Indeed, they contribute individually and specifically to non-verbal communication. "I saw it in his eyes" or "Her eyes told the story" .... Statements that describe a 'look' we can all relate to. Our eyes convey attention. We are more apt to listen to people who are looking directly at us and we will feel more intimately connected when making eye contact with other people. Intimate connections convey trust and belonging.

People who find it hard to make direct eye contact with others may be challenged in a variety of areas. It's very difficult to keep a gaze when we are being dishonest. Darting eyes can be an indication of a false story. People who are fearful of being judged may also find it hard to make eye contact. And, because our eyes communicate so much information, people who are masking emotion may not allow themselves to make eye contact for fear that their eyes will disclose too much information.

If you find it difficult to make eye contact - ask yourself why. Perhaps it would be helpful to seek guidance for any insecurities or fear. If you realize that your effort to avert a gaze is simply a bad habit, make a conscious effort to work on it. Eye contact can be overdone, it's not natural to stare constantly at someone so practice moving your eyes aside from time to time; side to side movement is the least disruptive to communication.

If you want to improve your connections, your communication, and ultimately your confidence... Make eye contact.

#320 Stop arguing

Arguments are rarely 'won'. At times there are things that need to be debated, but most of the time, it just isn't productive. You may want to argue the point, but what do you get from a useless debate? The more important question is what do you lose? I say you lose effective brain power.

Too much arguing creates a habit of looking for arguments more than for facts. We tend to get more deeply rooted in a rut as the defense continues and even avoid opposing evidence that may validate the other's view so that we can be 'right'. Ultimately, digging a rut and dismissing evidence doesn't make us better thinkers at all; it diminishes our power.

Some things we argue about are based solely on fact and while we may think we are helping the other person learn if we have our facts correct, we're just challenging them. Sometimes that completely backfires. If I say the earth is closer to the moon than the sun but you disagree, we're either headed for a science lesson or a tug of war and chances are that the misinformed person will have negative feelings after the debate.

On the other hand, if I say that nature is more important than nurture and you think it's the opposite, we can opt to simply respect one another's position. We could argue all day on defining "what's important in life" without any winner; especially if our perspectives differ. If we learn to simply listen, it's likely we'd learn something. Additionally, we'll be doing the only thing that's ultimately logical, kind, and compassionate

To break the habit of arguing, ask opinions and questions and then listen without judgement. You can ask for clarification but it's best not to offer contrary ideas. This isn't always easy to remember but with practice, you're likely to be in less hot water and get to know people better.

It's just a good idea all around in the effort of increasing your happiness and living your best life to …

Stop arguing.

#321 Create a romantic roadmap

Did you have a year-end review with your boss? Did you review goals and set new ones? Do you have a workout plan? Have you made a commitment to work out or lose weight? Are you in school? Do you know exactly what classes you need to complete in order to meet your objective? These are common ambitions at the beginning of the year and yet I find that very few people turn the same attention to their romantic relationships.

Your relationship is a long-term objective. It requires nurturing and effort. As such, it will benefit from all the energy you commit in designing a plan for its own specific growth and development. Indeed, those that are ignored, rarely flourish.

Where do you see yourself as a couple? What do you have in common? What are your individual growth aspirations? How are you supporting one another in achieving them? When do you spend time together and what do you do? How have your needs changed? Do you have savings goals? Projects to complete? All these questions can be a springboard in helping you design your relationship roadmap.

Of course, in designing this roadmap, you'll want to do it together. You may want to individually craft ideas to save time and then blend them together in a more organized manner that moves you toward a common theme. The most important element of the roadmap is a clear plan to grow your relationship. Failing to define dedicated time together is the most common mistake that couples make and it's apparent when they show up in my office for relationship counseling.

We seldom end up in new places randomly. It's important to have a plan and follow it - even if you get sidetracked. In fact, it's helpful to have a plan B or contingencies that will offer breathing room for you to get back on track. We can't always plan for the things that life dishes out but knowing that we've dedicated some energy on how to stay focused on the end game is helpful.

Grab your partner, a tablet and pen, a cuppa coffee or glass of wine, and devote a few hours to designing the map of your romance. Keep it alive and well by...

Creating a romantic Roadmap

#322 Develop more empathy

Empathy plays a major role in our ability to be socially competent. It is a key trait found in healthy relationships. None of us can exist on our own. Societies thrive when their citizens embrace the values of helping one another. While it's true that we are all responsible for our own actions, it can also be easy to forget just how much the desire to understand others and to work on their behalf matters.

When we think of being empathetic and doing compassionate deeds, our emphasis is usually on what the person in need, or who is receiving the assistance, gets. It's rare to look at what you can gain through working on behalf of someone else. Of course, you get the satisfaction and warm feeling of helping caused by an increase of feel-good neurochemicals. Performing compassionate deeds lowers our levels of stress and improves our health.

Empathy for others influences our social growth and competence, as well. Such actions force you to look beyond yourself and broaden your perspectives. Doing so can lessen your own emotional issues such as depression and anxiety. Reaching out to others in times of need builds social connections and enhances interpersonal skills necessary for healthy relationships.

Those on the receiving end of your empathetic efforts gain the sense that others care, which can go a long way toward improving overall mental outlook and sense of self. They gain trust in the outside world and feel seen. When others show compassion, it can lead receivers to believe that they are being perceived as worthwhile and have value. They feel more trusting and are often more motivated to work toward self-improvement goals.

We never know how the empathy we express may affect the person who receives it. I'm not sure we can have too much empathy as long as we are establishing healthy boundaries along the way. Empathy, compassion, and perspective work hand in hand to make great relationships better. If you're seeking more growth you can work to....

Develop more empathy.

#323 Practice a ritual

Sometimes, practicing a ritual can be an extremely healthy way to manage anxiety or stress. By definition, a ritual is "a sequence of activities involving gestures, words, and objects, performed in a sequestered place, and performed according to a set sequence". For the purposes of this discussion, I'd like to expand the idea of ritual a bit and allow for it to be something we do the same way each time with intention and purpose.

A Catholic Mass falls into the category of a ritual. Unless you are a priest of course, you won't be conducting the ritual but you may find that attending mass and engaging in the mass ritual offers the same benefit. Going to the gym at the same time every day and moving through the equipment in the same way with the same motivational music in our earbuds - is a ritual as long as there is focus and intention with the movements. Rituals differ from routines with focus and intention.

A ritual allows us to engage in an action consciously. Whether we are holding our hand over our heart and reciting the Pledge of Allegiance or kneeling in prayer at bedtime, they often signify meaning. Many brotherhoods, fraternities, and sororities practice rituals as a way of bringing their membership together; strengthening a sense of belonging. Some families have the ritual of a family dinner on Sundays or in our house... it's Mimosa's and Monkey Bread on Christmas morning. It's those things that unite and remind us of what's good. Mr. Fred Rogers shared his ritual of putting on slippers and changing into a cardigan as a way of getting comfortable each day; allowing us to feel as though we were at home with him.

Engaging in a regular ritual may energize you and create space for happy feelings. They demand focus and intention which, allows you to immerse yourself in your life. Routines that are mundane can be elevated to ritual status by engaging in them differently. Being deliberately present in those things that take little thought and experiencing them completely will change them from an unconscious pattern of movement to something that serves a positive function; something from which you may experience great pleasure.

If you don't yet have one, think of an action that is meaningful, intentional, and can be achieved on a regular basis. Perhaps it's sitting down with a journal every evening or meditation before you get out of bed in the morning. It could even be a Friday evening happy hour or date night with someone special. Self-care rituals may be the perfect starting point for those of you with busy lives and never having enough time. A ritual can reduce anxiety by providing a period of certainty in your day or week.

No matter the details, your life can be enriched greatly with the simple act of ...

Practicing a ritual.

#324 Reevaluate culture

What do you think about when you hear the word "culture"? I imagine that most of us think of ethnicity or the list of 'isms' that are currently politically correct (sex, age, gender, sexuality, etc.) and of course, those are in and of themselves... cultures. But the term culture can be expanded more broadly. I am of the belief that if we re-evaluate our thoughts about 'culture', it will help us to understand people better. Additionally, it creats more opportunity for developing empathy and offering compassion.

Remember the television show Wife Swap?? It was a program where the wives of two households traded places for a week. To make it good (and dramatic) television, the households were often dramatically different in sub-cultures (a suburban Atlanta businesswoman exchanged places with a Vermont stay-at-home mom who practices Wicca, for example). Each of the families are exposed to the different 'cultures' of the wife and they attempt to learn something from one another. It occasionally goes well.

I've never officially taken or performed sensitivity training, but I've had diversity training both in graduate school and in professional development coursework. I can't help but wonder why they aren't a part of our traditional curriculum at this point. And for those programs that do include diversity training, is there discussion about the granular aspect of diversity? An individual who grows up with socioeconomic privilege, in a one parent home, or with well-developed emotional skills is diverse from the person who has significant exposure to the opposite positions.

For a lot of the couples who sit in my office because of distressed relationships, it is frequently rooted in these diverse elements that are subconsciously at play. What was the 'conflict resolution culture' in your childhood home? It will matter when you attempt to resolve conflict in your adult relationships. What was the 'division of labor culture' in your childhood home? Again, it will matter in your adult relationship. Why is your coworker passive aggressive about your Jimmy Choo shoes? Did they grow up in a poverty-stricken community? Do they have strong 'cultural' bias about frugality?

We tend to make assumptions about people who share our physical traits and adopt a belief that they are culturally the same.

Likewise, we tend to believe that people who look different ... are different. At the end of the day our assumptions prevent us from asking important questions.

By reevaluating our idea of culture, nothing about the person sitting next to you can be assumed. It forces us to ask questions and see the individual nuances about him or her that compose their individuality. Your friend may have Asian features physically but was adopted into an African American home with a Jewish spiritual tradition. If you don't ask questions to understand the impacts of all those sub-cultural experiences, you're apt to totally misread who they are.

Our world - and the people in it - isn't broken into nice clean sections. If you really want to know someone and understand how to communicate with them successfully, you'll have to start by...

Reevaluating culture.

#325 Overcome self-doubt

Do you ever doubt yourself? Do you doubt you can do whatever it is you've set out to do? It's perfectly normal. We all do it. Self-doubt is something everyone faces at some point in their life. And for some of us it can be a real struggle. Self-doubt is defined as the lack of confidence in oneself and one's abilities. When it keeps us from doing what we want to do and from reaching our goals, it's time to act and work towards overcoming it.

Since self-doubt is caused by a lack of confidence, the solution is obvious. We need to work on becoming more confident. But how do you go about boosting your self-confidence?

By acting confident, you can trick your mind into becoming a more confident person. Stand up tall, talk with conviction and take some action. Act like a confident person until you become just that. I'm serious. As odd as it sounds this works. It's the old 'fake it 'til you make it' theory.

If you're the kind of person that thrives on praise and gets a big boost in confidence whenever they receive a compliment, go find yourself a cheerleader. Talk to a friend, find an accountability partner, or hire a coach or mentor. Let them know that you work well with praise and ask them to cheer you on as you work on your confidence.

There are probably dozens of things that you've accomplished over time. Make of list of all of the challenges that you've mastered, the goals you've reached, and the problems you've solved. This list will act as a reminder that you've been here and done that; that you have a track record of accomplishments.

Setting and reaching a goal is another big confidence booster. Set a challenge. It doesn't matter what it is or what area of your life it applies to. Then tackle it and rise to the challenge. Reaching your goal – whatever it may be – will boost your confidence overall and help you in all areas of your life.

And don't stop there… throughout your daily life pay attention to your confidence. It won't take you long to get out of the habit of doubting yourself and becoming the confident and productive person you've always wanted to be when you use these tricks to …

Overcome self-doubt.

#326 Try stand-up comedy

I can only imagine how many people snub this suggestion as a way to improve your life and laugh out loud because it may be the farthest thing from something that sounds fun. I suspect there are only two basic perspectives here... one being that "there's no way in hell I'd stand up and try to be funny because I'm not" or even if you think you could be funny... "there's no way in hell I'd stand up in front of strangers". And still... I stand by the recommendation.

Everyone has a funny side or at the very least, comedic memories; stories of times when the absurdity of life found you belly laughing. The longer you've lived, the more relatable experiences you have. But you don't have to be on the older side if you are a good observer. There's a lot of funny in the world and your ability to see it and describe it to other people is what makes good comedic material. In many of the basic struggles that we experience as humans, there is a humorous perspective. Some of the most famous comedians have been able to elaborate on the light side of everyday conflicts; relationships, work, raising children, proposals, traffic, etc.

Where many of us lose the momentum is between writing the ideas and crafting the 'script' of the story. The website CreativeStandup.com offers some great advice about "understanding the principles of comedy" versus "applying rules and techniques". In some cases, it's better to record yourself telling the tales and then have the recording transcribed and begin working from that point. In that way, you are breaking the creative process into two distinct pieces but allowing the 'material' to flow naturally.

Once you have a few ideas and a routine you're comfortable with, try an Open Mic night at a local comedy club. It's a great way to face any fear of public speaking because people are 'supposed to be laughing at you'. It's a great night out with friends if everyone is participating and an awesome way to work on confidence and esteem.

You've heard the phrase 'everyone's a comic!' - although notably it may have been a sarcastic expression at the time but there's a little bit of truth in most sarcasm. Use this as fuel to recall some of your most memorable personal experiences, tell the story with as much absurdity as it can support, and ... Try standup comedy.

#327 Sing karaoke

Several years ago, a Japanese research team published a study indicating that people who got together with friends and sang, were less stressed, had better cardiovascular health and were less susceptible to heart disease. I take this to mean that Karaoke reduces stress - no matter if you can carry a tune.

The point of Karaoke isn't necessarily showcasing vocal talent - although it does certainly serve that purpose. We are generally entertained when someone is able to carry a tune and has a little depth in their vocal range. But even if you can barely make it through Happy Birthday, gathering a group of friends and joining in on a collective rendition of 'Sweet Caroline' is great fun.

Perhaps one of the best physical benefits of singing is that it forces us to control our breath and breathe deeply. It tests our memory which, is exercise for our brain. It strengthens throat and palate muscles which, may improve snoring and apnea. It supports good posture by forcing you to stand upright, allowing for better breath control. And, it may be a natural antidepressant. People who sang regularly in church were found to have higher dopamine levels than those who did not.

Karaoke is an ongoing opportunity to gather with friends whether it is in a public forum or someone's living room. It gives you rhyme and reason to connect. If you are a 'regular' on open mic night, you may develop a following; fostering confidence and esteem with likeminded people.

There doesn't really seem to be a downside to this recommendation except for the fear you may have revolving around judgment, rejection, ridicule, or failure... all derogatory and ultimately unhelpful; totally worth staring down. A great way to face your fears while having a great time inside a supportive environment is to...

Sing karaoke.

#328 Send emails to the future

The website futureme.org focuses on encouraging you to send a letter to yourself with the header: Dear Future Me. Some of the letters are available to read publicly (you have the option to make it anonymously open) and are akin to reading diary entries. They can be used as encouragement, reflection, or inspiration for the life you are now living. It may be a great avenue to recall important emotional moments in your life as they happen.

Here is the real inspiration: There are many things that I've wanted to share with my children, friends, or other family members that maybe they weren't ready to hear. Or, perhaps I wasn't clear enough to share when the moment was at hand. Some things need time to talk about. The opportunity to share a reflection years later when the emotions have retreated can be a wonderful thing.

I recommend this to people who are born 'helpers' - people who can't seem to help themselves in the extension of advice whether or not it was solicited. There are many times when that advice is not the helpful support for which it is intended. Having the ability to write a letter to be delivered at some point in the future is a good outlet for the advice giver and may be relationship saving in the long run.

It is said that "time heals all wounds" which, is a misnomer of sorts. Time allows wounds to scar but some scars are always tender or downright painful when touched. Some relationships are simply not repairable. The ability to write a letter and have it delivered at some future point may be just the thing that can help the parties involved offer forgiveness. It can also serve as an apology without the energy of the pain associated with it.

Perhaps the most special part of this service is that we can share now, things that we may not be able to share at some future point. Certainly, I want to convey the love, admiration, and pride that I feel for my children today and I do make that effort but I feel good knowing that no matter what transpires between now and 10 or 20 years from now, they can receive a bit of mom encouragement then too...

I find comfort in the hope that people I love will receive a little surprise in their inbox at some future point because I took the time today to... Send emails to the future.

368

#329 Have a photo shoot

You may be part of the population that has an annual family photo shoot for the purpose of sending Christmas cards. Perhaps you've hired a photographer to take generation photographs when the family is all together, but have you ever just had a photo shoot for fun? A professional photographer is not required. All you need is a great location, a willing subject, and a smartphone or nice camera. The new iPhones take better photographs than the $1000 camera that is only a couple of years old.

This activity is often full of fun and laughter; especially with a bunch of friends or someone special. You can take turns using the camera to capture funny faces, funny poses, and action shots of all that silliness. Afterall, sometimes, the best photos are the ones that are completely spontaneous.

How about a sexy shoot with class? - that's the idea behind a Boudoir shoot. It's *not* pornography and *does* capture the inner sultry of whomever is the subject. They make wonderful gifts for both men and women.

You could fashion a backdrop and 'stage' a session for your shoot but a natural environment where your camera operator is able to capture candid images is often much nicer. Find a playground, a creek bed, or another favorite outdoor place to take your pictures. You might even have a friend follow you while you engage in your typical daily activities so they can seize any moments that find you immersed in your truest self.

If you can't get the shot you're going for, try Glamor Shots, a franchised photography studio that specializes in 'glamming' you up and posing you in an effort to capture your best features. They offer props and backdrops of all kinds to 'set the stage' for dramatic and beautiful photography. In some cases, they offer makeup, wardrobe, and styling services. Think one-stop-shop for professional photography.

It doesn't matter if you take this suggestion and go professional or if you grab a friend, your smartphone, and get out of the house. You're apt to have a lot of fun and permanent memories if you take the time to...

Have a photo shoot.

#330 Learn to juggle

Laughter promotes a sense of happiness and if you've ever watched someone attempt juggling or tried it yourself, you know the potential for fun is prominent. It's amusing to watch someone try and juggle and also fun to watch when they've mastered the skill. Juggling is the kind of 'sport' that works your body, mind, and soul.

Juggling is a great exercise for hand to eye coordination. This kind of activity builds neural pathways in the brain which, is important for people of all ages. In addition, it promotes better dexterity.

It forces your attention and physicality into the present moment which, we know is a treatment for people with anxiety. If you're not paying extremely close attention, you won't be able to manage the coordination and so it is necessary to pull all of your mental and physical resources into the present in order to juggle.

Lastly, you can't juggle without good posture. Practicing juggling on a regular basis will help you keep a straight stance - adding to the health benefits overall.

As mentioned, it takes great focus in order to juggle successfully. Some reports suggest children and adults who learned juggling experienced less expression of their diagnosed attention deficit disorder (ADD).

Some people posit that juggling qualifies as an 'active meditation' since you are present, focused, aware of your surroundings, and aware of your body all at the same time.

If you feel inclined to learn how to juggle, I am going to suggest starting with YouTube where there are a number of videos explaining how to start. The most important part of this process of course, is practice... as with any other thing that utilizes dexterity, coordination, and mental concentration - practice makes perfect.

If you've hit a wall... a plateau... or just have some spare time on your hands, it may be helpful for you to completely switch it up and get into something new by...

Learning how to juggle.

#331 Masquerade for a night

Have you ever thought about escaping your life? Have you ever wondered what life might be like if you were? I suspect we all have at one time or another. If you opt to don a mascaraed for an evening, you may surprise yourself at how good it feels to step outside your reality for a brief escape.

Keep in mind, it's not a permanent coping mechanism. It is a way to give yourself a 'break' from the stressors and/or responsibilities that you may need some distance from. This 'escape' is best played out with a partner or friend and can actually stimulate intrigue, curiosity, and excitement as you both engage with a new persona. It's your chance to role play or pretend for a few hours; an activity often recognized as helpful in spicing up an intimate relationship.

Masquerading and role playing are great ways to play out emotional fantasies such as having increased courage, being more sultry, or having more confidence. Sometimes, if we don't have the inner belief that we possess a particular trait, it's helpful to 'pretend' that we do to 'try it on' and get a sense of how it may be to experience that element. It's a way to "fake it until you make it".

Something as simple as wearing your hair up or wearing makeup if you don't typically do either one - can create a 'shift' in the way you think of yourself and hence, offer a different perspective in public. Getting out and doing something in juxtaposition from your 'norm' while dressed up or made up completely different from what's typical may add just the spice to your life that allows you to have a little breathing space.

So, don those hair extensions and add a pair of glasses or ditch the suit and tie for a pair of jeans and a Hawaiian shirt - grab your partner and ...

Masquerade for a night.

#332 Learn martial arts

While this is an activity that is often introduced at an early age, it's also an activity that we are never too old to learn. If you are willing to move your body, practice patience, and you won't throw up each time a ten-year-old advances past you... you are able to learn a martial art.

One of the primary benefits of knowing a martial art is the ability to practice self-defense. A solid karate chop will set back almost any average offender. We're never too old to defend ourselves. Self-defense is an essential life skill. When we are able to think quickly and react as such, it is a skill that transfers to many other aspects of our life.

Your martial arts activity will be good for your overall health. Just the fact that you're getting regular exercise has all the traditional benefits. Martial arts training is specifically good for your heart and bones. Some people even believe that engaging in martial arts can reverse the aging process!

Learning a martial art can be as good for the soul as it is for the body. Challenging oneself to push physical boundaries increases esteem, confidence, and trust. The increase in physicality will encourage you across all areas of your life.

There's a lot to gain from taking the time to...

Learn martial arts.

#333 Stash some cash

Remember the last time you went digging through each coat pocket in hopes you'd find a forgotten ten-dollar bill? It's important to have a cash stash for those moments when an ATM isn't readily available or as a way of tucking away a little savings ('little' being the operative word here as it isn't good financial advice to deny yourself any earning capacity your savings may have).

Many of us have 'change jars' or a container that is a collection place for the random change we accumulate. It's amazing how quickly a few cents here and there add up over time. You may be surprised at how much accrues by holding on to the coins we come home with at the end of the day. This is the principle behind apps like Digit who sweep very small - unnoticeable - amounts of cash from the account you give it access to.

This suggestion is more about having the cash in hand however. Once you fill your container with change, turning it into bills is easy with the sorting machines you find at grocery stores and banks. Although, those machines do keep a small percentage of your savings as payment for doing all the work. In my opinion, it's worth it unless you enjoy sitting for hours to sort, count, and roll all those pennies, dimes, and nickels.

As you are saving, you need a safe place to tuck away all those bills. Unless you are tremendously disciplined, I'm recommending it's out of sight to avoid the temptation of spending it. The big question is where to hide it so that you'll remember where it is, but it won't be easy to spot in general. There's no need to tempt people with shaky principles.

After winning a large lottery once, I brought home the cash and tucked several $100 bills on page 100 in several different books on my bookshelf. I believed - at the time - that it was a brilliant way to keep it at distance enough that I wouldn't spend it all at once. The first problem was that I didn't record which books I put it in - that was a huge error of judgment. The second problem was that I had *a lot* of books. I never did find all of them. There's either still a book in my home with a hundred-dollar bill in it or someone else got a big treat as I often donate books that sit around for too long.

Try to pick a spot that's not obvious but one that is safe as well. Here is a list of ideas that I've heard about through the years:

An empty food box or canister in your kitchen pantry

An empty container in your refrigerator

An empty container in your freezer

In an envelope taped behind a piece of furniture or wall decor

Folded into socks or undies

Tucked into shoes or boots

Under seat cushions of furniture

There are obvious problems with all of those ideas as none of them except possibly the refrigerator or freezer, will keep your cash safe in the event of natural disaster or fire. In those cases, the best hiding place is a fireproof safe hidden from plain sight. And... I'm certainly not recommending that you stash too much - a number that is very individual but probably doesn't need to exceed a few hundred dollars. Banks are the best for larger amounts.

In any event, it's often good to know that in a dire situation you won't have to worry about a tank of gas or a loaf of bread because you've made the effort to...

Stash some cash.

#334 Start a business

Many of us are entrepreneurial from the time we are small. Maybe we built a lemonade stand in our front yard, sold Girl Scout cookies, or joined Junior Achievement. If you have a great idea or make a great product, think about starting a small business. It's never been less expensive to bring your thoughts or wares to market.

As with anywhere you want to go, the first time it's easier to get there with a roadmap. A business plan is a roadmap for your business and it's the first place to start. There are probably thousands of blogs, websites, and organizations online that will teach you about a business plan and guide you in designing one. Business.com is one of the free and useful websites offering information about how to do this.

The most obvious opportunity is to go online. There are dozens of easy to use avenues from Etsy and Shopify to building your own website quickly on Squarespace or GoDaddy. Getting your services or products on the web can be accomplished with less than $100 and some of your time.

The world wide web is a massive place and your business is a grain of sand there. As a newcomer to the market, you'll need to grab some attention in any way that you can - professionally speaking of course. This is the make-it-or-break-it key to becoming successful.

Once again, there are dozens of places that you can go online to learn how to market your product. Some of those places are free of charge if you are a good self-study. If you want to dive right into the heart of the matter, it may be better to spend some of your working capital money in this arena and take a marketing class that can highlight the most important aspects of promotion. And then, don't stop… market your business relentlessly to everyone who will listen and give them a reason to tell someone else about you. Light a fire everywhere you go, and it will organically spread if there is a wind.

If you are one of the fortunate ones, you'll begin to make money. The best thing you can do in the beginning is to reinvest profits in your business. So many of us are tempted to spend it on those extra things we want - after all, we're working extra hard - but it's important to grow your business while it has some momentum and that generally takes capital investment. Even if you've only made a few hundred dollars, think of how that money can be spent to market more widely, improve your packaging, or build your inventory. Is there a trade show or a conference that will offer education or networking opportunities? Go to that.

Yes, many small businesses never make it, but some would tell you it's because the business owner wasn't persistent enough. Remember the Little Engine That Could and go that extra mile... pushing past where most people back down. Don't stop - not at least until you've reached the capacity of your investment in time, money, or resources. There is a time to call Uncle. But until that time has come - work hard and smart.

If you've been wondering about your ability to market a product or talent... this may be your year. Right now, may be your time... so why not...

Start a Business

#335 Get five-star treatment

When was the last time you were treated like the Queen of something? Or the King? Have you had white glove service? Flown first class? Have you been waited on pool side? You deserve to and it doesn't have to cost an arm and a leg - or anything at all if you are super lucky.

We are all deserving of being spoiled and attended to from time to time. Whether it is a spa day where our bodies are pampered, a five star restaurant where a meal is prepared and served with perfection, or a day at home where our every need is anticipated... it's nice to know that someone in the world - at some point in time - is there for us.

Exactly what constitutes five-star treatment? Most of us agree it's when we feel attended to, important, and/or special. It's when service is entirely focused on the pleasure and satisfaction of the customer. And, sadly - it's not available everywhere. Indeed, five-star service is so exemplary that it's difficult to achieve.

Five stars is a mentality according to Dr. Williams in an article in CSM magazine - a way of working. He explains that it's an attitude and discipline that denies mediocrity. And while we intellectually know that "perfect" isn't consistently possible - the persistent striving toward that goal is what sets the tone of five stars.

A five-star experience is when every detail is anticipated or provided for and it's not necessarily only at expensive establishments. There are spas, restaurants, markets, shops, hotels, and resorts that are reasonably priced and demand excellence from their staff. Finding it can be challenging at times and if it is affordable for the average consumer, there may be a significant wait time for service. Websites and apps like Yelp and TripAdvisor can help in your search.

There's something special about being treated as if you are the only person in the world for an hour, a day, or longer. Especially for those of you who are devout caregivers, it's great to provide exemplary care and maybe even nicer to be an occasional recipient. Why not treat yourself by making an appointment or reservations to ...

Get five-star treatment.

#336 Rent a sports or luxury car

In the spirit of treating yourself as a king or a queen by making opportunities to enjoy some of the 'finer' things in life, why not drive something a little different? Remember when you rented a limo for prom or a wedding? It was a special occasion that called for a special vehicle. Your birthday, anniversary or the third Tuesday of May can also be considered a special day if you want it to be. Allow yourself to consider this for a moment, would it be a sporty convertible or a luxurious sedan? A rugged Jeep perhaps?

If you live in a cool damp environment, perhaps sporty is the way to go. You might consider a weekend in a warm and dry region where you can rent a convertible coupe and spend the weekend exploring the region with the top down and the wind in your face. If you normally drive a SUV or truck and rarely get the opportunity to sit close to the road - consider something small that can take a turn tightly.

In the few markets that I investigated, you can rent a Porsche or a Maserati for under $300 a day. I know a few men who would be downright giddy to get on the road behind the wheel of that dream car. What a great gift idea for a big birthday!

Likewise, if you've been fiscally conservative in your vehicle choices through the years, it may be nice to go luxury. There's a certain kind of pleasure when your body sinks into temperature-controlled leather seats that conform to your body shape in a car offering more than necessary legroom as you absorb sunshine through the edge to edge sunroof over your head.

A Cadillac Escalade ESV or a Mercedes S450 may be the perfect ride if you're in the mountains or exploring a cold city; especially if you need those great features of four-wheel drive and traction control. There's something comforting about having the girth of a large vehicle protecting you when the road conditions are less than supreme. What's more luxurious than driving to the slopes in the comfort of a roomy, temperature-controlled ride filled with all the mind comforting safety features one can wish for?

If you're scheduled to take a vacation or if you have a special occasion coming up, why not treat yourself and ...

Rent a sports or luxury car.

378

#337 Know your worth

Without a sense of self-worth, happiness may be unsustainable. I will often ask clients to think about the last infant they saw and imagine the baby smiling with big eyes, back at them... what about that child right there and then isn't worthy? That sweet human is entirely deserving of all life has to offer - love, liberty, and success at the very least. And so is every other person on the planet. This is a universal given. And then... as we move from infant to toddler, from childhood to adulthood - we come to believe otherwise.

Those beliefs develop in a variety of ways perhaps starting with our home environment where a long list of 'should's' exist and value statements are transferred from one generation to another without examination. They develop as we perceive societal and cultural expectations and begin to compare ourselves against the published 'norms. As we are told or as we determine that we haven't or don't meet those expectations, we begin to internalize a value of self and an inner dialogue begins; sometimes under the surface of our level of awareness.

We fail to distinguish the quality of our behaviors from the quality of our Being. The resulting shame from behaving badly or making mistakes is wrapped around our self-worth until it is so intertwined that it feels as if it is one piece. And we deny our worth.

The antidote to a broken sense of self begins with untangling the value judgements and seeing oneself as a human being just trying to make it through the world. Most of us wake up each day with the intent of living a good day, of being decent, of connecting. Start there. BE those things. Connect with people, be decent, and make the day count in some way. Get to know your own heart and values; live by them. Look at the big picture and put things in context.

Practice self-compassion. Practice loving kindness on yourself every day. Use "I am" affirmation statements that validate your worth. "I am kind", "I am a hard worker", "I am a good friend", etc. And each time those old tapes play in your mind - those messages that were adopted when you didn't know any better - move your attention to what you know is true now...

Maybe the most important step in the pursuit of happiness is understanding that you are now and have always been 'worth it'.

Don't let another day go by without working to discover or making the effort to validate your value. Living your best life is at your fingertips when you...

Know your worth.

"The difference between misery and happiness depends on what we do with our attention." —
Sharon Salzberg

#338 Compete in something

If you engage in some type of sporting activity, you are most likely competing which, as it turns out - is good for you. If not, think of something you can do that will offer an opportunity to compete and win. When we win, the dopamine rush that happens may be important to our happiness.

We are biologically designed to be rewarded for "coming out on top" ... for winning. In fact, low serotonin levels are often the result of denying ourselves the opportunity to win. If you find that you avoid competition or don't try to succeed when given the chance, it may promote depressed feelings

When we win at something, our bodies produce a surge of testosterone - temporarily providing a rush of 'strength' in both men and women. In addition, dopamine - the happy chemical - courses through the area of our brain that is responsible for pleasure and positive emotions.

Competition isn't just about winning, however. There are great benefits to be a part of a team when it comes to those competitions that require cooperation and coordination. Learning to share energy in an effort to accomplish a task is an important life skill.

Competitions tax our body and/or our minds. Whether we're competing in a triathlon or playing Euchre, we are using energy in the pursuit of playing. Our brains are constantly at work in an effort to figure out how to maximize our performance. It also promotes creativity as we vie to 'get out front' and win.

Some people have negative reactions to social competitions and some, broken perspectives from poor experiences in the past. In these cases, I recommend competition against one's self. Beat your best at anything; strive to do it faster, or earlier, or bigger. Anything that you can do to promote the sense of "I did it!" will induce similar chemical responses in your body.

Competition is good for you so the next time you have a chance to play a game of anything or to personally challenge yourself... just do it. You'll be giving yourself an opportunity for some great chemical rushes should you win. After all, the only way to win... is to...

Compete in something.

#339 Interview a person you admire

The point of this suggestion is to take some time to ask questions of a person whom you deeply admire. It may be a high-profile person, a town celebrity, an old teacher, an executive of your company, the pastor of your church, or it could be an elderly Aunt that you've never 'really' gotten to know.

The goal is to garner information that you may not yet know about living a good life. How did they become someone worthy of admiration? What are their takeaways from their own experiences? What perspectives helped them through tough times?

When we take the time to listen - we learn. Sitting with someone with whom you'd like to emulate offers a tremendous opportunity to get into the life lesson fast lane. While their experiences are undoubtedly different than yours, the perspective and skills may be generally applicable.

I'll assume that most of us will be interviewing someone who has had some success either in their professions, in their spiritual journey, or in their relationships. How did they do it? What goals did they set? What steps did they actively take to reach those goals? How did they handle the challenges? What attributes allowed them to persevere? Did they fail? What did they learn from failure?

In this era of instant gratification, I know many of us don't want to work through all the kinks that learning presents. We want to be successful now. Knowing how others accomplished the pinnacle of the mountain you're climbing may offer a more clear path to the top. Take the time to learn the tips and tricks they used to get there.

I don't see this as a 'one and done' kind of activity. Because our lives are always changing, there will most certainly be people in our lives frequently with whom we can have these conversations. It may be a great tradition to practice annually. Choose someone in your life with potential to 'teach' you and invite them to lunch or dinner. Pick their brain and then record the essence of that conversation for inclusion in your own life plan. No matter where you are currently in your own journey, there is someone there you may learn from. Take the time to look around and...

Interview a person you admire.

#340 Expand on what you know

As a therapist, I am frequently talking to people who feel stuck in their lives and relationships. Sometimes, we can trace the 'stuck' feelings to the fact that people keep doing the same thing repeatedly. It always reminds me of the old quote...

"The true definition of insanity is doing the same thing over and over with the expectation of getting different results."

Of course, much of the time it is a behavior or action we continue because we just don't know what else to do. We move through the actions almost rotely, unaware of our limited knowledge. I am sensitive to the fact that we only do what we know because we 'don't know what we don't know'. Change only happens after awareness had been initiated.

The solution is simple: expand on what you do know - assume there is always something more to learn. It's my belief that we stagnate when we've adopted the notion 'been there, done that' and stop investigating. Learning isn't just about the depth of our knowledge... it's about the breadth as well. Most educators already know this as it applies to children's education. It's one of the reasons that the team approach works well - incorporating reading, history, and English together with the arts can help a child maximize their understanding of a topic. When they are composing poems or writing plays about the period of history they are studying and painting backdrops they researched in books... you get the idea. It fosters a much richer educational experience than a single liner assignment.

We can do this in our day to day life as well. If you like plants, build a garden with landscaping and make it bird friendly. If you like organic food - grow your own. If you are creative, make things and sell them online; build a website and expand your technical skills. If you enjoy cooking, experiment with recipes and ingredients to reshape the original into something unique then start a blog. If you like to build things, find ways to repurpose things you have or items you've gathered from yard sales and then donate them to organizations where you spend time volunteering. If you like to write, build a story and write a book... use resources from the internet to research and add character to the plot.

Growing your body of knowledge doesn't have to cost a dime or require much physical effort. It's as easy as visiting the library or hopping online. Most university libraries will also offer the public free or very inexpensive access to their facilities - opening the door to more learning than can be obtained in a single lifetime. If you know how to read - you can learn. It may not be easy if you're a more 'hands on' kind of learner but it's possible with dedication. Time and desire are the only mandates as proven by the amazing story of Maria Beltran when she taught herself English and went on to become a lawyer while raising six children as a single mother. If she can do it, most of us will never have a valid excuse.

There's no reason for your life to be stagnant... you already have a bank of knowledge. All you must do is...

Expand on what you know.

#341 Give some a homemade gift

A handmade card is lovely, and a handmade gift is often just as appreciated, especially when it is made with the recipient in mind. How about someone's favorite cookie, pie, or cake? A member of my family prefers to receive baggies of my well-known shredded pork barbeque (nothing special really) anytime it's his birthday or if I draw his name for our Christmas exchange. Knowing that you have a home cooked option in the freezer after a long day of working really is a 'gift' at times.

When we offer something we made, it frequently symbolizes that we spent time and energy thinking of the individual; crafting something specifically designed for the person receiving the gift. A friend of mine is involved in a community gift exchange every year and they make something that is reminiscent of the community in which they reside. It might be a collection of leaves from the trees specific to their street, another year it was made from driftwood that washed up on the shore of their community. Later yet, it was something crafted with the motto of the neighborhood. All of the gifts were specific to the broader connection between the giver and the recipient.

There are tens of thousands of ideas on the internet or in the aisles of big box stores catering to crafters such as Michaels, AC Moore, and JoAnn's. It can be cooked, baked, knitted, crocheted, stitched, sewn, painted, drawn, stamped, burnt, carved, glued, built, burnished, adorned, or woven - just to cover the basics. There are classes upon classes if you need ideas or support. There are how to videos all over YouTube not to mention basic instructions on almost anything you can imagine in blog posts and articles in the Do-It-Yourself genre.

Really, there isn't any excuse or reason one may offer to avoid the sentiment of offering something homemade the next time there is a gift-giving occasion. Now may be the best time to put on your thinking cap and start a list of ideas so that when it's needed, you can...

Give some a homemade gift.

#342 Sit with yourself

Do you know someone who can't sit still? Or others who are uncomfortable with being alone? Are you able to go to a movie or eat in a restaurant by yourself? Learning how to be comfortable with yourself turns out to be a critical component to true happiness. Having alone time is important.

Spending as little as an hour or two each day is all it takes to improve your sleep, your attention, your commitment, and your stress level. It doesn't matter if the hour or two is in one fell swoop or if it is broken into segments. Perhaps it's only a half hour at lunch four days a week. Maybe it's getting up a half hour early or going to bed before everyone else. At the very least, it may be an hour on Sunday evening while the rest of the family is watching a movie or reading.

The kind of alone time that is suggested here is being 'still' with yourself. It's not intended to be a time where you clean, work, or talk on the phone. It's not taking an hour to scroll through social media or even read or watch television. It's quiet time; sitting and being. It's for introspection, creative thinking, and thoughtfulness. It's for mental planning, self-nourishment, and emotional recharging.

Doing so may be the antidote you need for the stressors of daily living or a stressful work environment. It may be the time you need for the creativity spark that will help you finish a story, inspire a painting, or adopt an idea. It may settle your mind long enough so that the solution to a problem becomes crystal clear. It will likely help you find your voice - to sort through your thoughts sufficiently enough that you are able to articulate more fully in the process of communication. It will likely help you hone into your perceptive energy, encourage deep thinking, and hence, improve your relationships all around.

There is much to be gained when you commit to spending time alone where you just...

Sit with yourself.

#343 Realign yourself

This suggestion is about realigning your behavior with your value system. You see, as the driver of our lives, we do many of the same things we do when we drive our cars... we hits bumps in the road; we go too far without routine maintenance; and we can spin our wheels so long that we get worn out along the edge. When that happens on our vehicle, we take it in for an alignment and this post is suggesting that we do the same for our mind/spirit/body connection.

You know when a car needs an alignment because the steering is a little wobbly and it won't go in a straight line when you take your hands off the wheel. It takes more effort to steer. The same is true for life. When you despise going to work every day - or home... when your stomach turns each time the phone rings or mail gets delivered... when you run into someone you know or when you get invited to a party - any negativity that arises may be indicating that your action(s) may not be consistent with your value system.

Our bodies are great barometers for when our actions are out of alignment with who we want to be. We feel bad, guilty, or ashamed. We get defensive, argue, and raise our voices. We may get headaches, have stomach trouble, or back pain. We may even break out with zits, pimples, or hives.

Let's say you decide to value honesty but you - out of habit - told a series of 'white' lies in an effort to avoid confrontation... or you go to work every day to a department that has historically reported jacked up results to look good... or you volunteer with someone who helps themselves to product when 'on duty' - all examples of dishonesty. The migraines you began having last year soon after you committed to be a more honest person may be indicative of the discord between your value and the dishonest environment in which you find yourself.

Or perhaps you've made a commitment to have a closer relationship with God by living the doctrine of your faith more passionately. Now, you find that every time someone uses the Lord's name in vain or curses up a storm - the hairs on your neck tingle. Or perhaps those are habits that you are finding difficult to break. The angst you feel getting up each morning may be your body reminding you to pay close attention today - to the commitment you made.

As we grow, mature, and experience life, as too do the values that we hold dear. As a young twenty-something, I valued parties and social variety much more than I do today where sharing a bottle of wine with one or two friends in a quiet, relaxed environment is my idea of meaningful engagement. If I were to step out and try to 'party' every weekend, it would be inconsistent with my current 'value' and I may find that I am 'off'? If I keep doing it... If I keep dishonoring the value that I've adopted, being 'off' turns into something more obvious and I am left with the need to figure out why I have developed insomnia or a bad attitude.

Just like you do when the steering wheel starts to wobble... step back once in a while and take stock of your values - matching them against your actions and behavior. Pay attention and notice when it is time to ...

Realign yourself.

#344 Create a "make me happy" list

When my children were young, I made a list of things that "made mama happy" so that if they wanted to ask me for something such as running them to the basketball game after I'd gotten home and put on my jammies, they could look at the list and do something nice for me in return. And, while I don't generally promote a 'tit for tat' attitude in most relationships, it's no surprise that humans are more apt to concede when their needs are also met.

What is it that makes your mama, your partner, or your roommate happy? [know that the word "makes" is being used in the context of 'generates' - what 'generates happiness for your partner, etc.,]

There's an old fable that goes like this:

A man and a woman show up in a counselor's office after 40 years of marriage stating that they were on the verge of calling it quits. The counselor asks, "why after all this time are you opting to end the relationship?" The gentleman replied with a frustrated and loud voice "Every time she walks by me, she pats my God Damn head. I've asked her a thousand times to stop and she won't. I'm done!". The counselor looks at the woman who is sitting demurely and asks "and you? What's your position in this?" to which the woman replies sadly and softly... "he never pats my head."

The point here being that she patted her husband's head as a way of telling him she loved him... and because it irritated him so - he never considered that she may actually like it. We each have a different way of understanding and feeling loved. It's the premise behind Gary Chapman's Five Love Languages and a common problem in many relationships. We are inclined to treat our partners and family members the way we want to be treated instead of stopping to recognize how they want to be treated.

One simple way to have your needs met is to blatantly tell those who matter - what it is that generates happiness for you. Are flowers important to you or would you rather have the house cleaned? Do you value a romantic dinner or a couple's massage? Does it bring you peace when the kids pick up their shoes and put away their backpacks? Or when they empty the dishwasher? (assuming you need to choose).

I am suggesting that you make a list and tape it all over the house... on the mirrors in the bathrooms. On the back of the bedroom doors. In front of the PlayStation or to the top of the laptop. Wherever it is most likely to be seen most.

You don't use the list just at those times when you want a favor however... if that's the only effort - it is manipulative. You use the list when your partner has had a bad day, feels sick, or has gone above and beyond. When a child feels appreciated, they will often step up without being asked so know what is important to them as well.

Finally - be sure to be appreciative! We only have so much to give without a consideration of appreciation before we adopt a sour attitude. Even though appreciation isn't the motivation - once again, we're human and unless you are a strongly evolved individual - you probably have limits on how much you are willing to give without any acknowledgement of the effort.

A simple and effective method of having your needs met and meeting the actual vs. perceived needs of others to have everyone in the household is to...

Create a 'make me happy' list.

#345 Host a clothing swap

Were you ever dismayed to find out that your friends' sweater - the one you loved - got sent to Goodwill? Are you in the habit of dipping into your roommate's closet more often than your own? Are you on a budget but tired of your wardrobe? The solution may be as easy as hosting a clothing swap.

This is an activity that moms often engage in when they have friends with children just under or over the ages of their friends. Kids, especially babies, frequently outgrow their clothes before they can wear them out and so it's financially prudent to swap clothes as you go along. Since we so easily think of this for our kids, it's equally sensible to do it for ourselves.

It's easy.

Clean out your closet just as you would if you were going to donate clothing to charity. Invite a few friends over after directing them to do the same, open a bottle of wine, and take turns choosing something from one another's discards. Don't limit the items to clothing. Jewelry, shoes, bags, and other accessories will also be "new to you". These items are key considerations when inviting friends who may not be of similar size and are unable to wear the clothing. Whatever is left can then be donated.

This suggestion hits the mark on all levels by promoting recycling, inspiring financial sensibility, upgrading your wardrobe and boosting the happiness that ensues from all of that.

If you're looking to refresh your closet, why not invite a few friends over and have a fun night by...

Hosting a clothing swap.

#346 Practice self-discipline

One of the most important elements of maturity, emotional intelligence, and good health is developing self-discipline and engaging in it more often - than not. Self-discipline is the thing that allows you to control your impulses and stay focused. It helps us establish the habits that drive us to obtain the goals we set in life.

Self-discipline is most difficult where our weaknesses are concerned. It's important to understand our weak points so that we can develop strategies which work. It's not hard to get up at 6 am if you are a morning person but if you are a night owl, you will need to acknowledge that mornings aren't your thing before you can effectively manage discipline in that area.

Self-discipline is a learned behavior. It's the practice of doing the same thing with purpose over and over. It's the practice of denying yourself the thing that prevents you from reaching your goal. Because of this - learn self-discipline the way you learn anything else... start at the beginning, take small steps, and build up to the harder chunks.

Research has demonstrated that our belief about our ability to practice self-discipline will ultimately determine how successful we are. Imagine that you are building your personal capacity for discipline as you move forward; giving yourself the opportunity to expand your belief.

Almost a century of research indicates that we are likely to perform better if we are rewarded. B.F. Skinner demonstrated the theory of Operant Conditioning where learning occurs most efficiently when there is a positive reinforcement. Building your capacity for self-discipline can be accomplished in this same manner.

If there's a goal you've been working toward and haven't been able to quite get there, consider redirecting your focus and make the effort to ...

Practice self-discipline.

#347 Eliminate these words from your vocabulary

After years of working with couples in crisis and helping families communicate better, I've noticed a pattern of vernacular that is a part of most dysfunctional relationships. Our language mattes. The words we use are important and paying close attention to your vocabulary will help you communicate better... improving your relationships and your overall sense of happiness. Here are the primary culprits:

Should

There is a suggestion entirely devoted to eliminating the 'should's in your life and that was mostly from the perspective of identifying the internal expectations that guide you. However, they often interfere in our relationships as well because we think others "should" do something. When we impose our own 'should's on others, we are really attempting to convey an expectation and it's better expressed that way. Instead of "you should take a day off so we can spend time together" you might eliminate the word should and offer this: "It would be great if you could take a day off so we can spend time together". Simply replacing the word 'should' with the word 'could' - makes all the difference.

Right & Wrong

"Do it the right way", "If you did it right the first time", "No, you're wrong" ... all those phrases are likely to incite a defensive reaction almost as soon as they are spoken. When someone is defensive - they probably aren't listening and so, the conversation is broken at that point. When we understand that 'right' and 'wrong' are generally spoken about perspectives and values and that they are different for different people we can shift the way we speak about them. Try to adopt the ideology that there is no right or wrong - only differences.

Instead of the phrases above, try these: "I was thinking it could be done this way", "Generally, I do it like this", "I'd like it done this way", "that's an interesting perspective" or "I don't see it that way"... notice that in each of these statements - you are using the "I" voice and describing *your* thoughts/perspective. That's the key.

393

Make

In the English language, we often use the word 'make' to mean cause' which, is one of the secondary definitions and yet when it is in reference to feelings or behavior - it creates a problem of responsibility. Under the assumption that we - each of us as individuals - are personally responsible for our behavior - no one can force us to behave in a particular way. Literally speaking - WE are the cause of our behavior. Thinking anything different is deflecting responsibility and handing away our personal power. Each time we utter the phrase "you make me..." or "you made me..." etc., we are inferring that the responsibility for *our* behavior is on another. That is simply untrue. While it is true that we may react to another person's behavior - it is still *our* choice on if, when, and how we react.

When we feel something and react - that happens inside our own being and is *our* responsibility. Try these phrases: "I get really angry when you....", "I feel really disappointed when [that] happens", "I have a lot of feelings about..." - notice that in each case again, the communication is about what is happening for *you*. It's always about communicating your experience from your perspective.

When we pay close attention to the language that we use in our communication, we can significantly reduce the amount of defensiveness that is generated by...

Eliminating these words from your vocabulary.

#348 Lean into fear

Maybe one of the hardest things in life is to face those things that we are afraid of. Perhaps it's important to begin by understanding fear. It's the thing that our brain uses to move our body in such a way as to improve its chance for survival. No matter if it is physical or emotional... fear lets us know that danger is pending. Sometimes though, the problem is that our fear is based on a perceived danger, a false danger, or an imagined danger. That's right... the danger doesn't have to 'actually' exist for us to literally feel fear. We just have to believe it exists.

Because our very existence depends on surviving, and surviving means that we must avoid great danger, we are hardwired to constantly be on the lookout for things that are wrong. (It's one of the reasons we may not notice the 'good things' in life.) It's literally in our best interest to be fearful of those things that we don't know or that aren't certain.

Having said that... fear can be very limiting and deny us opportunities to enjoy what life has to offer. A fear of airplanes may prevent you from visiting places you want to go. A fear of heights may prevent you from seeing amazing views. A fear of animals may prevent you from walking along magnificent forested trails.

What does it meant to 'lean in' to fear? It means moving toward it instead of backing away. It means allowing the discomfort to encompass you instead of resisting it. Leaning in means taking a risk with that thing that you fear. Feeling uncomfortable and accepting risk takes courage so the idea of leaning in means to act courageously.

We can often learn about our fears when we look to our emotions. Anger, anxiety, frustration, hate, bitterness, and resentment are the consequences of fear much of the time. We may be afraid of failing, of letting someone down, of not being accepted or loved. Perhaps we are afraid of disconnecting, of leaving, or of staying. When we zero in on our fear we will know exactly what to 'lean in' towards.

A best life is when you are living the most authentically - that takes courage. It may also require you to...

Lean into Fear.

#349 Argue effectively

When you live with someone, you're bound to run into conflict and the solution isn't to avoid the confrontation, but to approach it effectively. The following eight suggestions - when followed - will allow disagreements to be addressed with respect and maturity.

Use "I" statements only. Explain your position, your role in the conflict, and your expectations. Identify your triggers, explain your needs, and describe how you will work to bridge the gap in the conflict. Concentrate on *your* perspective and work hard not to engage in finger pointing or blaming.

Step back from your ego. In supportive partnerships, it is important to embrace our differences with respect and develop acceptance for the ways that our partners are different. There are mostly differences between us - not always rights and wrongs. If you feel you need to fight for being 'right' about something, ask yourself "why?" If it is only ego based, drop it.

Be present. Don't focus on the past (unless you are reflecting for the lesson it is teaching you) - or worry about the future. Try and stay right there in the present moment and focus on what is happening there. Don't allow your baggage to overwhelm the issue at hand.

Pay attention to the issue and why it is important to or distracting you. Is it a failed expectation? Something you didn't know. Are you defensive? Why? Exactly what are you feeling and why?

Don't interrupt your partner. You can't be a good listener if you aren't allowing their complete thought to be articulated or expressed.

Make sure you understand what you are hearing, and the intent involved. If necessary, restate what you hear - paraphrase it - based on your understanding so that you get on the same page.

Remember that most of us have good intentions. Try not to jump right to the conclusion that your partner is being an ass. Consider that they are experiencing frustration and give them space to talk about how they feel.

Do not raise your voice or walk out. If you need a break from the conflict - honor that it remains unsolved and ask for a time out. Don't threaten. People who feel attacked or threatened will get defensive almost immediately. Once that happens, the discussion is doomed.

Communicating with respect is probably the most critical aspect of a healthy relationship. Remembering that we each come into a relationship with different experiences, worldviews, expectations, and methods will go a long way. Resolving conflict is more easily accomplished when you know how to ...
Argue effectively.

If you want happiness for an hour, take a nap. If you want happiness for a day, go fishing. If you want happiness for a year, inherit a fortune. If you want happiness for a lifetime, help someone else.

Chinese Proverb

#350 Ask for help

Far too often I find myself talking with people who are overwhelmed because their life has turned temporarily chaotic and they do not stop to ask for help. Frequently, it's because they think they 'should' be able to handle it and asking for help feels like a weakness. Other times it is because they don't want to 'bother' people. We tend to deny ourselves village support by not asking for help when we need it.

The phrase "It takes a village" is an African proverb speaking to the concept that an entire village is involved in the rearing of its children. When a catastrophe happens, it takes a village. When an illness strikes, it takes a village. When a move is imminent, it takes a village.

If you are in the middle of a major challenge and someone says "let me know if you need anything" - let them know! If they were just being polite, they can assume responsibility for setting their own boundaries. I find that generally, people mean it when they offer help and are happy to aid. When life takes a disastrous turn, it's hard enough to maintain the simple elements of our daily routine and personal composure, let alone managing the major responsibilities of daily living.

Sometimes, life's challenges are minor and mostly a nuisance. Your furnace goes out on a day when you have an important meeting... You get stuck in a traffic jam and can't get home in time for the school bus... You have a family emergency in the middle of the night... All these experiences are unpredictable and mostly out of our control. In those moments, it's imperative that we reach out to those people in our village to fill in the gap.

Sometimes, our 'village' takes on a different identity than we may have imagined. It becomes our neighbors, our children's friends' parents, our co-workers, or our church family. Remember too... it takes being a friend to have a friend who steps up when you need a hand although, it may not be the 'same' friend. Karma doesn't travel in a liner line.

Remember, it's not just about building the village - it's about *using* the village and making sure that when you need to, you...

Ask for help.

#351 Know 'your' colors

In the very early 90's, there was a product line distributed via the home party platform, called "Color Me Beautiful" based on the book of the same name by Carole Jackson. The principle of Color Me Beautiful is that everyone can wear any color but the richness and undertone (warm or cool) is better on one skin color over another. The idea was that you could have your skin tone assessed and that would direct the color of your makeup, lipstick, and wardrobe colors; because when you wear the 'right' colors - it highlights your natural beauty.

Once you know your 'scheme', it's suggested that you prioritize those colors in your wardrobe and base your makeup selections accordingly. For example, if you are an Autumn - you would want to keep things in the green/rust/brown arena. Springs would choose red, lavender, and teal. Summers lean toward blues, yellows, and pinks. Finally, Winters might choose purple, burgundy, and emerald green.

Additionally, the colors are broken into the categories of warm or cool; winter and summer are cool while spring and fall are warm. As stated earlier, it's the richness and tone of the color that either does or does not work with your individual coloring.

There's plenty of research telling us that when we feel attractive, we stand taller, smile more, and engage more fully in our communication. What could be easier than working with the base pallet we were born with? Most of us probably have an experience of wearing a color and notice that when we do, the number of compliments about our appearance is elevated. Maybe people don't say "I like that color on you" but the comment about how pretty you look or how nice you look. They may notice that you look happy or simply "good". It may be helpful to see if there is a correlation to the increased comments based on a color you wear.

The color palettes are readily available online and once you've taken the quiz to determine your 'season' - buy the palette and carry it in your pocketbook or keep it in the car so that when you are out shopping, you are matching your purchases to the colors determined to be a best match to your skin tone. It's as easy as that to look your best once you...

Know your colors!

399

#352 Go on a retreat

How many times have you wished you could get away from it all? Have you fantasized about sitting in silence or dedicating time and attention to your spiritual, physical, or emotional health? A retreat may be just the thing for you.

A retreat is an opportunity to temporarily abandon the typical distractions that become a part of our day to day life. It's an opportunity to deeply relax and allow enough time for an inner change to take place and be sustained. Generally, a retreat differs from a typical vacation in that it focuses on a developmental purpose. The examples include Yoga, Meditation, Massage, Spiritual, Mindfulness, Food, and Fitness; there are dozens of options.

Imagine a week of de-stressing in a relaxing atmosphere where your only concern is may be literally feeding your body, mind, or soul. A retreat can be effective even if it is for a weekend. The concept is getting away long enough to fix your focus on something that is healing.

From websites like Retreat Guru to Google searches such as "retreat centers in [your region]", there are literally thousands of choices around the globe that offer get-a-ways to recharge you. Depending on your budget, you can go local or halfway around the world.

A retreat is self-care taken to the next level. It takes you beyond a good night's rest or an evening with friends and dedicates an entire period to individual care - much of what you do on your own (meditation, yoga, spiritual) but with the time and space to accomplish what doesn't happen at home.

When life is too much or preferably before it is overwhelming, do yourself a favor and …

Go on a retreat.

#353 Make decisions

How decisive are you? Is it easy for you to set a course? To make decisions? To act? If you are not naturally decisive or you struggle to be so, the following suggestions may be helpful.

Information is power. It is the cornerstone to making decisions because we can only act on what we know. The more you know, the more confident you will be in choosing. Do a little research - or a lot - depending on the intensity of the decision.

With every decision there are pros and cons, even small ones. Nothing is perfect. Sometimes, they are almost evenly balanced and it's important to see your options clearly so outline them as granularly as possible.

Take time to imagine each of the options; or at least the top three. Try to visualize how each of the decisions may play out in your life. Notice which option feels more intrinsic.

Remember that you've made decisions before and even if there are some bad ones in your past, there are more than likely many good ones as well. It's important to recall that you have the ability to, and the history of, making good decisions.

If you can learn to be still and connect to your innermost self, any decision you have to make will be easier. We all have an intrinsic 'knowing' - some people call it an intuition or gut feeling. For most of us, it takes practice to connect to it; to feel it. Authentic decisions come from that place.

If you are attempting to build your decision-making skills, start small. Make decisions about dinner or what restaurant to go to. Build up to more permanent decisions like paint color or furniture purchases. Be prepared to make mistakes. Take small risks and reassess as need be.

Remember that once in a while, you are likely to make a poor decision or one that you become dissatisfied with. It's likely to be ok in the grand scheme of things. Forgive yourself and try again.

Learn not to be afraid and build your confidence about ...

Making decisions.

#354 Develop your EQ

You've heard about IQ - your Intelligence quotient - for sure. And, unless you've been under a rock, you've probably heard about EQ which, is the term for Emotional [Intelligence] quotient. There is a segment of psychological professionals that consider it more important, than traditional intelligence.

EQ was popularized in the mid 90's by Dan Goleman's book outlining research by Salavoy & Mayer. It is defined by the ability to "recognize, understand and manage our emotions and to recognize, understand and influence the emotion of others."

When we understand and manage our emotions, we are more likely to direct our thought toward positive affect. Unyielded emotions diminish cognition, impede our decision-making skills, and interfere with our ability to communicate effectively.

Very few of us have achieved emotional mastery and so we're likely to benefit from practicing on a regular basis by doing the following as often as possible:

Be super aware of your own emotions. Know them. Label them.

Consider perspective at every opportunity.

Be curious about how others think and feel.

Stop and think before you speak. Speak intentionally.

Stop getting defensive.

Use your voice with respect and responsibility.

Each of these suggestions are to be used in conjunction with one another in as many situations as you can remember to employ them; regardless of the situation. Indeed, it's when life presents us with the most difficult or challenging scenarios that we must dig deep and practice, practice, practice.

Emotional Intelligence has been touted throughout corporate environments for almost two decades, but it's not yet taught or developed in schools or traditional environments even though it impacts communication in the most positive ways. EQ is a predictor of success and has been shown to improve mental health overall in research. More self-knowledge leads to more happiness and that leads to better life satisfaction no matter who you are. Looking for more happiness?...

Develop your EQ

#355 Stop being defensive

We experience a sense of needing to 'protect' ourselves whenever we become afraid and perceive that we are at risk for losing something. Whenever we imagine that we are in danger of having less of or never having something... we also may feel afraid and we tend to want to fight. When we feel attacked, we want to fight back. Emotionally speaking, we aren't taught effective strategies very often and unless the other person we are speaking with is also equipped with similar strategies, the communication is sure to break down quickly. The conversation can resemble a war zone.

First, you must make the effort to understand when you become defensive and how it feels in your body. Does your blood pressure rise? Your shoulders? Is there a tightness in your jaw? Does your heart race? Notice that they are the same symptoms of fear. It's your parasympathetic nervous system getting ready for a fight.

When you feel your body tightening, that's the moment you know it's imperative that you step back. Take a deep breath. Count to five. Get Grounded. Remember who you are - who you want to be. Think about something you love or really like about the person in front of you. If it's a stranger or an estranged individual, remember that by engaging you are giving them *your* power. Stop.

Backing down from a confrontation demonstrates emotional mastery - not weakness. Think about how much intention it takes to get to this point after your fear or fight is activated. It takes great strength to step back and gain composure. Adopt the attitude that you will not engage in a confrontation infused with negative energy.

Once you take the defensive energy out of an interaction, you'll be amazed at how it dies down - it's akin to a fire without oxygen. Your confrontations turn into constructive discussions and problem solving when you get to the point where you can...

Stop being defensive

#356 Get insurance

Just after I first got married at the age of 22, a couple dudes in ties knocked on our front door and spent two hours or more trying to convince us that we needed life insurance. We were young and invincible, expecting our first child and naive about the realities of the world. We were also broke, so they left that day without a sale and we didn't really think twice.

Fast forward two years as I found myself a 24-year-old widow with an 18-mo. old baby and no life insurance except for the little bit of money that was automatically a benefit for a Navy Reservist. It was a hard lesson and yet it was a great testimony for the years that I ironically, sat at kitchen tables explaining why people needed to think about life insurance and financial planning.

You're never too young for life insurance - in fact, that's the very best time to buy it because the odds that you'll die are low - so insurance is cheap. You don't need much if you don't have many responsibilities - just enough to cover your debt and burial expense (which, can easily run into the 5-digit range). However, the more responsibility you have, the more insurance you need.

Insurance is explicitly for the purpose of covering your behind when life throws curveballs. Whether it's health insurance, disability insurance, long term care insurance, rental insurance, theft insurance, or life insurance... we never know when we'll need coverage.

Technically, you only need to cover those things that you are willing to risk. Certainly, I never considered it a 'real' risk that my 23-year-old husband would die; nor did he. But it happened. Accidents happen. We've all heard horror stories of people who were involved in an accident and many of us think it "can't happen to me". How much are you willing to risk?

Consider the risk you're willing to take and then speak to a trusted advisor about insurance. Everybody needs at least some. Think about your car, your home, your belongings, your income, your health, and your life and then.

Get insurance.

#357 Know your ancestry

It used to be that people were excited to get their 'palm' read - now it's trendy to have your DNA read. Just by spitting in a little tube, you can identify where your ancestral roots originated. Why bother?

Whether it's a family tree or DNA, your family history is important. It's the anchor of your ship... the chemical composition of your existence. It offers information about your great-great-uncle Joe or connect the dots between your English and Irish heritage centuries back.

The most elementary part of knowing your ancestry is to record your direct lineage. Your father, his father, his father and so on... Do the same with your mother and hers... Connect those lines as far back as you can. When you run into a stumbling block, try the DNA route to run the lines as far as they can go.

Whether you choose 23&Me or another service, researching your cellular structure offers even more information. Instead of learning that your great, great, great, great, Aunt Florence was the first woman to captain a ship out of Naples, you might discover that your Italian heritage is closer to the French than it is to the Baltic even though she was the hero of that port.

DNA even allows you the genetic history of disease influence. No matter if your ancestry stems from Jewish, African, European, or Middle Eastern roots - the results can indicate propensity for issues carried by others in that gene group.

At the very least, knowing your ancestry is a tool to help you construct your 'story' - the story of you and of how you came to be. It's a more advanced version - a 3D illustration - of you. Knowing a little about the people that came before you gives depth to who you are.

Can you imagine all those souls that were in front of you? Do you know their story? Their contribution to your being? It's possible that you'll be forever changed if you take the time to ...

Know your ancestry.

#358 Learn how to shoot a gun

This is an emotional topic for some and yet it's a skill set that - at the very least - might save your life at some point. Perhaps you are already adept in this area and the following will validate your position. In either case, there is a certain amount of security that results when you know how to properly [safely] handle a gun.

Because a gun is a tool that has the capacity to kill, it is imperative that anyone handling one learn safety and responsibility. Just like the automobiles that we drive - it is a piece of machinery that deserves respect. Likewise, developing skill requires training, practice, and patience. When addressed properly, a gun is simply another tool or piece of sporting equipment.

Knowing how to shoot a gun can generate self-confidence. There's a certain amount of accomplishment and pride when the target you were aiming at gets obliterated. Whether it's a clay that you hit in midair, a can on top of a bail, or a bullseye on a clip at 50 feet - knowing that your hand was steady, and your eyesight keen offers a sense of satisfaction.

Target practice is a fun thing to do on a date night or with friends, especially if you're a little competitive. Think of it as an extreme dart game. Clay shooting is another target activity that gets you outdoors in the fresh air. Because alcohol cannot be part of these experiences (liquor and guns are never a good combination), it's an opportunity to gather and enjoy the experience of each other's company without all the silliness and obnoxious behavior that alcohol tends to conjure.

Shooting a gun with intent and purpose is an empowering experience. Not only does it foster self-confidence but also attention, focus, and reactivity. All of those elements contribute overall to the sense of empowerment that supports individual esteem. It exercises brain and body muscles - all potentially leading to better physical and emotional health.

I'm not taking a side on gun ownership or gun laws in any capacity, only suggesting that knowing how to safely handle a gun - at the very least - may save your life if you happen to stumble across a loaded one. God forbid we ever 'have' to shoot one for self-preservation but if we do, the first step is to...

Learn to shoot a gun.

#359 Make a movie

Creativity and imagination are some of the things that came naturally to most of us as children and for some, they develop - for others, they morph or die. Why not try your hand at combining creativity and imagination again by making a movie? It's easier than ever and there are several smartphone apps that practically do it for you. In fact, several of the movies presented at festivals these days are entirely filmed on an iPhone. An idea and some ingenuity can go a long way.

The most obvious choice is to make a home movie. Many of us have a collection of video clips that we've accumulated from special moments that could be strung together in a fantastic memory video. If we don't have anything to start with, it's super easy with phones, tablets, and portable video cams that are inexpensive and easy to use. It could also be a 'movie' that's simply a collection of photographs with title cards and sound effects; a live photo album of sorts. This is a standard these days at weddings, graduations, and funerals but why wait? A collection of Johnny's little league days is just as much of a keepsake as his high school graduation.

My family has hours upon hours of Christmas day videos. We propped the camera on the tripod and let it run for the 4 hours it took to open presents. Watching those things is almost painful. Digitizing the tapes and editing them to create something worth watching is a chore to be sure, but also a pleasant treat that will be treasured for years.

You could also create a storyline, employ some actors/actresses, and direct your first feature film. You could be part of an elite group who is recognized early in their career process who has raw talent. It may be as easy as going with your gut and allowing creativity to flow through you. Why not? If you play the lottery, the odds may be just as good.

The point here is to step outside of your comfort zone, create memories, have fun, take a risk, embody creativity and honor your imaginative side. With any of those efforts, you are enhancing elements central to the happiness principle. So, go ahead and step out of the box…. Make a movie.

#360 Practice mutuality

Mutuality is defined as...

"The sharing of a feeling, action, or relationship between two or more parties."

It's a reciprocal exchange of intent, energy, and commitment in friendship, familial relationships, and marriage. The pinnacle of mutuality is when your interest is in the love, respect, support, and trust of another individual. We do this in friendship. We encourage, support, trust, love, and respect the autonomy and independence of our friends.

You may get up every day with the goal of helping your loved one have their best day ever. Your focus is on supporting them to achieve their highest goals, to be their best selves. You do this no matter what, and it can be hard in those love relationships that endure day to day stressors and get more complicated over time as we combine finances, raise children, and try to balance home and work.

Mutuality is based on the concept of reciprocation. You have my back... I have yours. Do onto me what you would have me do onto you. Etcetera. When I feel supported, I am willing to support. When I feel loved, I am offering love back. When I am respected, I respect. When I am appreciated, I will be appreciative. It works beautifully under those conditions and it fosters great respect. Without reciprocation, mutuality takes on a whole new look.

In the best example of mutuality, both people in the relationship are focused on one another, respecting the space, independence, goals, and autonomy of the other. If you are in a relationship where it is not reciprocated, then the key is to kick self-respect into high gear and practice mutuality personally.

In this case, it may look like this... "I respect you but if you can't be as respectful of me, I must practice self-respect". "I am encouraging you to reach your goals but if you can't encourage me than I must encourage myself". "I am supporting you to be your best and will continue to support myself to grow and learn". Sometimes, the mutuality you engage in is with yourself by setting boundaries that demonstrate a respect for self.

The self-respect examples I list are more often for those relationships that you don't necessarily choose; family, boss, neighbor, etc.... In a romantic relationship, the practice of mutuality is one of the only ways to foster a happy and healthy bond. It creates an environment where both of your needs for love, respect, support, and autonomy are being encouraged and developed. You are building one another up - not with hot air, but with energy that binds. It will 'feel' good.

For best results in every relationship, it's important to ...
Practice Mutuality.

---

*"The more man meditates upon good thoughts,
the better will be his world and the world at large"*
— Confucius

#361 Play a practical joke

Life is just better when there's laughter, isn't it? I know I am guilty of getting locked into a serious mood from time to time and a practical joke is just the thing to bring me out of it. Before we go much further though - perhaps we can take a moment to define 'practical' in the interest of keeping it funny.

The literal definition of a practical joke is to "trick someone in order to make them look foolish or amuse them". I strongly suggest we avoid the 'looking foolish' element and strive for amusement. Here, it may be important to understand how the person you want to 'trick' - is amused. While some slight forms of discomfort or embarrassment can be funny - there is great variability on our perspectives of this. For the sake of this suggestion, the intent of a practical joke is to promote laughter and levity.

Perhaps the epitome of the kind of stunts that may be considered 'harmless' are the kind used by the famed television show Candid Camera. The tricks of mind and eye - the ones that leave us wondering about our sanity; tricks of the mind.

Because the goal is to create amusement and for everyone involved to have fun, there are particular limits that must be respected in the pursuit of practical joking. In particular, no physical harm. No property damages. No significant inconvenience (i.e., creating situations that may make someone late for work - their boss may not think your joke is funny). And remember, what you're willing to tolerate may not be the same as your target so - keep it light. Laughter elevates the most necessary chemicals in our body required for a sense of well-being. It provides a dopamine rush and helps us feel better by pulling us into the present moment. Remember, have fun but be thoughtful as you …

Play a practical joke.

#362 Go on a picnic

Throughout this book I mention picnicking as a way of experiencing a variety of suggestions (i.e., spend the day with a friend, get outside, etc.). I assumed that everyone had some element of experience with the concept and then I met someone who had never actually experienced what I would consider a 'true picnic'.

In my world, a classic picnic is outdoors, sitting on a blanket, and eating a meal that you brought with you. In the movies, the blanket is red checkered – in my life it's old and fuzzy. In the movies, the food is carried in a nicely woven wicker basket – in my life it's a reusable bag that's probably a little dirty and worn. In the movies, the food is organic and especially prepared – in my life it is entirely based on what was in the refrigerator.

There are about as many varieties of how to picnic as there are families and there is no right or wrong way to do it. A picnic can be about romantic conversation at dusk, a family frisbee championship, or a solo reading adventure. It can be laid out on a picnic table in a state park, by the side of a road along a creek, or on a blanket by a lake.

The value of picnicking isn't the eating…. It's the outdoors. It's about the presence of the sun, the fresh air, and the absence of a need to do anything else. Perhaps today is a good day to…

Go on a picnic.

#363 Try acupuncture

Wikipedia classifies acupuncture as "quackery" and reminds us that it is not based on scientific knowledge. While I have not ever experienced acupuncture personally, I know people who swear by it.

It's a form of traditional Chinese medicine where thin (sometimes long) needles are inserted at pressure points in the body. It's based the concept of refining the flow of "Qi" (life energy). The theories vary, but it is thought that acupuncture may stimulate the release of natural pain-relieving endorphins. Any benefiting result is generally associated with a placebo effect. And yet, for thousands of years people have claimed to benefit from its course.

Proponents of acupuncture tout its effectiveness for ailments ranging from arthritis, chronic pain, and headaches to fatigue and reproduction issues. While the scientific research is inconclusive – it's been a thriving profession for thousands of years; presumably an unsustainable proposition if it didn't ultimately work.

There is a potential of serious side effects (like anything else) and they can be serious, so it is imperative that treatment be conducted by trained and licensed professionals. Certification is generally accomplished through the Commission for Acupuncture and Oriental Medicine (NCCAOM). Be sure your practitioner is accredited.

If you're experiencing pain, depression, or another ailment purported to benefit from acupuncture, it may be worth a try. Alternative medicine can be a wonderful adjunct to traditional medical treatment. But remember, it's always necessary to check with your physician before you...

Try acupuncture.

#364 Spend the day on the water

Notice that this suggestion is to spend the day *on* the water – not *in*. Those of you who are boaters know the joy of hanging out 'on' the water all day long, but you don't need a boat to accomplish this task. Rafts, tubes, and floating piers will provide the same benefit and it doesn't matter if it's on a creek ten inches deep, a lake in the center of Arkansas, or the great Chesapeake Bay.

When we spend the day on the water, we are generally engaging in behavior which, is substantially relaxing with perhaps the exception of people who are white water rafting. In all of the examples that I can think of, it is a fun way to spend a day; when we have fun... we feel happier.

Even if the only option you have is to visit a water park and hang out in the lazy river for an hour or two, you'll benefit from the vitamin D that gets absorbed from the sunshine. As long as you remember the sunscreen so that you don't burn, you're likely to walk away from the experience with an overall sense of well-being (this does not consider anyone dealing with cranky, tired children).

Some people suggest floating in the water reminds us – at a deep intrinsic level – of being in our mother's womb. It's a sound rationale for why slowly bobbing up and down on the water is so soothing. It's about as close as we can come to staying suspended in a weightless sense.

Whether you do it with a group of friends or family, or you go solo, you'll feel relaxed, produce more vitamin D, and connect with nature in the most natural way when you...

Spend a day on the water.

#365 Support Community Theatre

The next time you want a night out, why not consider supporting a local drama troop. Community theatre is a delight. Aside from watching some of your neighbors and friends who have great talent, you'll be entertained with wonderful stories.

Community theatre is the way that the average individual can participate in theatre arts. It enriches the members of the troop, the members of the community, and the community-at-large; primarily because it represents a diverse range of individuals who understand and appreciate the art form.

Community theater generates opportunities for talented individuals and curious parties to realize potential without the strict and limiting parameters of professional organizations. It is a platform for young and old alike. It nurtures new artists and offers unrealized dreamers a venue for honing or mastering skills. It fosters confidence and communication. It introduces valuable and necessary skill sets to youth in a manner that traditional education may not.

Theater supports the concept of storytelling in a way that can connect with some people more than books. It allows imagination to thrive in areas where it may be stymied.

Local theater strengthens a sense of community in the most basic of ways. It brings people together from a variety of directions for a common good; supporting business, residents, and the arts; any of which would be benevolent. Benevolence fosters happiness. There just isn't a downside when you …

Support community theatre.

Happiness comes when you believe in what you are doing, know what you are doing, and love what you are doing.

Brian Tracy

Made in the USA
Lexington, KY
24 October 2019